Forget Me Knot

5 Step Guide To Tie You To Them

By
Dr. Aviva Boxer, OMD

Publishing by Healthy Notes, Inc.
214 Barbour Street
Playa del Rey, CA 90293
(530) 238-5649

Publishing in association with Motivational Press
7668 El Camino Real, #104-223
Carlsbad, CA 92009

Copyright 2015 © by Dr. Aviva Boxer, OMD

Cover Design: Taylor Nelson and Chelsea Spann
Interior Design: Taylor Nelson and Parnell Cordor

All Rights Reserved

No part of this book may be reproduced or transmitted in any form by any means: graphic, electronic, or mechanical, including photocopying, recording, taping or by any information storage or retrieval system without permission, in writing, from the authors, except for the inclusion of brief quotations in a review, article, book, or academic paper. The authors and publisher of this book and the associated materials have used their best efforts in preparing this material. The authors and publisher make no representations or warranties with respect to accuracy, applicability, fitness or completeness of the contents of this material. They disclaim any warranties expressed or implied, merchantability, or fitness for any particular purpose. The authors and publisher shall in no event be held liable for any loss or other damages, including but not limited to special, incidental, consequential, or other damages. If you have any questions or concerns, the advice of a competent professional should be sought.

Manufactured in the United States of America.

ISBN: 978-0-9863433-2-2

Library of Congress Catalogue Card Number: 2014922227

1.Religion, Spirituality, Mysticism 2. Legacy 3. Death and Dying 4. Dr. Aviva Boxer, OMD

Table Of Contents

Dedication ix
Foreword xi
Introduction xix
Chapter 1:   Step 1 - Your Thread And Life Pattern 1
Chapter 2:   Step 2 - The Chine Or Knick Points Of Life 49
Chapter 3:   Step 3 - Expressions/Responses 99
Chapter 4:   Step 4 - Your Essence 147
Chapter 5:   Step 5 - Make Your Mark! 197
Conclusion 229
Acknowledgements 244
Index 246
Love My Life-o-graphic 5 Step Televideo Course 252

Did you know that <u>Forget Me Knot</u> is just Book 1 in the Baby Boomer End-of-life Series?

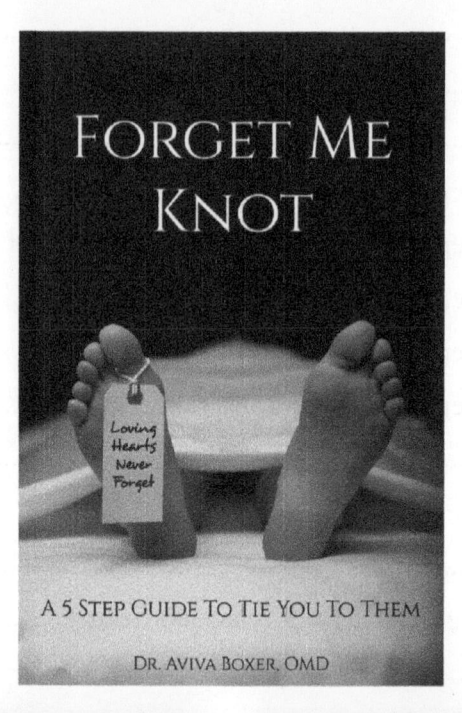

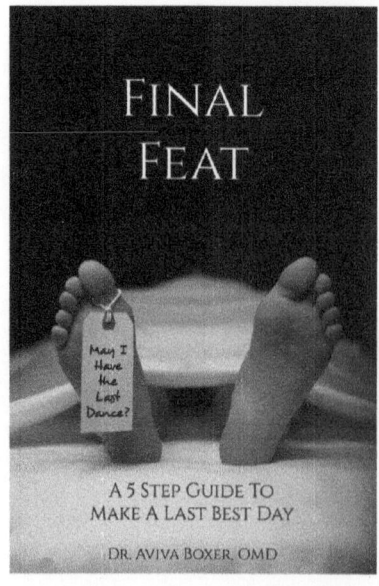

Forget Me Knot
A 5 Step Guide To Tie You To Them
Dr. Aviva Boxer, OMD

Final Feat
A 5 Step Guide To Make A Last Best Day
Dr. Aviva Boxer, OMD

Funusual Funerals
A 5 Step Guide To An Unforgettable Finale
Dr. Aviva Boxer, OMD

Book 1
<u>FORGET ME KNOT</u>: A 5 Step Guide to Tie You to Them

>Your one-liner legacy bonded with their 5 senses and triggered by an everyday symbol that activates the lives and hearts of your loved ones.

Book 2
<u>FINAL FEAT</u>: A 5 Step Guide to Make a Last Best Day

>Your day to allow them to heal, bond, love, and escort you through the portal into the hereafter using simple, sacred, ancient natural healing methods that soothe you, heal them, and open wide your spiritual ascent.

Book 3
<u>FUNUSUAL FUNERALS</u>: A 5 Step Guide to An Unforgettable Finale

>Your last customized, legacy-driven gift as an honorable and delightful send-off, filled with gratitude and reassurance for loved ones left behind that you are complete and at peace, but still spiritually connected.

If you would like to be notified when Book 2 and Book 3 are published in the Baby Boomer End-of-Life Series, please share with us your contact information at:

DRAVIVABOXER.COM

ELEVATING AND CUSTOMIZING THE END-OF-LIFE EXPERIENCE

DEDICATION

To my beloved mother
Rita Marie

You were always a shepherd, never a sheep.
You were consistently true to your own self
and never false to another.

The modeling of your soul's core life message
was my rich inheritance.

I live off your never-ending intangible dividends every day. This book is an example of my being a shepherd and being true to myself. I carry your core life message forward everywhere.

You live on in my heart and now in the hearts of many.

Sparrows know not the dreams of swans.

FOREWORD

THE DREADED CALL

The phone rang at 5:45 a.m.

"Your mother is taking her last breaths. So come here as soon as possible."

The thoughts rushed through my head: "Was it her time? Was this it? What is death? How do you say good-bye to a mother? My daughters are watching and modeling me. How do I look strong and at the same time feel the feelings I have? I am scared, yet I have to lead the family right now. I can do this. I can do this for my beloved mother."

There are no instructions on "how to," no maps showing the way, or to get one's bearings on death. There are no signposts to yield, merge, dead end or no 'u turns'. Absent are hints or clues that my senses could get a glint of what to do, or what was to come next from the imminent impending doom of death. That night's dreams, if I was actually lucky enough to sleep, delivered no help or peace that what was to come was finality of a life, as I had known it. There was no escape. The only sense that the Grim Reaper was at hand was this eerie sense of silence, similar to the quintessence of quiet one hears when flying in a hot air balloon on the ribbon of a wind shear. There was also a type of stretching of time, so the pace of time seemed somewhat slow motion and warped out of sync.

If it weren't for my mother, I would never have veered off the conservative beaten path in life. I would never have been willing to be different. I would have become a pediatrician instead of a Homeopath and Doctor of Oriental Medicine. I would have been a teacher rather than a healer. If it weren't for my mother, I would never have felt I could do anything I set my mind to if I wanted it badly enough. If it weren't for my mother, I wouldn't have the compassion for my fellow man and have the sensitivity to try to understand what it would be like to walk in his shoes. If it weren't for my mother, I wouldn't trust after betrayal, or hope after adversity. She was a person who modeled a life of character and talked about it only briefly afterwards when asked. She didn't ever have to toot her own horn, because the band of excellence and honor was always playing loud and clear wherever she would go.

I remember asking my mother in my late teens when I had my very first boyfriend, "Mommy, how do you know if you are in love?" Her answer was, "When you don't have to ask that question, my daughter." My mother spoke spiritual language her whole life. She let her conscience be her guide. I was the lucky one who got her as a mother to guide me through my heart and my head. She taught be how to be a woman. She gave me the courage to write this book. She was human love.

The best I could do was to show up to this day like I had any other day, wondering what would come next and trusting that I had enough in me to respond with authenticity and do the best I could with what I had. There is no 'winging' it in the dark of death and the unknown. To be swept forward into the abyss of it, all I could do was be present with my best faith and courage that whatever is the meaning of this abrupt shift in my life would reveal itself if I stayed present with all my wits, heart, and volition. I gulped, took a big breath in, and moved into the mode one does when they have to give CPR or the Heimlich maneuver. Just react. Just do 'automatic', one foot in front of the other.

FOREWORD

I was flying higher than I thought possible, like a seagull, feeling and doing hard things that I never thought I could do. I was giving it my all, staying present with all the focus and attention I could muster. I came with my sense of curiosity and wonder to the end process of death. I had been near others who had passed over before. This time it was different. It was my mother. This was my beloved mother with whom I had shared an umbilical cord of nourishment and life. This experience was different, and I knew it was an auspicious moment.

My three sisters and two daughters knew what an early morning call like this meant, so by the time I'd hung up the phone they had already thrown on their clothes and were ready to go.

In a voice unfamiliar to my own ears, I heard myself speaking the words, "It's time." Everything seemed slow motion. We packed ourselves into my minivan and, in somber silence, set out for the 35-minute freeway drive to the assisted living home. As I drove as fast as possible, the thought of one of the last conversations I had had with my mother was replaying in my mind, until a sight on my right interrupted it.

THE LAST CONVERSATION

One of the last times I visited my mother in the assisted living care home, I found out she was in excruciating pain, while sitting hunched in her wheelchair. The pain was even beyond my mother's extremely high tolerance for pain. My mother, who was called 'Mew' by us children, looked at me in the eye, with her stunning transparent Mediterranean blue eyes. She said to me, "You know I am dying soon, don't you?" I said, "Yes, Mew." I had no idea why I knew it, but I did. I said, "Mew, I will miss you terribly. How will I contact you and talk to you when I need your wisdom, your love, and your comfort when you are no longer here?"

My mother said, "I am already in you. You have only to look inside. I am also in your daughters. Look into their eyes. I will always be with you in spirit. You know that I love the story of Jonathan Livingston

Seagull. That story and the birds will always be there to guide you with my presence."

JONATHAN LIVINGSTON SEAGULL

Jonathan Livingston Seagull is a metaphorical story, written by Richard Bach, about a seagull that had the courage to fly higher and faster than all the rest, even though it was forbidden and impossible. Instead, he was an outcast for making it his mission and destiny to practice and fail, then practice some more to soar to heights, past the taboo of limiting beliefs and public opinion. Jonathan Livingston Seagull accomplished his dream of flying higher and faster than any seagull had ever done in history.

Even though ostracized, Jonathan Livingston Seagull remained true to his dreams. He stayed consistent to himself and his vision. He flew higher and faster than any bird had flown. He flew to where spirits are free and love is the atmosphere. It is where there are no words, just being. Jonathan Livingston Seagull had to fly his way. He was driven. Nothing could stop him. His spirit yearned for the freedom and space, even if it meant leaving his community behind.

This too was the story of my mother's life. Though told she would never amount to anything, and never have anything, her life proved otherwise. As a child, my mother experienced more adversity while seeing the ugly side of life and human nature than any person, young or old, should endure. Nevertheless, she triumphed by leading her own flock, her own children, to speak the language of compassion, generosity, creativity, integrity, and determination through hard work. Her modeling set the bar of humanity in the same ethers as those that Jonathan Livingston Seagull soared, no matter what the naysayers squawked. Her life's meaning was how she lived her life authentically and modeled the congruity of her message for us children. She lived her truth.

My mother's last conversation ended with, "You know my philosophy is to rise to a level and fly free with the truth of your being and your individual gifts, no matter what anyone says and what the naysayers might believe, Aviva. To thine own self be true, and you can be false to no man. Remember to always be a shepherd, not a sheep so that you can be master of your destiny and captain of your soul. The birds will always be representative of my presence. So be at peace. I will always be with you. And never forget, I love you."

THE COFFINS

As I came back from the daydream of my last conversation with my mother, the most unbelievable sight passed before all of us in the car, as we drove toward her.

Out of the blue, there was the strangest sight traveling right next to our car, in the adjacent lane, as I drove along on the freeway. My mouth dropped open. In disbelief, wondering if I saw what I thought I was seeing, I quickly looked over at my sister sitting in the passenger seat to see if she saw it too. By her look, and her glance at me, I know she was thinking the same thing. We both immediately looked at the digital car clock in the car console. I said aloud, "It is 6:14 and I think Mom has just passed." We all were silent. The sight we saw next to us, in the adjacent lane, was a 16-wheeler truck with uncovered, untethered cement coffins in full public view: five 8-foot caskets stacked high, eight of them long, on the flat bed of the truck. What was especially odd was that they had not been covered or secured with ties. I had never seen anything like it, and the timing was beyond coincidental.

When we arrived at the assisted living home, we found we had not made it in time, and that my mother had already passed. I asked them what time she had passed. It was exactly at 6:14 am, the same time as we had observed the cement caskets on the truck. My sister and I looked at each other as if we already knew. We believed our mother had been trying to say goodbye to all of us in her own way, so we didn't feel badly that we hadn't made it in time. Whether it was shock, denial, or it just hadn't sunk in yet; my mother still seemed to be around. I felt her presence in the room. The best I can describe it is the feeling you might have when you are watching TV in the den and your mother is making dinner in the kitchen. You don't have to see her, or hear her to know she is there. A mother's presence is very large in a child's heart. The room I talk about for myself is not just the physical room I can see and touch. The room is the place within me that has a place just for the bond I have with my mother. It is always there, even when she is not. It was a curious feeling to know I was witnessing the finality of life, but the sensation did not have a closed, locked off feeling associated with it in the bonding place in my heart. I still felt connected. This was a new feeling to me. I did not expect it.

THE RAINBOW GOODBYE

When we came into the room we saw her still body. It was still warm. It was eerie. She was here and not here at the same time. She seemed so much at peace.

She didn't look like she was sleeping. It was different. No more pain, or living in limbo. Finally, it was freedom for her spirit, just as she had wished. She had let go of her disintegrating body.

One by one, each of us took our turns sitting on her bed to say our last goodbyes. We all wanted to tell her we loved her in our own way.

When it came to my turn, I sat on her bed, curious, heart wide open, and I clasped my mother's warm hands. I locked on with her as I stared at her closed eyes. Then, all of a sudden, two things happened that seemed surreal. Suddenly, a vision I will never forget happened. As I focused on my mother's closed eyes, I saw a ribbon rainbow of colored fumes rise off my mother's body like the heat waves off hot coffee. The colors were a vibrant wave of rising, rippling color. I blinked several times thinking it was my contact lenses clouding, but the brilliant color continued to rise. I was in jaw dropping awe.

At first, I was going to glance over at my sisters and exclaim, "Did you see that? Isn't it beautiful? Isn't it amazing?"

FOREWORD

However, loud and clear, in a voice that was not my own, but my mother's voice I heard loudly, "No! This is for you and you alone. Pay attention. Stay with me." Then, secondly, I heard my mother's voice say to me, "You are not like your sisters. You are different. Embrace this. It belongs to you. You will do something very wonderful with the gift that is yours. I love you."

In a barely audible whisper I breathed, "I love you, too, Mew. I love you."

As we waited for all the last arrangements of my mother's body to wrap up, my thoughts returned to my last conversation with my mother, interrupted by the casket sighting.

The tears were finally rolling down my face as I recalled the elegance of how she said goodbye to me with such reassurance, and strength. There was no one like her. I was so lucky to have been her child.

Ash Scattering

Later, as the human remains of my mother sat piled into a heap of ashes surrounded by a flower ring lined basket, we cast them off into the water and out to sea. The flowered ring remained floating in the water as the gray ashes dissipated into the deep blue sea. It was just as she wished; flocks and flocks of seagulls came to pay their last respects. One seagull in particular perched himself on the top of the boat and stayed there until we were safely docked and disembarked. We knew it was Mom's spirit with us, thanking us for doing it just as she would have wanted.

Moreover, as time passed, her words came to be just as she had said.

Birds Surrounding The Moments We Needed Her Most

At every celebration: graduations, weddings, birthdays, health problems, and every challenge, for all her children and grandchildren, there were birds present, and not just one or two. We children knew it was my mother's presence because the behavior of the birds was unusual, not what birds usually do around humans.

When my sisters and brother would get together, we would share "Mom and the birds" stories. We all had many stories. We all felt that my mother was around us all the time. Each story was unusual, and just as clear as the day her ashes floated out to sea.

I, too, had my own stories on a constant basis. Every day that I walk around the high school track, my mother would leave a feather for me with a coin right next to it. In my home, I have a shelf that has hundreds of feathers from my mother to let me know that she is with me and supports me. It is so comforting. I feel loved. I feel her spirit around me all the time. I say her name, I hear her wisdom coming out of my own mouth, and the certainty of her spirit is with me. I feel blessed that her legacy lives on just as she had said to me in that last conversation we had.

I would want everyone to have the spirit of their loved one who has passed, with them in the pocket of their heart, as I do, my sisters and brother do, as do all that knew my mother.

Julie Andrews, in the film *Mary Poppins*, sang of the spiritual connection to birds: "Though her words are simple and few, listen. She is calling to you."

With a feather in my hand, I am calling to you. Let's fly above the naysayers that say it is an impossible feat. Let us be shepherds, not sheep. Let's do what many say can't be done. Let's change the idea and experience of death as it has always been. Together let's bring light to the last experience of death as a dark abyss. Let's change the way people look at death. Let's put a knotted red string on forgetting so our children and their children can follow our path of light and find their way home.

Don't call the doctor after the funeral.

INTRODUCTION

I can hear it coming.
Can you?
The loud sound is getting faster. Closer.
I wish I could run from it.
But I am certain it will overtake me.
It will run right over me, strike me down. Just like the rest.
I am a Baby Boomer.
And it is coming for us.

We are dying.

The pervasive dark cloud of grief hanging over our loved ones and ourselves is accumulating.

If we think we were grief stricken over JFK's assassination, or the shock of 9/11, we ain't seen nothin' yet; or should I say our loved ones left behind ain't seen nothin' yet?

It is happening fast.

More death will happen in the next 10 years than in all of history. The Baby Boomer bulge in population is ending. Everyone will feel its effect. Because of this tsunami of death, one way, or another, it will touch young and old. The luxury of denial, fear, avoidance, fantasy, procrastination, impotence, apathy, shock, and delegating it to another is no longer an option. We cannot afford to be 'deer in the headlights'. We can no longer leave it to our animal instinct, or perceive it as God's territory where no man has a choice. We can no longer see it just as finality where everything stops, and the season for life has come and gone. We can no longer play the ostrich, with our head in the sand wishing our death to be quick and painless, when we don't know when it is going to happen or that it is happening at all.

We can override our all-encompassing fears with our will and our yearning to have a part of ourselves live forever in the hearts and minds of our loved ones. Our automatic default to avoid even the sound of the word 'DEATH' can shift with our permission, interest, and intent. This book is a calling to your hearts and minds to let the best of you live on forever. So that those who follow you have a chance, in a way you did not, to speak a spiritual language that unites and amplifies the best of each other and elevates our species in all of life, and in all of history.

We are ill prepared for death. We have no manual, no map, no tools, and no plan. We are asleep. Moreover, because of our passivity there will be a great, big gray atomic cloud of 'get in fetal position' grief. This is an all-encompassing cloud of grief and loss, instability and fear that will cover the earth, in our place, when we are gone. That is, unless we Baby Boomers do something different from what people have done before, about death, passing, and the end of life. If not, we will litter the earth with grief because of our 'Que sera, sera' attitude.

The Baby Boomers have a desire of peace over war, natural over manmade, and equality to all men and women over segregation and double standards. Baby Boomers think outside of the box with critical and creative thinking. Boomers want to save the earth for future generations, and to leave the earth in which they lived the

INTRODUCTION

same or better for having been there. Baby Boomers are expanders, globalizers, and space travelers. Boomers are risk takers and dreamers, where all seems possible. Boomers desire to put their spin on the past way of doing things.

If we can do all that, can't we also take on the perception of death and turn it upside down to make the most of it? Doesn't the idea of reframing and redefining death itself fit all of the attributes that endear the Boomer generation? It has peace, natural, equality, and thinking outside of the box, creativity, legacy, expansion and dreams all wrapped up in this mission. It is an untouched frontier for eons. We can rally together, look past anti-aging and long life, and use the platform of inevitable death to elevate our species.

As Baby Boomers, it is our time to put our spin on the last terrain of life…end-of-life. If not, once more we will leave the clean up and the responsibility for our selfishness on the generations after us to wade through, sort out, and come to terms with the unexplainable. It is just plain selfish, and reinforces the Baby Boomer generation as 'The Me Generation" in neon bold. Our lack of foresight will create paralysis and emotional obstruction to our future dream makers. Our family line will suffer, if we don't wake up and reconfigure how we will modify and rethink the death experience for both them and us. It will leave a bitter last taste in the mouths of generations who think about our Baby Boomer generation.

We Baby Boomers changed the world's eye view. We did it with war. We did it with love. We did it with space exploration, globalization, and expansiveness. We did it with communication. We did it with introspection. We did it with innovation. So until we make it our mission to tackle the last territory of the human soul, death, we will end our era flat, inhumane, making every gain we've made, suspect to ulterior motive and self-gain.

Another reason for us Baby Boomers to awaken and reframe the experience of death is so people remember us, our way. While death is as human as birth, Baby Boomers have redefined all that they touch, and put their mark on it. Some have likened Boomers to locusts, using all the resources and leaving everything picked over and scorched. Perhaps it is human nature for all of us to want recognition for our unique contribution in life, but Baby Boomers took it to a new level because of the sheer numbers of people competing for being unique and noticed, all at the same time. It became the norm to want to personalize everything and to become famous in one's own right, and anonymity became the exception. This was something different from the Great Generation, the parents of the Baby Boomers who achieved greatness by 'walking softly, but carrying a big stick'. As individuals and as a group, Boomers, if misconstrued, very possibly inaccurately, by future generations with hindsight perceptions, Boomer meaning could be described in a way that negates the actual value of their era's footprint. Boomers can define their death, just as profoundly as they defined natural childbirth and defined their presence here on earth. Boomers don't want to be just some nameless person in a photograph two generations from now, whose value is only that they share the same shape of nose or color of eyes.

Birth Dearth

Birth Dearth is the opposite of a population bomb. It is a population bust. It is when a decrease in population happens as the older population dies off. The young have no idea that they are about to be hit with the cloud of grief. Their parents, the Baby Boomers, the 'helicopter parents' have fed their self-esteems and tried to protect their children from any conceivable disease, adversity or malady, so much so that the next generation feels permanently invincible, capable, and safe. However, the next generations are not immune from the grief of death that is coming, at least not this level of grief. The next generation has lived through 9/11, school shootings like Columbine, the Oklahoma bombing, and Sandy Hook. In some ways, with video games, horror movies, Harry Potter, and the vampire themed stories, to the next generation it all seems so unreal, almost play. Death and grief are just fantasy. The belief is there will be a sequel that will make the ending all okay.

INTRODUCTION

For these innocents, they will feel a sharp dagger in the heart. They are a dependent generation. When their parents die and they become thrown into independence without the experience or tools of emotional independence, the effect of grief will hit even deeper. There is no one to turn to for safety. There will be no one to tell them that they are invincible. Not only will the people who shored up their self-esteem die, but also, all the ideals they espoused will crumble and be up for scrutiny to this next grieving generation. How do the young achieve the dreams of which they are capable while shock and grief immobilize them? Multiplying that shock and grief exponentially, so that everyone can talk about their grief, in some degree or another, the effect will permeate society in all facets. People find it almost impossible to achieve anything when the devastation of grief hits. They go through the motions like zombies, or empty shells. Then the horror films or video games the young people have watched their whole lives become real, and they themselves are horror characters in a real life horror of grief.

We Baby Boomers bought the idea in the '60s of 'Zero Population', that the way to save the world and not create over consumption of the earth's natural resources was to reduce the number of children we bore to just two. "Two will Do" or "One for Mum, One for Dad, One for Nation" the slogans told us. Just replace yourself and your spouse for the next generation. If we all had fewer children, there would be more wealth to share with the next generation. That was the idea. We would be making more elbow-room or space, which would mean more freedom, more privacy, and fewer rules. We would be saving the earth by just replacing ourselves.

The problem is that Zero Population is a failed theory. It was supposed to keep the population constant. Instead, we have pollution, violence, loss of values, and individual privacy. The opposite of what we wanted. The unstable lowered population rates have led to drastic changes. The theory ignored the idea of migration and globalization. It did not take into consideration that in order to have a higher number of young people to run the world as the aging get ill and retire, the younger people have to have children. There is a large time span between birth rate and death. When the population falls below the death rate because of a time lag, there is 'Birth Dearth'. The young people have to support the older generation, which is top heavy, until they die off. It is getting even more serious as there is an increase in life expectancy. It is a real twist in the Zero Population theory. It hasn't even hit the next generation in the eyes yet. Nevertheless, it will. As this next generation wakes up, at the same time they will also be in the midst of a huge cloud of grief, which could send them into a type of PSTD. Unprepared and in shock, the next generation will have to heal while surviving and reproducing.

Baby Boomers were born right after an atomic bomb dropped on Hiroshima. They were born at a time when there was not only a massive amount of destruction of human life, but also destruction of the earth's structure and resources as well. Additionally, there was a destruction of ideals. Boomers wanted to solve problems differently than their parents had, so they made new rules for the game of life for themselves. Boomers redefined the life rules of their parents with regard to frugality, loyalty, separate but equal, and patriotism. The biggest fear of Baby Boomers is aging, pain, dependence, memory loss, and turning to dust at death. Many Baby Boomers see themselves as having the divine right to be perpetually young and all the dreams that go with youth. That is one reason, at least at this point; there is no talk or interest in death to the Baby Boomers. The attention is on prevention, denial and fantasy, not reality. Boomers are such a force, they could use it to shift perception about death and have their greatest impact of all, going out with a bang and a burst of new thought, hope, and possibility. In this way, they can remain forever young, reverberating their impact on the future of humanity.

The key point to all of this 'Birth Dearth' is that it is becoming impossible to preserve Baby Boomer cultural traditions as ethnic diversity and inter-culture births become more common. Worse, the population can no longer provide for itself with less able-bodied contributors. The result is very possibly that we fall to famine; at the very least, certainly emotional famine, where overwhelming feelings obstruct goals and dreams from becoming reality. It is sounding

INTRODUCTION

similar to the movie, Soylent Green, a cult favorite in the Baby Boomer era, where our very existence is threatened. This is not just the death of some small, obscure aboriginal culture. Baby Boomers are still a force to "be reckoned with," in death as they were in life. In addition, like locusts, we have changed the landscape of the world, as we know it. It is happening again in our death. We have the power to change the direction to where it leads.

We Baby Boomers are dying. Our values, ideals as a culture are dying with us. Does that mean all the alternative ways of living will be lost, just as the Great Generation, our parents, are slowly vanishing from our children's memory? In addition, as we vanish are we taking our children's opportunity with us into the grave? Statistics show that after two generations have passed most of the plots in cemeteries have no visitors. When we read their epitaphs, no one knows who the people are or what they stood for in their lives. They have disappeared from memory. This is happening to us. Cultural Extinction is happening right here, right now.

CULTURAL EXTINCTION

Cultural Extinction is the destruction of the moral character, human behaviors, values, language, point of view, contributions, and skills of a culture. Just like animal and plant species in nature becoming extinct because they no longer can reproduce their kind, the Baby Boomers and all they stand for can be dust in the wind, as their bodies die off. For instance, the Great Generation, the parents of the Baby Boomers are slowly going extinct. Values like conscience, one's word being their bond, being a good citizen, rags to riches, frugality of resources, loyalty, and simplicity are often associated with the Great Generation. Many of these qualities are considered old fashioned and irrelevant to the present generation. The Great Generation and all that it represents are dying off into a cultural extinction. The Baby Boomers, who hold the memories of their parents values, are the ones that remember but are not carrying forward those values because they are not their own. Boomers redefined the values on their own terms. In so doing, there is no torchbearer to hand those values to the future generations. The same demise is certain for Boomers unless Baby Boomers redefine the last frontier: death and end-of-life.

The tables will turn soon. The small will rule the large, if they have the strength. The next few generations will be the 'David' wrestling with the Baby Boomer 'Goliath', the children of the Baby Boomers taking on the emotional litter of their parents.

The United States has never been quite sure on what to do with vanishing indigenous peoples. They have restricted them to reservations; have initiated programs to assimilate them into our dominant culture. These types of programs to assimilate were disasters and created people who were neither 'fish nor fowl'. They no longer fit into their ancestral culture, and are not accepted by the dominant culture either. Now assimilation by the dominant culture is no longer an option.

It seems like such a waste for all the Baby Boomer talk about equality, fairness, gender rights, race rights, children's rights, victim's rights, being ecologically responsible, etc., and yet they have not been fair to their children or their children's children by leaving an emotional mess for them to clean up. We have not been fair to our own. Rightfully, they will call us hypocrites. At our death, when our children must face independence and look back at Baby Boomers, they will call our Baby Boomer generation hypocrites that talked a good game, but didn't incorporate those same values and ideals for their own. Baby Boomer parents will leave their own children not only with the spoils of irresponsibility, but also without tools to handle it themselves and fix the emotional mess that was their inheritance. It is time to recognize the inevitable effect of mass dying on our children. Use our foresight for them, not just ourselves in our moment of finality. It is time for Baby Boomers to be fully responsible to the beliefs and values we supposedly lived. We need to leave a map, path, tools, and connection for our children and their children at the very least, to have a chance in their evolution. This 5 Step Guide to tie you to them is a good start to help our young.

Now that this dominant culture, the Baby Boomers, is dying, with it goes our cultural distinctness. Our own values will be unknown to children born two generations from the year 2025. People will remember Baby Boomers as material gluttons or self-indulgent cultural capitalists, rather than for changing values, introspectiveness, innovative in communication, science, or technology. Forgotten will be that Baby Boomers were risk takers in space and expansiveness, attention to the natural or ecological, and the demand for equanimity between gender and race, or for peace. Gone will be gratitude for the development of global cultural tolerance and curiosity outside our borders.

The Unknown And Forgotten

In Los Angeles under the crisscrossing of two to three major freeways resides The Chinese Cemetery. I found myself there when I lost my way and ended up on a dead end street. I noticed in this cemetery hundreds of headstones, two feet by three feet, nestled close together like shoeboxes, one after another. I looked to see the names and inscriptions. There were none. Not one of them had any name, date, or a mark of any kind in English or Chinese character. They were all the same, just a slab of stone.

I inched in between slabs, carefully, so as not to knock anything over with my shoe. I didn't want to be disrespectful stepping on someone's grave. However, there was no room between them. Finally, I noticed there on the top of the stone slab, chiseled on a thin strip was a date. No name. No birth. Just a date. Then close by, I found a small plaque further down at the end of the row. Evidently, these Chinese souls were the individuals that built the transcontinental railroad across the United States. Oftentimes they just died without anyone ever knowing their names. They died without anyone knowing who they were or what they stood for. They were nameless, faceless heroes that no one can thank for selflessly creating the transportation and means by which our country grew and thrived. There was no way to give these souls our attention and gratitude. They were nameless, faceless slabs.

Everyone deserves to be more than dust in the wind. We all carry magnificent light and unique gifts. It is up to each of us to say, "Thank you," to each other every day, not just at Thanksgiving. To recognize the individual gifts and contributions in another is to recognize it in us and in the unifying force of all that is, as well. As naïve as it sounds, when we give equal time and attention to the good of creation of mankind, of what we do well, instead of its destructive capability, there will be a wave of more good in the world and humanity just because we are looking for it. We will evolve our spiritual footprint within others and ourselves, too. As you look for the good of creation everyday, realize that right next to all creation is death. For every choice we make, there is a choice we let die. Therefore, at the same time notice the death that surrounds life, and the life that surrounds death. Intertwined with life is death. Just as Baby Boomers made their lives bold and unique, so, too, can they make their death and end-of-life unique.

In the case of those buried in the Chinese cemetery, no one will visit his or her grave. No one will know his or her gift or his or her spirit. Nevertheless, they gave of their lives for the greater good. Still, no one thanks them in history. This story horrified me. It made me sad. Their souls go to seed unnoticed. Yet we owe them so much. We could learn so much from them about integrity, commitment, tenacity, strength, loyalty, survival, and faith. Instead, they go anonymous for all they were and all they stood for in life. The silence will have to be the whisper of their legacy.

I wish that anonymity on no one. No individual. No group. No culture. It is a mental, emotional, physical, and spiritual reckless waste of human spirit and knowledge. That is one important reason to make sure, for oneself, to recycle at least one key bit of wisdom, character or value that we've distilled from our fully lived lives. That is the purpose of *Forget Me Knot A 5 Step Guide to Tie You to Them*. Stop the extinction of the Baby Boomer culture.

INTRODUCTION

WHAT'S THE HURRY? DEATH CAN WAIT!

As I previously said, more people will die in the next ten years than in all of history, more than the plague, the Holocaust, or any World War. The reason is the worldwide Baby Boomer bulge in our population. Statistics of death and debility start to mount, as Baby Boomers turn 50-years-old. Some form or another of grief and loss by death will touch young and old alike. Unlike the past when the experience of death was mostly a quick read in the obituaries section of the newspaper, it is not so right now.

To clarify, I am not advocating being "okay with death." The standard traditional emotional definition of death includes grief, denial, anger, shock, sadness, abandonment, paralysis, indigestibility of reality, sleeplessness, and heart angst for the living. There is nothing okay about any of those feelings. It feels like never ending torture when it happens to you. Yes, you and I have to go through them and feel those feelings in waves, some more intense than others at any given time.

However, death itself, for the dying, is another experience. We as a society have left death in the taboo arena where we deal with it on a 'need to know basis,' or as little as we possibly can and only when necessary, and by doing so we have left great riches there undiscovered. Wherever there is uncomfortable, disowned, ignored, disgust, revulsion, and dislike, this is also where great, powerful things are buried, and untouched in their original form. When we mine for minerals like gold, often we must go through caves and soil to reveal the gold. Under most taboo are great riches. Death is no different.

There is no 'okay' to expect or to desire about the physicality of death. It hurts terribly to lose those you have loved. However, if you separate all the expected natural, physical, and healing emotions that help the living to heal from loss and grief, you can see death in its own right, as a spiritual graduation, with meaning and expression. Death is a moment that brings you to the immediate present, in energy and with an infinite expanse of thought, as we know it. Only then can you enter the spiritual domain with the same opportunity as you did when you exited the birth canal at your beginning. You can have a different experience of death. The spiritual domain does not give you immunity from feeling what you must when death happens. However, the spiritual domain does give a larger more inclusive viewpoint that allows other emotions that also can give peace, calm, and even love, especially in death.

At this point, you are a salmon swimming upstream with the weight of the collective viewpoint about death and its finality. Your quest could be just to entertain the possibility that death can be more than a clump of fear, emotional pain, a horizon of unfathomable sadness, void, and destruction. That is the common point of view. It is a piece. It is not the whole. The possibility of experiencing the connection between life and death, and increasing your spiritual language before your own death is not only a possibility, it is an inevitability if you keep a spot of yourself open to something different about death and act in ways that support that possibility to be a fluent spiritual speaker.

THE BABY BOOMER REALITY STATISTICS

DEATH

There are 1.8 Baby Boomer deaths per second worldwide. Out of that number, every 49-58 seconds a Baby Boomer dies. In the last 24 hours 1,491 Boomers died, with the number rising. Only 6.6% of Boomers are dead and there are 77 million Baby Boomers still alive waiting to hear the silent steps. Now one out of every nine Americans is over 65 years of age. Americans have more 65-year-olds than the entire population of Canada. It is hard to believe that for the first time in history, people 65-years-old will outnumber children under the age of 5-years-old. In fact, there are more 65-year-olds worldwide than the entire population of Russia, Japan, France, Germany, and Australia combined. By the year 2030, out of 55 countries, 65+-year-olds will be 20% of the world's population. The majority of Boomers will be

INTRODUCTION

dead by the year 2025. Then the tsunami of death will start to subside. However, its effect will have repercussions for a very, very long time.[1]

As seconds and minutes pass emotionally, Baby Boomers are dying, leaving so much that is valuable and useful about themselves and their life left to be dust in the wind. Baby Boomers are not leaving a way to connect to their loved ones even after death, so they reinforce the idea that death is all about grief and loss, denial and abandonment. Boomers have an opportunity to redefine death, as society has known it. However, up until now death is just as it has always been, finality intertwined with grief, loss, and abandonment.

With the statistics known, we can no longer pretend we don't know. Those numbers are the realities for Baby Boomers. The diseases we are experiencing in our degrading bodies are heralding what is right up ahead for us. Our physical bodies are readying us for our transition. Heed the call. We cannot forestall the inevitable, but we can have a say in the process of how it is experienced and what will be the aftermath once we have gone. The numbers are the alarm clock. It is time to wake up. There is no snooze button to get a few more minutes of sleep. It is our time right now to proceed to the next and final stage of our evolution. We can harvest our bounty and can it for the next generations, or we can leave our bounty to die in the field because no one picked the fruit. It is up to us. Nevertheless, ready or not, the time has come to pay attention to the physical becoming the spiritual.

DISABILITY

If the promise of death is not overwhelming, the promise of debility is worse. Consider being alive, but a walking zombie with a body and no working mind. Think of President Ronald Reagan as an example of living with Alzheimer's. The expected life expectancy of most males is 78-years-old, and for females it is 82-years-old. Even though Boomers are aging, 74% look forward to retirement for freedom. That may be a fleeting opportunity. Surveys have found that the number one fear of Baby Boomers is the possibility of forgetting or losing their minds. Not financial ruin. Not cancer. Not heart disease.

It is the fear of mental decline and the potential development of dementia or Alzheimer's disease. These fears are not without reality. Chances are very good that Baby Boomers will not be able to avail themselves of that cherished freedom in retirement they so desire. Because one out of two Baby Boomers, or 10 million, will have Alzheimer's, and 24 million will have dementia. Most will receive a diagnosis of dementia or Alzheimer's in their lifetime. Alzheimer's is the fifth leading cause of death in 65+-year-olds, and 70% of 70-year-olds are dying of Alzheimer's.[2]

Can you honestly ask yourself if you were at your own day of reckoning, at your 82nd birthday today, if you would you pass your own personal litmus test about your best use of your life? Would you have been authentic to your own spirit and lived out your destiny in its fullness, as you had hoped that you would, as a respected and treasured elder? On the other hand, would you be dependent on others, becoming infantile in thought and deed, paused in God's waiting room just waiting for your turn to return to oneness and wholeness? Alternatively, would you take the opportunity to redefine death as you have known it, or as society has insisted you experience it? Now is the time to choose. You do not have to wait until you're 82-years-old. Who knows, you may not even live that long to ask that question. The time is now.

LONELINESS

It may now not be a matter of how long you live, but rather how quickly you die. It is not just being a walking zombie, but a dependant zombie yearning for the freedom of the afterlife. With the dismal statistics, it may be wiser to plan your farewells and funeral before weakening takes over your desires. If the theory called *Dunbar's Number* is true for the Baby Boomers, then it claims, at the most, the number of relationships, including family, friends and acquaintances, any one human can handle is only 150 people in their life. This is because the neurons of the brains limit the number of connections one can make. If that is true, then by 63-years old Baby Boomers will have only 2/3 of those relationships left. That

INTRODUCTION

means, for most of us 67 people will be at our funeral, if you are the average guy, and 75-years-old at death. Slim, lonely pickings! There will be 67 mourners at your funeral to carry on the core meaning of your life the way you would want them to remember you.[3]

Not only do your relationships dwindle in number as you approach death, but often the quality and frequency of your connections with loved ones become diluted in the physical experience of them because, naturally, you have less physical energy to respond to others as you approach death. Your living loved ones, seeing your reduced energy, pace, intensity, and inability, often don't know how to connect or adjust. They remember having had a close relationship with you in the past. It makes them uncomfortable to be with you, the dying as you move toward death. They want to remember you in vitality not in degradation. When you are dying, your loved ones don't know what to say or how to handle the time spent with you. They feel helpless. It also makes them think of their own mortality, and that is scary. It brings up all kinds of fear about death.

Many of your loved ones avoid you as you approach death, because as you are close to death, it can make them uncomfortable or guilty around you. The things they have in common with you are harder to access and enjoy. Somehow, it feels like there is an estrangement with you, a loss of how it was before when you had more in common with them. All this is felt but unsaid, creating loneliness. Loneliness is the biggest blight of the aging; possibly because the living loved ones don't know how to relate. When the dying feel more and more alone, they start to get more introspective. As you approach death you review your life, when there is no one with whom to connect. Loneliness is the result. It can be a sign of emotional death before the body has become ready for transition at the end of life. The life review begins when one is lonely. It is one more step closer to the finality of death. If you wonder, you have only to visit an 'old people's home' or an assisted living facility to see for yourself.

Sorry to be the bearer of bad news. If you are not dead, then you might have lost your mind. If you haven't lost your mind, you might have a big problem with memory. Therefore, any way you look at the equation, it equals loneliness.

SUBSTANCE ABUSE

Death cancels all engagements. Death is in your face if you are a Baby Boomer. Eighty million Baby Boomers face death of parents or a spouse. Of that, 5 million will be suffering long-term grief and loss that goes with death and divorce. One in 6 of those adults are binge drinkers, and are often more likely than any other age group to suppress feelings of some of the loss of family and friends with alcohol. The alcohol use increases cognitive decline and memory loss. Therefore, we go full circle with dementia again. Eight million older adults exhibit substance abuse symptoms, 1/3 of which are older adults over the age of 65 years, addicted to some form of substance due to the challenge in life transitions. These Boomers attempt to cope with loss by abusing alcohol or medications. There is no more "Peace-Love-and-Happiness" any more, is there?[4]

Gertrude was a character at 75-years-old. She loved her Newport cigarettes and her beehive hairdo, which was touched up platinum blonde, teased, and lacquered every Thursday at the beauty shop, come rain or shine. She was a devout Republican with strong political opinions and an animal lover. She always said, "I love animals better than people." She had her old, small, wiry terrier with an aging white snout called Zandra that she carried everywhere she went. She kept Zandra in her lap as she wheeled around in her wheelchair.

One day, Gertrude fell asleep mid-day in her wheel chair. This wasn't a catnap. It was after her fourth martini, a chain of 'smoked to the filter' half pack of cigarettes, and two doses of tranquilizers. It happened to be Martin's and her anniversary. He had died suddenly with a widow maker heart attack three years prior. She was devastated. The grief had just been too great to bear. After his passing, her spunk and spirit became morose and hermit-like. The only interaction she had with the outside world was her Thursday hair appointment. When Gertrude fell from sleep to coma, Zandra

INTRODUCTION

nudged her mistress. She barked and barked. Zandra went to the windows where the couch bumped up against the wall and screeched a pleading bark for help. No one came. No one helped. 'Leave me alone,' had been Gertrude's request, heeded by family and friends. When the postman saw the build up of mail in Gertrude's mailbox, he called the police. Gertrude had died in her wheelchair 2 weeks prior. Zandra, having had no food or water for 2 weeks lied on her lap, head nestled under a stiff pale cold hand, also had passed along with her. It was a very sad story.

The life stopping grief that Gertrude experienced will not be the exception in the next 10 years. It will be the norm. Those closest to those who die, the spouses of many years will be affected the most. Many of them will turn to medication to numb the pain, loss, and grief. In addition, with the self-medicating for emotional relief, some of them will die, too. To die from a broken heart is a death that stretches our very being to a breaking point. This *Forget Me Knot 5 Step Guide* gives the tools so that there is a connection of heart beyond the physical body. Had Gertrude used some of the steps in this book, she could have felt Martin around her all the time. Maybe he wouldn't be there in physical form with all the little cues. Nevertheless, his essence would surround her and comfort her. He would trigger her sense of love and understanding. Gertrude did not have tools, a map, or a path. Gertrude fell through the grief cracks of life. It does not need to happen this way.

ACCIDENTS

If dementia or Alzheimer's, substance abuse or loneliness don't get you, once you are over 65-years-old, and you still think you have a little "Harley" left in you, think again. More and more motorcycle riders over the age of 40-years-old are dying in motorcycle crashes as they try to regain their youth and freedom of days gone by.[5]

Gary, a 67-year-old supervisor in a transcontinental oil pipe company took up motorcycle riding after his life-threatening bout with melanoma. He joined a club and faithfully shined his baby with Meguiars wax. His touring Harley was a midnight blue with fringe hanging off the leather seat. He would play '60's and '70's tunes on his souped-up surround sound, every Saturday while he waxed. He took pride in his Harley. He decided to buy one after reading the Douglas Adams book, *The Hitchhiker's Guide to the Galaxy*. This particular day he was riding with his riding club on one of the winding back roads around Yosemite, California. The scenery and smells were hypnotizing. The fall colors were hard to match. As the curve came up on the right, Gary took it a little wide and crossed over the middle yellow line just a tad too much. At the same time, in the opposite direction came a fire engine red Mini Cooper at a rapid downhill speed. They clashed in a blink. Gary saw everything in slow motion as his motorcycle hit the Mini Cooper and his body flew up over the car 40 feet into the bushes, camouflaging the edge of a deep ravine. Bones crunched and blood spurted. Gary lost consciousness. After many surgeries and medical therapies, Gary went back to work to finish out his last 2 years until retirement. He sold his motorcycle and now sits in his recliner, with his remote, watching *The Grand Prix Speedway* on television. Gary felt older and sadder, but he was glad to be alive to see his grandchildren.

FIRE DEATHS

Try as they might, as they try to rekindle the romance in their lives with candles and warm fireplace hearths, the rate of home fire deaths are twice the national average for people over the age of 65 years, and three times that for 75-year-olds. That is 32% of Baby Boomers dying of fire deaths. Add to that the fact the Boomer may not even remember they lit the stove in the first place! So much for the idea of bringing back that lovin' feeling.[6]

Sonia, 65-years-old and Lithuanian born, had been a looker in her day. She had the curves, cleavage, and the long eyelashes to prove that she could make many a head turn. One day, she was at her community watering hole, *The Valley Inn*, where everybody knows your name, your political persuasion, and your favorite drink. Though most of the regulars were retired, Sonia prided herself on the fact she could pass for a woman 10 years younger, and would exercise her skill in

INTRODUCTION

attracting the younger men. This particular evening she 'went fishing' with a younger attractive man, Steven. At *The Valley Inn*, there was no smoking in the bar. Therefore, people who smoked would have to move outside of the bar to have a cigarette.

Sonia went outside to have a smoke with Steven, a paralegal from a prestigious law firm. She and Steven started to light up a cigarette. Sonia bummed a smoke and put it to her glossy red lips. Steven tried to light her cigarette as a gentleman might. However, the lighter did not spark a flame. He flicked and he flicked. Nevertheless, he was unable to 'flick his Bic' lighter for Sonia. It was then the accident happened. Sonia offered to make the Bic lighter produce a flame. Sonia took the lighter between her long red lacquered fingernails and, voila, produced a flame. Unfortunately, Sonia had on a polyester flowery blouse that had feminine frills on the cuffs, round the collar and down the front horizontally, hiding the buttons. The spark from the Bic lighter flew onto Sonia's frills and caught fire. The polyester fabric was like gasoline. The fire took hold quickly and flamed up into Sonia's face burning the tissues of her face and hair. Sonia almost died from that fire. To this day, her beautiful face is but a scarred memory, even after multiple operations to restore her looks. Now, Sonia sends old photos of herself to the soldiers in Afghanistan. She flirts with them via letters. The soldiers think they are pen pals with a younger woman their own age that has all the right stuff. Sonia carries on her charade, even though she is maimed and disabled. It is her secret and her link to the part of herself she loved most.

BLIND OR DIMINISHED VISIONS

To make things worse and reinforce the seriousness of the plight of Baby Boomers who yearn for the freedom of their youth in retirement, one in three Americans have some sort of vision loss or become legally blind by 65-years-old. It is especially noticeable in the 85+-year-olds. That is before anyone knows the long-term effects of laser surgery, especially if one has cataracts! There is a lessened ability to cope with activities of daily living when blind. Freedom and autonomy fly out the window, replaced by dependence and depression.[7]

Ninety six-year-old George, a retired attorney, self-defined pack rat, and information junkie found himself blind after taking a drug for his heart arrhythmias. George was on a cruise to Alaska. He was to disembark from the ship in Juneau and he saw a black shade drop half-mast over one of his eyes slowly, until he could not see any longer in that eye. He flew home immediately, only to find out he had damage to the optic nerve and he would not be able to see in the one eye. George continued his arrhythmia medication as prescribed.

Meanwhile in Canada, the drug company that made this drug had sent letters to doctors claiming that the drug could cause blindness in some patients. They had not sent this letter to doctors in the United States. George's doctor did not have a clue the drug he had been prescribing for 35 years could cause blindness. Therefore, he did not stop George from taking the medication. Three weeks later, George lost the vision in the other eye. Several months later, the doctors in the United States received the letter about the drug's capability of causing blindness.

George sat for years in his apartment among his stacks of unreadable newspapers dated over 15 years. He did not want to throw them away in case the medical profession found a cure for his blindness. George tried to get legal representation to sue the drug company for medical malpractice. However, because of the laws that limit malpractice to $200,000 judgments, no attorney would take his case. They said the resources of the drug company would far exceed the payment of the $200,000, so it would cost George more to try the case than the benefit he might receive. The drug company did not want to have a judgment that would open a can of worms for other patients who also lost their sight from the arrhythmia drug. How ironic that the very place George had worked his whole life to achieve justice could not provide justice for one of his or her own.

Cost Of Dying

Death industry businesses loom like vultures over Baby Boomers. They are the ones who are seeing the oncoming tsunami of death.

INTRODUCTION

It is big money to the embalming companies, casket manufacturers, florists, cosmetic companies, automobile industries, cemetery associations, insurance agencies, tombstone manufacturers, and funeral homes. The average cost of a funeral without the added cost of the funeral plot is $6,500. A plot on Craigslist averages $1,000. In Japan, 98% of the Japanese have cremation, because the average cost of a Japanese funeral is $40,000. In Britain, 72% of the British have cremations and in America, 32% of Americans have cremations. There are 22,500 cemeteries across the United States for those who want to have a burial in the ground.

The cost of dying makes many people angry because some say there are those in the funeral industry that exploit the grieving loved ones, by taking advantage of the vulnerability of their grief and loss. The protective internal censor the grieving usually have when they are not in grief and are able to comparison shop, does not operate when in the shock of loss. Many who are grieving, maybe even feeling guilty, want to spend more than they can afford to make up for their perceived faults to the deceased. Though not always true, to many it looks and feels like people in the death business who make their income from the dying are looked at as vultures nourishing themselves off the flesh or carcass of the dead. In the coming years, the death industry will be exponential in its reach, because there will be a need for services surrounding the end-of-life.

Because of the stigma of death, planning, and looking ahead to make passage easier on our loved ones it is not a popular subject. We do not like to plan for death. Somehow we think when we plan for death we affirm its existence, and in so doing subconsciously give permission for death to enter our life. The fear of dying stops us in our tracks. The funeral industry is lumped into that same category of our minds to avoid, deny, and pretend it will never happen to us or to anyone we know and love. We believe that until it is proved to us, the idea of death just isn't so.

When you add it all up, after 65-years-old you will be deaf, dumb, blind, burned, drunk, high, broke, or dead. When you decide you want to leave more to those you leave behind than your money, statistics, your biography, or your resume for your obituary, then think what a difference you can make to those that come after you. Therefore, the time is now to think about finding the meaning of your life and leaving it for your next of kin and those generations that come after you.

As the common quote says, "The only thing you can be sure of is death and taxes." Death is inevitable. Statistics or not, the method of your exit is unknown, but the fact that you will leave this earth is certain.

FORGET ME KNOT INSPIRATION

Once you plan your Forget Me Knot core life message as described in this guide, with one inspirational message you can relax, breathe easy, and just let the destiny of your life take its course. You will be able to reinforce your core life meaning in every way you can to the people who will be delighted to carry forward the best of you. In so doing it will be making you immortal.

In this way, you get to put the lid on your own pot, the punctuation mark on your own life sentence, the Wikipedia entry in your own life's work, or the last nail in your own coffin. On the other hand, you can leave it to the clergy to weigh in on your share of the Seven Deadly Sins versus the Seven Heavenly Virtues. Not only may you be possibly misunderstood or remembered wrongly, but also your wise core life legacy will be dust in the wind. You can also let the kids or your siblings describe the dash between the dates of your birth and death dates, from their own eyes, experience, and opinion of you. However, you also risk the possibility of the true you being lost in the ethers with no real sense of the meaning of your life for the generations to come in your family line. Your funeral might end up sounding more like an obituary entry, a resume, curriculum vitae, or even a roast.

Further, if your last bit of wisdom is finished, and translated into a one-liner, you can start bonding it to your most important meaningful loved ones right now. It will make it easier on your passing.

INTRODUCTION

In summary, we are entering a period where we are ill prepared for the tsunami of death and debility that is coming our way. We can no longer keep it in the taboo whispers, the offices of trained psychotherapists, or blogs of catharsis. We need facts, tools, maps, and strategies. We need to see how to weave it into our lives, include it as part of our life rituals and passages so that we waste not one ounce of wisdom, lesson, or value from the dying individuals that might have garnered true meaning in their life.

We can harvest the life meaning of the Baby Boomers and the few remaining great generation souls that will pass over in the next ten years, so the generations to come can navigate their way with valuable tools and a map in a world that has become more and more solitary, isolating, and complex in a digital social network.

WHAT IS A CORE INSPIRATIONAL LIFE MESSAGE?

A core inspirational life message is one thought, idea, or saying that encompasses what made you 'tick'. It comes from the lessons of adversity, hard work, character, and values. It can be a proverb, quote, 'ism', oxymoron, saying, endearment, definition, mantra, theme, song verse, movie line, sound, poem, etc. One line of wisdom that is the most important thing a Baby Boomer wants personally to be the way people remember him or her. It should be wisdom for those that come after him/her. It is a crumb on the path of life for others to find their way home to heart and character. It is a way to recycle and pass the torch of goodness that came from surviving life's trials and tribulations.

WHY DO I NEED A CORE INSPIRATIONAL LIFE MESSAGE?

We need a core inspirational life message of wisdom to leave a legacy. We need to know we mattered and what we lived mattered. We have to know that the every day man or woman needs to leave his or her mark with clues on how to get through life's erosion of the spirit. Everyone who has breathed has a core inspirational life message. It is a distillation of the essence of us, and our meaning on earth.

One of my mentors, Dr. Sidney Yudin, a Medical Doctor turned Herbalist, was in a prisoner of war camp during WWII. During that time, he learned all about herbs all over the world and their healing capabilities: Chinese, Native American, South American, German, etc. He was such a wizard when it came to healing and herbal medicine that he received what was equivalent to the Nobel Peace Prize in herbal medicine. He was brilliant. He could just as much look at you and know what herbal preparation you would need. He founded *Little Herb Company* and educated western and holistic doctors on how to use herbs in their practice. It was his life's work. Dr. Yudin came up with an herbal formula to treat HIV and AIDS using an herbal medicine protocol, before the drug cocktails were even available. His formula was amazingly effective in reducing the disease to be asymptomatic in patients. It was almost too good to be true. Dr. Yudin himself eventually died of stomach cancer after having successfully lived with an animal stomach transplant for many years.

Dr. Yudin taught me many things. However, the one that had a wide spread life long implication happened one fall day when I confronted Dr. Yudin. I had been treating a patient for thrush in the mouth and systemic Candida as one of the steps in her treatment of chronic fatigue syndrome. The patient not only got well, but her whole outlook, attitude, and zeal for life changed at its very core. I was amazed. I couldn't believe that these herbs would have an overall effect on the essence and demeanor of my patients.

I said, "Dr. Yudin, you did not tell me that these herbal formulas would have a May Pole effect, where all the ancient symptoms would dance around and shift my patients at the very core!"

Dr. Yudin, peered over his black horn-rimmed, coke-bottle thick glasses and said, "Aviva, always remember, the answer is always within 25 miles of the problem."

I looked at him quizzically. "Dr. Yudin, do mean that when you are bitten by a snake that the antidote is within 25 miles of where you have been bitten? Or are you talking about the emotional effect?"

INTRODUCTION

Dr. Yudin just lifted his eyebrows, smiled, and turned around to leave, leaving me with my own conundrum to prove for myself.

To this day, I call it "The Ruby Red Slipper Effect." Our answers are always close at hand, right under our nose, or under our slippers, if we can just change the way we look at things. Dr. Yudin's Ruby Red Slipper wisdom gave me the courage to keep searching for a medical answer even when things looked impossible, incurable, and very bleak to say the least.

His wisdom gave me the tenacity to take on very difficult patients, even very sick babies. Because now, from my own experience, I know that the answer is always within 25 miles of the problem. I thank you, Dr. Yudin. Your wisdom continues into the hearts and minds of my readers. In this way, Dr. Yudin and all that he is and stands for lives on in the world even though he has long since passed away. While you did not know the herbal wizard, Dr. Yudin, now you do know about his tenacity, his optimism, his creativity, and his willingness to express and share his wisdom. I cannot look at a plant now without thinking of this gifted man. He left his mark in me and on humanity.

How Is It Different From An Epitaph, Obituary, Or Eulogy?

A core inspirational life message is a personal choice. It is our own personal ten commandments rolled up into one. It is our nickname and trigger to let others know to pay attention in their lives; that the wisdom we impart would be appropriate for them in that very moment. The core inspirational life message is our voice, our connection with the living. It is the telephone lines for our own emotional and spiritual life across the ethers from the dead and gone to the living. It breathes life, not stagnancy. It is portable and is for anywhere, any time. It is not in past tense. It is in present tense with applicability in the now.

I remember a famous epitaph of a known hypochondriac who died and was buried in a Florida cemetery. The epitaph read, "I told you

I was sick." We laugh and find the epitaph unique and funny. If the deceased wanted to make sure we remember her sense of humor and use it when we least want to laugh at serious moments, then she has left her message, motto, and premise to all those who read her epitaph. She keeps herself and her message alive when tours of the cemetery bring her story to life for visitors. Most epitaphs do not have that skill to embody the message of their life on an epitaph.

Ask yourself if it is enough for family and friends to remember you as a "beloved wife, mother, and sister"? You can probably find hundreds of thousands of epitaphs that have that same worded epitaph on their grave. Nevertheless, what else makes the souls that lay beneath that epitaph unique from all others? What else would these souls want the generations that come after them to remember so when they most needed it, the future generations could have a bit of wisdom from you, for a successful life, and feel prepared to meet life head on? Having a generic motto to cut, copy, or paste on any number of dead souls' graves robs the deceased of their opportunity to stand out in death. In many ways, such a generic definition of the dead is no different from being a nameless, faceless gravesite, with no differentiation, not too unlike those buried in The Chinese Cemetery.

WHY ISN'T IT MY LOVED ONES' RESPONSIBILITY?

You can leave it to the living to surmise what your core inspirational life message is. Very often relationships that were clean, pure, and involved in your life can easily come up with your core inspirational life message. In addition, if you were repeating your mantra, your theme your whole life long, it will not be hard for the living to understand what you stood for. Nevertheless, even in those instances, the living will not have the symbol or trigger, or spiritual ringtone to let them know you are calling with your core inspirational life message. Assuming you know is not the same as knowing for sure what another wants. Most of us have many gifts. Our loved ones may not know which ones to choose, or even choose the wrong one of which we did not want to be known for in perpetuity.

INTRODUCTION

WHAT DOES IT TAKE TO MAKE A ONE-LINER?

It does not take long. It is quite simple, and it is free. It is actually fun. It doesn't usually cost anything but a little effort of attention and introspection. The possibilities are endless; you can choose ideas from entertainment, books, magazines, newspapers, television, movies, songs, or the Internet. It does not mean you have to be a writer or a brainy university graduate. It means you just have to have passion and certainty, and the intuition to recognize what is just like you, even if it is just the polar opposite of you.

WHAT IF IT WON'T COME OUT RIGHT?

In this simple guide, each step builds on the next. Anyone can do it. It usually is quite revealing and gratifying to know what makes us tick. It feels good. There is no single correct core life message that fits you. What matters is what YOU think is the core life message that you want your great-great-great grandchildren to know even if they don't know what your face looked like.

WILL I LOOK STUPID OR FEEL EMBARRASSED?

A core inspirational life message makes you look like a wise sage. It will reveal to your loved ones that your life had meaning and that they understood it. It will be the weaving of your own emotional DNA, done your way. You will look smart because you will be speaking the language of character that all of humanity has spoken since the beginning of time.

Many cultures have traditions that may seem absurd to outsiders in other parts of the world. For instance, in parts of China, parents will find single deceased mates for their deceased single adult children. The parents will advertise for dead mates and offer dowries. The will have a real wedding for their deceased loved ones with all the wedding works: flowers, music, clergy, etc. The idea behind this wedding after death is to marry them off. They believe that by marrying their dead children, the souls of these children will not haunt the parents in their homes and their lives. Once the children are married off, they will give peace to their souls and a new home for their deceased children's soul to reside. Now, this may seem odd to us, but it is perfectly logical and honorable to the Chinese culture.

Another example of cultural differences in death customs is the burying tradition of the dead in a certain area of the Philippines. They bury their dead in caskets that hang on the shear vertical decline on the side of the cliff at the ocean's edge. The wooden caskets hang on a vertical shear in open air, not underground. This may seem strange to you but for the people of the Philippines it is an honorable tradition. Something may seem absurd to some and sacred to another. It is subjective as to what is stupid or what makes one embarrassed. If it makes sense to you and fits your perspective of the world, then it is your signature on the lives and loved ones left behind.

WHY DOES THIS NEED TO BE DONE IN ADVANCE?

It is best to complete your Forget Me Knot message in advance. The sooner, you complete it, the better. Better because you have more memory the younger you are. Better because you can shave away the unimportant and irrelevant themes in your life and concentrate on reinforcing what makes you tick with every relationship you make in your life from that moment onward. Better because you brand yourself your way for as long as you are able. We will sing a song by heart more easily the more often we have heard it or sung it aloud. Your core inspirational life message is no different. It is the pledge of allegiance to your own flag.

WHAT WILL MY LOVED ONES THINK OF IT?

Your loved ones will love you even more for knowing what makes you, YOU. It will be your signature. They will reinforce it while you are living, right now. They become your present day foot soldiers for your core inspirational life message. You can see the result of your life message on the living, hence you will receive the rewards now.

INTRODUCTION

It will make them feel good that they 'get you', and they can serve you in their own way, even if it is not an exchange of the tangible material kind. It is far more powerful when there is an exchange of the intangibles; where others will put their attention and actions. It is an act of love to translate the core life message of someone you love dearly, explaining it to another to keep the flame of life in the message. It is contagious. It is the original viral methodology.

Imagine a world that looks like the Christmas movie, *It's a Wonderful Life*. Imagine a world that never knows what hard-earned pearls of wisdom and experience that helped you through many of your adversities. What will happen if your pearls of wisdom are able to help future generations in your family line? Future generations could benefit from your pearls, helping them as much as it helped you. Imagine that not all the hardship you endured was in vain. The future generations will thank you, praise your name, and remember you in their everyday life. In a way, you will become immortal in your family line by remaining fresh in their minds and hearts. The other benefit of leaving a core inspirational life message or motto is it is a healing link for your immediate loved ones. It is your very closest loved ones who grieve and need an intimate connection to you in the first months of your passing. Having a core inspirational life message or motto provides a type of security blanket for them to feel your presence and it softens the shock, even when you are in the hereafter. A core inspirational life message helps to make your transition to a different reality just a little bit easier.

We all know the meaning of empty, void, grief, and loss at death. We can do nothing and have more of the same heaviness. On the other hand, we can look at death anew. The choice is yours. I look forward to the day when we all know there is still a spiritual connection to those we love even if their physical body is no longer with us. I look forward to more people speaking the spiritual language of character, values, and love in their everyday lives.

DON'T MY TRIUMPHS SPEAK FOR THEMSELVES?

In this *Forget Me Knot* 5 step guide, you are not your achievements or your triumphs. You are who you are, not by what you chose, but by what you did NOT choose. It is the part of you left behind that becomes the fossils of who you are, what you chose to live, and what you choose to let die. It is the carving of your spirit. Your core life message is not a curriculum vitae, a resume, a medal of honor, a Boy Scout badge, or a job title in a company. It is what you said NO to when push came to shove. It is where you delineated your being and your signature. Nor does your adversity define you. We all have adversities, many of them the same. It is the choices you did NOT make that made you who you are today when adversity hit. It is the NOTs and the NOs of your life that define you, not what sits for the world to see in the sunshine. Your truth lives in the dark and the forgotten shadows of your life that you had to face solo in the narrows of your life.

CAN YOU GIVE ME SOME EXAMPLES?

In this guide, there are examples throughout the 5 steps. You will not be left behind. In the story of my own mother that I shared in the Foreword, she is just one example. Even with this book, all the readers will be foot soldiers for my mother's core life message: "Don't be a sheep. Be a shepherd." Or, "To thine own self be true and thy can be false to no man."

Because I have shared her message with you it will now come up for you readers when you see a feather and realize that when it gets really hard to be a tall poppy in the flat ground cover of life, try to stretch even higher toward the sun. You, the reader, know that I am the foot soldier for my own mother's core life message by sharing the unique, new concepts about Baby Boomer legacies at end-of-life, even when the subject seems gruesome, scary, and dark to most people.

INTRODUCTION

WHY SHOULD YOU TRUST ME?

I have used some of the principles used in Homeopathy in this *Forget Me Knot* 5 step guide, though the principles are changed and molded for the end-of-life. As a Homeopath, I see each patient as a magnificent creature of nature, just like the remedies I use everyday. My curiosity is aroused and I marvel at the way patients have escorted their spirit through their life. Their answers, responses, ideas, feelings, expressions, and experiences are amazing, even in disease and ill health. I would not want any of these human creatures to go extinct without leaving their wisdom and healing behind, for the rest of us, just like all the remedies in my pharmacy.

In some ways, each of us, you and me, we are walking, talking remedies for each other with a healing and catalyzing force. Some of your relationships heal, while others amplify your strengths or weaknesses. Some people even instigate a response within you. However, in all the years of medical practice, I have seen many human beings face adversity on the mental, emotional, physical, and spiritual levels. Like their counterparts, plant, animal, and mineral, they lived to 'tell the tale' and to become a healing agent to mankind. I do not want to see each one of us become dust in the wind, with all that healing capability lost and mixed into matter in nature once again. I would like to extract the essence of our spirit, before our physical bodies degrade, and let the essence of our spirit be healing, in its own right, for those human beings left behind.

Unlike what we Homeopaths have available to us in books like the *Materia Medica* and the *Repertory*, you and I do not have a book on the healing capability of man's spirit as a remedy. So it is with this *Forget Me Knot* 5 step guide that I hope for each of us, individually, to define just what we have healed within ourselves, and to offer that to others, even generations that come later, ones we have never known. I believe man can make his own vibrant *Materia Medica*, defining the healing of his spirit that has come about for him from adversity, predator, prey, weather, erosion, catastrophe, war, disease, pollution, and mostly from man himself.

It is in this vein that I write this *Forget Me Knot* 5 step guide. I have a vision for us all to leave the best of ourselves behind, as our healing essence, and never go extinct. Instead of what Homeopaths call a "Delusion" from which we prescribe remedies, I believe you can prescribe on your "Core Life Message" as the healing component and essence of yourself. You are the only person that will ever truly know what your own healing essence is to leave behind for humanity.

Read further to Step 1 and discover the patterns of your life that have been evolving since you were born. It will be an eye opener that your destiny is so clear from this bird's eye view of your life. Step 1 allows you to be introspective and observing at the same time. It feels good to know you are that clear to yourself. It will give you peace and purpose for your life.

1. http://www.agingstats.gov
2. http://www.alz.org
3. Dunbar, R.I.M. (1992). "Neocortex size as a constraint on group size in primates" Journal of Human Evolution 22 (6) 469-493
4. http://www.ncadd.org
5. http://www.ncbi.nlm.nih.gov
6. http://www.cdc.gov
7. http://www.cdc.gov

INTRODUCTION

When you are finished reading *Forget Me Knot*, in 5 steps:
- You will know just what three main life choices influenced your core life message.
- You will know the way you respond best to the world through thought, feelings, doing, or envisioning.
- You will know which of the five senses leads your life experience.
- You will have a one-liner, core life message.
- You will have an everyday life symbol trigger that you can use to anchor and match your core life message.
- You will have a multimedia Life-o-graphic™ that 'glues' your core life message to their hearts and minds.

Forget Me Knot's 5 steps are one method to prevent the extinction of the best of the Baby Boomer era. It is a type of character autopsy so that each and every Baby Boomer can select the one most important bit of wisdom he/she would like to pass on to others to make sure the life lessons are recycled for others who come after us.

The **5 Steps** are:
- **Step 1 Life Segments**: 9-year life cycles, decisions and patterns.
- **Step 2 Life Decisions**: Chosen & Unchosen at three major ages: 27 years, 54 years, and 81 years.
- **Step 3 Life Responses**: Thinker, Feeler, Doer, Dreamer, and the 5 Senses.
- **Step 4 Life Pattern Anchor & Trigger**: One-liner of wisdom and an everyday trigger symbol.
- **Step 5 Life-o-graphic™**: 9-year patterns of choices with a core life message in a multimedia format.

Forget Me Knot
5 Step Guide
To Tie You To Them

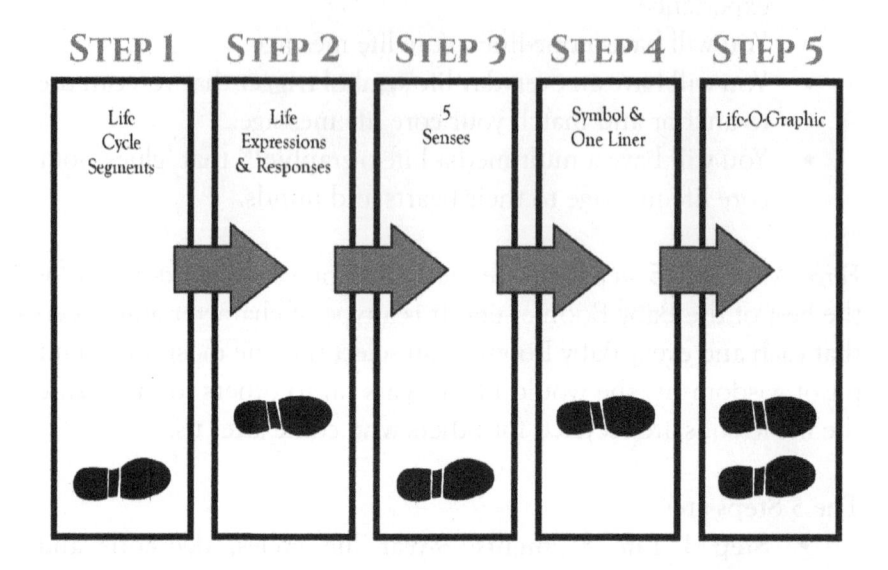

STEP 1	STEP 2	STEP 3	STEP 4	STEP 5
Life Cycle Segments	Life Expressions & Responses	5 Senses	Symbol & One Liner	Life-O-Graphic

He who is free of faults will never die.

CHAPTER 1: STEP 1

Your Thread And Life Pattern

Your life has a thread and a pattern from beginning to end. It is what makes you tick. It is how people understand who you are and how to relate to you. We all have a pattern. If we follow that pattern backwards from today to birth, we can see where and when the major decisions were made and not made that reinforced this pattern. This pattern goes with you wherever you go. It is part of every memory, every decision, and every response. It is the fingerprint of your being. How and where you use it will make you feel like your existence had value and you mattered. It is your core life message. It is your motto, your personal proverb, and your 'ism'. A core life message is with you when you hit the turmoil of adversity, groan from growing pains, delight in curiosity, or focus on introspection. You look through these 'rose colored glasses' when you must make any choice. At life's end, your message is clear as a bell.

You Are Already Famous In Your Own Mind

You don't have to be famous to leave your mark, byline, postscript, and fingerprint on your life for the living left behind at your passing. You don't have to have had degrees, medals, or honors, either. You just need to be you. In fact, you have an advantage over celebrities and other famous people. You don't have to fight the idea that you do not match your "public" face, like famous people do. You have one face, your face. Oh, you have a personality that doesn't always reveal your vulnerable place that you share with your nearest and dearest. Nevertheless, even your personality has connection to the inner core life pattern of you. Not so with the famous; imagine being type cast like actors. Frequently, they have played a role so well or so long, people look at them as that character everywhere they go, in their work and real life, too. It frustrates many actors.

Take for instance, the actor Larry Linville, in the series M*A*S*H as Major Frank Burns. He was a very well read intelligent man, but he could not get any part that did not have the same personality as Major Frank Burns, a man who masks his serious shortcomings with his superiority and dismissive attitude toward others. Paparazzi and exploitive magazine journalists follow people who attain fame, fortune, and accolades, to look for the holes and missteps of their public face. Your advantage is being remembered, in your family's memories, for what and who you want to be. The road to your core life message is cleaner and clearer than the famous, which must honor both their public and private face. Anytime you split your will, something dies. Inevitable, for the famous, what dies is the authentic part of themselves that only very few get to see. People remember the famous for being someone they were not.

Anyone who knows me in any of the hats that I wear, knows that I love the simple, authentic individual truths we all live by. I am not so concerned with whether the truths you live by are right for the masses, but if it is right for you, it inspires me that you put your mark, expression, and light on that idea or truth, however it comes out. My curiosity and delight is to see what you did with that truth in your own life.

That is one reason I have always been charmed with Dr. Seuss. I cannot tell you how many times I light up with joy when I meet a patient for the first time. It is as if I see the original light in them that they were born with, and that which they walk around with, as if they have their own movie marquis, in lights. These same patients may be coming to me for some difficult disease or impeding symptom, but the light they carry is undeniable to me. Therefore, if I had to say I had an 'ism', I would say it might be something I remember Dr. Seuss saying so simply, "You are you. Now, isn't that pleasant?"

Oh, I have had judgment, gossip, and taken things personally, but this undeniable light supersedes that humanness we all share. It is sheer bliss recognizing that special and unique light and its expression in each one of us. It is the reason I have written this book. I do not want that special light, which holds your core life message, to flicker out for anyone. I want that core life message sustained in you, as well as fueled to new heights when others take it on and carry it forward. In this next step, you will discover how to find that core life message in that spectacular light you carry; your motto, personal proverb, and your 'ism'. It is a fun and delightful journey. I know you will agree after our time together.

Core Life Message

Your core life message is the premise, the principal, and the point of your life. It is your motto. You made many of your life choices by this yardstick, and it is the compass to determine the direction of your life, as you know it.

When you know your personal core life message it is often hard to tell where you stop and your core life message starts, and where you begin and it ends. The roots of you grow around your core life message in a symbiotic manner. It is your reason to believe, and the default by which you make choices in your life. Your core life message is a closely held belief or impression that you firmly maintain, despite contradiction by others, or what some consider generally accepted as common, valid, or even rational. Your core life message is what 'floats your boat', 'blows your hair back', or gives you 'the willies or goose bumps' on your skin.

We all have a core life message, not taught to us, but we do learn it. It can come from trial and error, watching others' mistakes or victories, reading, listening, and modeling behavior. Your core life message becomes your beacon or cursor of your life. It gives you your bearings in life when you have no sense of your environment or the situation or relationship is unclear. You have tested your core life message repeatedly. When you use your core life message, it seems to put the world right for you. You count on your core life message to help you navigate and make sense of your life. It has an intangible quality that needs no investment on your part. It just seems like it is and always has been.

Your core life message is an automatic part of your living. You probably never gave much attention to exactly what it is and how it ever became your guiding light. It just was. In this step, I break it down. You can see how it evolved and how it got ingrained and reinforced to become your core life message. You will finish this step knowing the pattern and the premise of your life. In addition, you will know what you want others to gain by using the same premise in their lives to gain value just as you did in yours.

My beloved mother, Rita Marie, had a core life legacy message, "Don't be a sheep, be a shepherd." She lived those words in her own life because no matter what adversity she faced, she was a leader with a guiding light. She made a decision and stood by those decisions until completed. My mother was a foster child, thrown from foster home to foster home, witnessing and experiencing horrible things; things no child should either witness or experience. However, it did not make her a hooligan, or taint the purity of her core life message. Oh, it could have, and many others have said it should have put a shadow on her heart. My mother learned her core life message from the underbelly of life. She wanted to see the expression of her core light in spite of the shadows in which she found herself living.

Finally, my mother found herself with her grandmother from England for three short years. Her long lost grandmother, a poet, businesswoman, and entrepreneur was ahead of her time in many ways. She supported and acknowledged the strength and leadership skills in my mother. She reinforced my mother's core life message about holding her head up high and carrying her light and gifts with strength. Rita Marie was never a victim no matter how dire the adversity she faced. She always lifted her head high even as she lived through the economic downturn of the Great Depression. People often called her "Duchess" because she had a regal flair to her presence. This regal flair was consistent with her insides, her actions, her beliefs, and her authentic self. Testing came early on with this core life message. It kept her in good stead so she taught it to her children. She would tell us, "Self respect knows no compromise. Like what you see when you look at yourself in the mirror every morning."

Mahatma Gandhi said it so well, "My life is my message." This was true for my own mother as well. Her words, decisions, and actions matched her choices.

Nine-Year Segments

Your life cycle runs in nine-year increments. Developmentally, you complete the parts of yourself mentally, emotionally, and physically every nine-years.

"Nine is the number which symbolizes primordial frequencies from which other frequencies derive resonance. According to my research, nine frequencies vibrate from the Great Emptiness, called the Great Paut. They are the forces of birth, growth, maturation, assimilation, creativity, suffering, pleasure, death, and renewal."[1]

Specifically, nine is your number of cyclic completion, periodicity, karmic completion, judgment, omniscience, wisdom, release, and the finishing up of all cycles. After each nine-year demarcation, you must again make a new choice, a new beginning. At each of these nine-year increments, you must choose one direction from the many. You must again choose something that separates you and defines you apart from what you have been. You willfully refine and choose your evolution in this way. At each of the nine-year increments, you must individualize yourself even further and refine your spirit. It is how you can uncover information about yourself, understand yourself, and evolve.

The nine-year increments are 9, 18, 27, 36, 45, 54, 63, 72, and 81 years. You refine, redirect, and let go of parts of yourself, at the very least, nine bold times in your life. Nine choices, because nine times you will bring a part of yourself to fullness and start again empty, just like the Moon.

At age **9-years-old**, you are sensitive and imaginative, beginning to see yourself and life in abstract terms, and how you fit into the world at large. You are noticing that you must be skilled at your own survival, so you are noticing just how your environment plays a part in your survival. You are impressionable, imaginative, and even generous. You look to have and give love. You are expanding your consciousness about humanity. Friends and getting along with others are very important to you. You make choices about how you will learn and hone your skill to survive, on your own, without the help of your parents.

At age **18-years-old**, you are feeling the independence of your beliefs and your individuality. You desire to be an independent thinker and it occupies a good part of your yearnings. You do not like to take a secondary position among your contemporaries. Your individuality is strong, and can even be bossy. However, it comes from an inner strength you rely on when the going gets rough. You are ambitious and you will let no obstacle deter you in attaining your goal. You are discovering how to use your individuality in the world and large masses, with whom you may work. You make choices as to whether you will stay in education or go to work, or both. You make decisions about whom you will love and where you will live from now on. You must make decisions to test the skills of survival on your own, independently, in a world without the help of adults as your safety net.

At age **27-years-old**, you have formed, conditioned, expanded, and tested your independence in the world around you. You have experienced a lot of trial and error. Now is the time for you to choose your piece of that world. It is time for you to develop your chosen piece of community, job, or family roots to see what you can do with it in a

CHAPTER 1: STEP 1

physical material way. You are now asking yourself to form your own single entity apart from the world. You are changeable, adaptable, and even indecisive. You like to be diplomatic, peacemaking, and compromising. You are receptive and can follow others at this time in your life, because you are seeking answers that align with your philosophies. You look for friends that can elevate or match your own intuitive inspiration. Big changes happen at this time. You make life choices about marriage, homes, jobs, salaries, entrepreneurial possibilities, health, and your physical looks.

At age **36-years-old**, you are conscientious concerning duty. You use your inspiration and imagination to achieve your goals and to help others. You are cheerful, optimistic, and working to make your dreams come true in the physical world. Giving and receiving love is important to you. You become satisfied and well adjusted in making other people happy. You are loyal to the ones you love and like the idea of the Golden Rule. You work hard to keep domestic harmony as your ideal way of life. You may seem smothering at times, to your immediate family, when they try to express their own desires and you don't agree with their choices. Your choices are to increase your material gain on the path you have chosen. On the other hand, maybe you've chosen to change and to take a more productive, profitable path with regard to home, family, job, and community.

At age **45-years-old**, you stay well organized and have some material success. You are practical and have a pattern of order in your plan for living. Your loyalty, balance, and dependability mean a lot to those around you. You know where you stand in your life. You feel any dealings should be fair and square in business, family, and romance. Your dreams come true because of your practical and planned view. You are proud of your accomplishments but yearn for something a little less predictable. Another part of you wants freedom and doesn't want to be limited in your ideals and way of thinking. You yearn to have a place for your self-expression outside of all the planned responsibility of which you are so adept. You are beginning to feel dull, listless with the desire for stimulation and a new outlook. You want to travel and believe an education will broaden your outlook.

7

You feel yourself falling into a rut and crave a vacation or travel for inner growth. You make choices in education, travel, relationships, job, or home at this time in the hopes of nurturing the other side of you that has remained dormant.

At age **54-years-old**, you have claimed the freedom of your earlier years, and now you want to feel the balance from the new outlook to see how it all fits in your life. You liked the free rein and accomplished wonders from throwing off the feeling of being limited. However, in the journey you have lost your enthusiasm, and now are accomplishing little and not a lot of material rewards to show for it. You have become interesting in your quest for discovering knowledge, and you enjoy the freedom of not feeling so tied down and responsible. Now you want to put a base on that experience and knowledge and order it with a system of conduct and morals. You want some conformity to the culture in which you live. You still want to provide for those within your care, and expect them to respond with dignity and respect. You are thrifty and don't like to take a chance unless it is a sure bet. You are seeking higher goals and want to achieve concrete results by facing reality and for practical reasons. At this point, the choice is to find meaning and purpose for the life you have lived. You seek to find the bridge between the spiritual path ahead and the physical/material path you just came from. The meaning of your life becomes integral in the choices you make.

At age **63-years-old**, you respond well to beauty, harmony, and peace. You are affectionate, sympathetic, and loyal to those you love. Your mission is to teach others to spread the idea of the Golden Rule even now. You work hard to keep this harmony and take your duty seriously. You have learned a sense of responsibility to your family and community. You are responsive to the needs of others and have compassion and understanding necessary to ease the burdens of those drawn to you. You do this in a creative, intellectual, and artistic way. You need to express yourself and see it manifested in your work. You like luxury and pleasure and feel you have earned it. You are happy with self-expression and freedom, but you must guard against becoming spread too thin, because your energy and

CHAPTER 1: STEP 1

attention are not as they used to be. Therefore, you find you have to specialize in one thing, but must do so without routine. You still dislike restriction of your freedom and so you sometimes like to work alone for your best results. Your decisions often are about how much or how little you interact with others and how best to use your energies on compromise and sharing your wisdom.

At age **72-years-old**, you have developed your mind and your wisdom. You have a strong intuition and insight. You may be an enigma to yourself and others at times. You like to read, think, and meditate. You are interested in your spiritual, even mystical connections. You love music and the arts because they give you harmony. You are drawn to the church, science, research, and analysis. You like to spend time by yourself and to be introspective. You are a support to others and help them to find the goals in their life. You remain behind the scenes. You have consideration of others and try to bring people together for a common cause. You are adaptable for most things that need finishing. Your choices are often how to balance your energies on the physical as well as your spiritual interests, and the meaning of your life.

At age **81-years-old**, you have become strong-willed, creative, and innovative by this time in your life. You have had courage and been a pioneer. If you have been dictatorial and stubborn, you may not like the life you have made. You do not like the rigors and restriction of domesticity, but you are managing. You are sophisticated and can head any social or commercial group. You connect to God intimately, and it has come time to decide your individual path in your spiritual development. You have had the brain and brawn. You have helped people to become successful in their own right. You have led and shown others by example. You have learned about power, authority, and money, and have the wisdom to show for it. You have achieved success for your family and your family name with pride. You want your offspring to carry on your name with honor and dignity. Your health and stamina affect your choices. You choose now, when, where and how much of your energy to spend. You ponder the choices facing you at death.

These nine segment choices may or may not be obvious to you if you retrieve memories about yourself at those times. However, when you select the defining memory, event, or moment you will identify what you chose out of the circumstance. Maybe you decided to take up a sport at 9-years-old; or go to work instead of college at 18-years-old; or to marry your high school sweetheart at 27-years-old. However, what you are not paying attention to is what you did NOT choose at those defining moments. You are not paying attention to the decision to work in a team or community, over solo individual achievement at 9-years-old. Out went solo individuation, and in went group belonging. At 18-years-old, you are not paying attention to application of your skills and expression in a job rather than accumulating ideas, theories, and enrichment of the intellect in college. Out went the safety of mind expanse and in came the doing of trial and error. At 27-years-old, you are not paying attention to giving up a relationship with yourself alone that needed no compromise, but instead to including another human being into the mix and the influence of compromise in your choices.

It is human nature to recede out of our attention what no longer is necessary for our survival or pleasure. Therefore, it goes, the choice not made is recessed. Notice I do not say forgotten. It is impossible to forget a choice not taken because it links directly to the choice made. You think in polar opposites: Yes-No, Night-Day, Black-White; the two choices link. The reason, value, or character-driven censor that helps you to make that choice is also the thread that helps to evolve you. That thread never goes away, even as you move on in your life and evolve with your age and development.

At every shift, you leave a little bit of yourself behind. That little bit of you is deeper than the decision you made at each of these nine-year demarcations. That little bit of you lays dormant underneath your decisions. That little bit of you is where the intangibles reside along with memories, conscience, beliefs, morals, and your authentic self. Those little bits are fossils of your soul. You don't usually look for these fossils unless you are forced to do so with some adversity, life-threatening disease, death, or a tumultuous adversity that is like an earthquake to your being and makes those little bits of you surface toward the light. In this Forget Me Knot process, I am going to take you there without the tumultuous event. I will take you, by the hand, gently, with safety but with profundity and honor. You may ask yourself why spend the time on looking for the invisible bits of yourself left behind? It is like looking in the cracks in the earth where a fault line exists without falling in. It is a short cut to what monks do when they meditate, or people who go on vision quests. It is a way to go from your head to your heart with a little assistance. It is a journey to your core life message and that, which makes you tick. The shifts in your life are the places to start your search.

SHIFTS

I have a special needs child. Any mother who has a special needs child knows that if problems are going to happen, it usually happens when there is a transition. Even 'abled' children can have the same problem. These children lose things when going from school to home, class to class, Mother's house to Father's house. They have emotional strife when they change from one school to the next new one, or their routines are changed. It is just as true for you and me. When the seasons change in the fall, you may end up getting the flu or a cold. When day turns to night, there are more traffic accidents at dusk or dawn. When things are shifting, things fall through the cracks causing a release of energy. This is when most mothers know it is necessary to pay very close attention to their children. You see teachers at day care centers insist on having the children hold a long rope with a teacher in the rear, as they make their way down the street, on a field trip. You see a goose waddling behind her babies to make sure transition happens smoothly. Things fall through the cracks in transition releasing energy, both positive and negative. These things are usually good clues to your core life message. So pay attention to any literal or metaphorical doorway, either going in or going out. Pay attention to those times in your life that were surprises, shocks, turnarounds, splits, blind spots, changes in direction, and culminations. Don't miss it when you sense something is unclear in the shadows or the change that can come after bliss and pleasure.

These important shifts will help you discover just where to dig deep for your core life message.

So often, we have energetic billboards that almost scream "Dig Here!" for your core life message. The human 'energetic billboards' have gestures, humor, signals, magnetism, or some other sensory picture. Digging can be fun, enlightening, and revealing. However, most of all, digging for your own core life message can give you peace in the depth of your being. It can give you the clarity of your unique imprint, and connection to others.

In this step, you will NOT be focusing on the two polar opposite choices you made at each nine-year increment. Instead, you will be discovering the discerning process that happens with your character, values, or evolving core life premise that determined your choice. The method of *how* you chose is more important than the content of *what* you chose, because that is what follows you your whole life. *How* is the part with which you build the pattern of your core life message with every experience. It is what you end up with at your deathbed. It is your spiritual language you choose to carry on, even after you have passed. *What* you chose will define you in the physical world. *How* you chose it will define you in the spiritual world. You can pass this spiritual part of you onto your loved ones that you leave behind at your passing.

THE DECISION OF NO

Most of us think we know each other by what we have chosen. They know us by what we have said yes to, and what we have allowed into our lives. It might be our name, job, stature, prosperity, religion, ethnicity, gender, education, language, country, or politics. This might be true on one level. This superficial knowing is not the whole story of who we are. You and I know that feeling of, "Is that all there is?" It happens when you and I have been living too superficially and we buy the idea that the superficial information about us IS all there is. Something in us knows there is more. We are all just a little bit lazy. Therefore, we organize our physical world and the people

CHAPTER 1: STEP 1

in it in superficial, but efficient, ways. We want the 'stats' on people like they are baseball trading cards to keep order and efficiency. To have the cliff note version of a person, or just to know their name is to pass over the diamond shining from their being. We can miss the most important part of them, and in doing so, we miss a part of ourselves too. We do it all the time. We treat each other as we treat the homeless man on the street. We know him by his attire, and the dog he pulls in tow. We know him by the brand of liquor on the empty bottle that lies by his side. However, do we know what made this man vital, bright, and alive in his time?

As I said, I have a special needs child. I had to look at the simplest actions and break them down to learnable steps. My child could not chew because the texture of food was too much stimuli for her system to handle. To have a child fourteen pounds at a year old is to worry about her survival. I knew I had to pay attention and go deeper for her survival. I didn't necessarily like it. I didn't even think I knew how to make the situation different. Nevertheless, somewhere, somehow I found a way for her to eat, and to thrive. I didn't take things for granted, and assume I or anyone else had the answers needed. However, I held steady with the intent to do the necessary work to go deeper and find the uncommon solution. Therefore, with my attention, the answer revealed itself. My child could live, and so she did. She even thrived.

When do you give yourself more attention than your profile, your resume, and your educational degrees on the wall? When do you find your intangible qualities that make you human? When do you give yourself credit for your incredible courage in growth and evolvement? When is your turn? Do you think this happens just before death? Maybe. Then it will be a different kind of experience, when your energies are waning, and the physical part of living is beginning to become vague, while the spiritual part of you is becoming more vibrant.

If you really want understanding, acceptance, and inclusion by others in your life, you must start with yourself and your willingness to know more about yourself than your name, birth date, and social security number. Moreover, while that seems an exaggeration it is not far off. Our public face, our personality, cannot and does not hold our full truth. Society and our culture would like to think it is so, so that our community structure functions faster and smoothly, in an assembly line fashion. However, if you take a firm stand against floating down this hypnotizing communal stream, you will honor and respect your soul in this lifetime. Life will have some form and pattern, and you will be skilled at looking at things deeper. The truths you find will have a rich, nourishing feel to them. When you look closer, you will find you are a small microcosm, a small universe of responses and reactions, experiences and expressions to bring your soul back to the totality of Oneness.

You are miraculous and unique. Doesn't it interest you to discover that you are a unique miracle? It does me. How do you expect others to know, love, and understand you if you never do it for yourself? Maybe if you do this digging within yourself with introspection and intent, you will be more interested in what also makes another tick, what makes them special. Alternatively, will you default to, "I know her. She is just like her father," or "I grew up with him. He will never change," or, "Avoid him, he is such a bore." Judgmental, superficial, and lazy, maybe, but also you will miss an opportunity to see how you respond, express, and experience your own polar opposites with them.

Your unique differences are getting harder and harder to find as you fit yourself into internet profiles, social networking, 140 character sentences, cryptic texts, and short attention spans. The constraint of describing who you are and what makes you different in a 30-second elevator speech, or a 25 words or less Hollywood pitch is accentuating the idea that you are all just stats on a baseball trading card. You are not pasteurized, homogenized milk that just blends in so you can get along and feel connected in some way. The way you can feel connected is to give yourself practice to revel in your personal differences and uniqueness. You can flaunt with pride and fun your unique parts that connect you by both your commonalities and your differences with them.

CHAPTER 1: STEP 1

The Forget Me Knot way of discovering your core life meaning, and anchoring it to a symbol that triggers the five senses, will give a shared experience and bond you to them. While you get closer to them, you get closer to your own spiritual side and the spiritual language that connects you to them. You move beyond the baseball trading cards idea. You can speak both physical and spiritual languages.

There is a way to stem the tide of an empty superficial feeling, and get closer to your spiritual side. You can feel real, authentic, and here for a reason by starting with your own self-introspection. Dig within yourself first before you go connecting with others. Look *in* before you look *outward*. You *are* the center of your universe. Start with connecting your own head with your own heart. Only then will you be able to connect with the head and heart of another.

Your stats and cliff notes of your being are true to the majority of the physical, material, and earthly world. Your close loved ones know it is not all there is to you. You have the spiritual side of yourself as well. You have the universally connecting side of you, too. Your physical choices do not define the spiritual side of you. Your intangibles, character driven, and non-measurable experiences define the spiritual side of you. Some examples of the intangibles would be imagination, curiosity, patience, industriousness, humility, vigor, piety, moderation, and respect, to state a few. These are spiritual words and experiences. It is what binds you to all of us. We all understand these intangible, character-driven, non-measurables no matter what culture, language spoken, or place of origin. It is a spiritual side of us we all share in our being human. Our intangibles can live on even when our bodies cannot. The non-measurables are the true wealth of our being, so let's go deeper.

Non-Measurables

How do you measure imagination or curiosity? How do you measure charm, chemistry, or kindness? For intelligence, we have an IQ ratio. For stress, we have the Selye Stress-Response Chart. For pain, we have the Wong-Baker Faces Pain Rating Scale. We measure everything.

In fact, once something is measured it becomes more important, more valid, and more reproducible. Somehow, in life, those things unable to be measured have been assumed to have less value because there is no way to measure how important they are to the rest of us. Are they really less important or valuable? Are patience, compassion, consideration, intuitiveness, and anticipatory or deductive traits any less valuable? My own personal connection with others and in prescribing remedies, I found these non-measurables *more* valuable. These non-measurables are what make you and me human, feel connected, and understood. You cannot get this from a Facebook profile that lists the status of your relationship. The non-measurable intangibles speak your spiritual language.

At each of the nine-year demarcations, you choose among these non-measurable spiritual intangibles. You choose to carry one of them forward into the next nine-year cycle. At these nine-year demarcations you might have said "No" to choosing this best friend over that one; "No" to this marriage partner over that one; "No" to this job over that one; "No" to this solution to a health problem over that one. At these demarcation points, these transition shifts, your internal censor is at its peak discerning power. Armed with your non-measurable intangibles, your discerning power runs your show and directs your destiny. A Forget Me Knot experience uncovers the inner workings within you that are underneath the "Yes" to one and "No" to another. At death, the end of all cycles, when the measuring stick is no longer physical, but rather an evolution into the spiritual, you will use spiritual language, the language of character. At death, you spend your spiritual energy and release it. When you pass into the hereafter, it is the language of character and conscience, which has evolved in the background of your life, and the language of your spiritual intangibles that define what you were all about in your life. The spiritual definition of you is what made you matter. The physical hurdles and accomplishments you experienced in your life were a means to help you experience your spiritual evolution. Your physical vehicle delivers your spiritual treasure back to the totality of Oneness.

CHAPTER 1: STEP 1

The reason we look to the spiritual intangibles instead of just the material, physical definition of you, is so you can live on in the lives and hearts of your loved ones even though your body has dissolved into matter at death. Your spiritual side can live on in the hearts of your loved ones. You just have to find a vehicle for them to house the spiritual spark of you: "a symbol, relic, or trigger." At death, you cannot make physical what is not physical. However, you can spark in another a memory or a sensation that bonded them to you when you were alive. This spark is the triggering of their bonded memory. It is the way to have them conjure your presence. By doing so it will feel, even in death, you are still with them.

At each nine-year demarcation, you can look at your physical choices. However, in trying to find the premise, principle, or point of your life, you need to look at your moment of choosing at each of the nine-year marks. It is clearest to see at these very points in life because you have culminated into one full cycle. Oh, we make decisions every second, minute, hour, day month or year. Each of these nine cycles, nine seconds, nine minutes, nine hours, nine days, nine months, etc. have meaning. Nevertheless, in trying to find the pattern of you, we will focus on the nine-year increments. It is much easier to snag memories there.

Interestingly enough, to find the spiritual intangibles, like fossils in an archeology hunt, you look NOT at the choices you made. Instead, what was it that you said 'NO'. What choices did you let go, and why? If you look to the choices you made, and said yes to, you will be assessing your physical being in the world. However, at death, that physical body is no longer. You want to understand the spiritual part of the soul so it is remembered, kept alive, and catapulted forward through the hearts and words of the living. 'No' choices help you to find the spiritual *how* in your life.

In the discerning process of each of the nine-year cycles, you chose some non-measurable character intangible in making your life choices. In discovery of the core life message, premise, and principal of your life, you want to identify and collect your choices on which you turned your back. It is your 'No' choices and the reasons why you said "No" that contain the spiritual language. The 'No' choices are what you need to see the pattern of you and what makes you tick over a lifetime.

You are more than your resume, medals, trophies, accomplishments, curriculum vitae, title, honorific, and degrees after your name. You are more than your name, fame, possessions, children, parents, or spouse's relationship. You are more than your intelligence, your emotions, your expressions, and the nouns of your life. Those define you in the physical world, but not the spiritual world. *How* you evolved through those nouns is what defines you spiritually. As you are evolving spiritually, you experience yourself as a changing verb and preposition, even after death.

You can take a snapshot of the evolution of your spiritual development every nine-years, like a spiritual MRI or a spiritual autopsy and see what made you individually unique and special. At 9-years-old, did you stop playing the piano and start playing video games with the new neighbor next door? At 18-years-old, did you decide to go to an out of state school because your girlfriend was attending that college? At 27-years-old, did you decide to get married to your current boyfriend because you felt your biological clock ticking and you wanted to start a family? At 36-years-old, did you decide to change job positions from being a paid employee to a consultant? At 45-years-old, did you leave your marriage for a younger woman and purchase a red sports car? At 54-years-old, did you choose robotics over conventional surgery for the removal of your cancerous prostate? At 64-years-old, did you decide to rewrite your will to include Guide Dogs of America instead of leaving all your inheritance to your grown children? At 72-years-old, did you move to Leisure World for like-minded companionship rather than move closer to your divorced, financially strapped daughter and your grandkids? At 81-years-old, did you move into an assisted living center because you can't quite remember the word that unlocks your door and are finding it difficult to swallow food? It all passed so quickly. You were so busy living; you never knew you were leaving little clues behind you. Large choices are easy to recollect. However, it was the decisions left behind, at each one of these nine-year demarcations that hold the information as to why your character chose what it did. The patterns of clues of you are what hold the key to your core life message. This is how you can discover your evolving spiritual fingerprint on this world.

Your spirituality is not your religion. Your spirituality is all that encompasses your spiritual and physical body and everything else. How it is experienced is personal. It can be through religion. You can experience it through nature, wonder, loving, or even adversity. However, it is more than your physical body. People, whose beliefs are different by religious affinity, can speak the same spiritual language, which is that of character, conscience, and compassion. Therefore, as I use the word spiritual, I do not mean any particular religious affinity, and yet at the same time I mean them all, because they all blend into loving at their origin.

Example Of No

Edgar Cayce, considered a 'sleeping prophet', was a devout Christian, a deeply religious man who used his psychic talents to heal and benefit his fellow man. Cayce would put himself into a trance and would diagnose those who he consulted, recommending healing treatment and cures. He was a healer, a religious man, and a spiritual man. Stories state, he had the ability to read the Akashic records. Akashic records hold every sound, thought, and vibration since the beginning of time. These records include the first sound vibration, which was called forth into manifestation. Cayce helped thousands of people to regain their health and conduct their lives in a more constructive pattern. (Edgar Cayce Foundation is a subdivision of the Association for Research and Enlightenment A.R.E. in Virginia Beach, Virginia.)

Edgar Cayce was born March 18, 1877 in Hopkinsville, Kentucky. His life's work was in taking responsibility for others, attend faithfully to duty, and make the best of any situation. He possessed common sense and foresight in order to make fair judgments. He believed service was the way toward mastery, and so he lived his life to prove that so. He proved it so by healing the physical body, the thinking mind, and the spiritual heart. Cayce loved to teach and serve others. He had courage and fortitude to face the adversities of life, and felt everything would work out with God's help and guidance. He was willing to work hard even at the expense of his own health. His core life message and premise was, "Let me ever be a channel of blessings, today, now, and to those I contact in every way." Therefore, it was that he dedicated his life to the betterment of humanity.

When we look at the nine-year cycles of Edgar Cayce, as an example of the nine-year demarcations we can see how this core life message of being a channel of blessing in the lives of everyone he contacted evolved and was passed on to us in this day and time.

CAYCE'S BIRTH TO NINE-YEAR CYCLE

According to Cayce's mother, even as a small child, he saw and talked with invisible playmates. At age 4, the death of a much-loved grandfather gave him grief and loss. A few months later, he claimed that his grandfather appeared and talked with him. Edgar Cayce was permitting his skills and gifts as a psychic to come through him.

At age 9 to 10, Cayce decided to involve himself with the church. At 10 years old, Cayce began to work as a church sexton, or caretaker of church property. This choice to be a bridge to the spiritual world was indicative of his future path.

What defined Cayce at this nine-year demarcation point in the physical world is that he chose the differentiating qualities of being in both the spiritual *and* the physical world. He chose to be caretaker of the physical possessions, relics, and objects of the church that had spiritual meaning, and had the ability to connect others to GOD through physical relics and objects. What Cayce did NOT choose is to be just about self, the material world, or just about the spiritual world either. He asked to be helpful to others, especially children, and that he could love his fellow man. At 9 years old he could have been a boy

CHAPTER 1: STEP 1

playing with toys, making friends, or curious about the workings of the physical world. Instead, he let all that recede into the background of his attention. He concentrated on being a bridge between the physical and spiritual worlds, even at that young age, and the praying through relics. He defined his spiritual language and part of himself by what he did NOT choose. He used the discernment of his character and closely held values, even at the age of 9 years old.

9-18-YEARS-OLD

At age 18 years, another nine-year demarcation segment of his life, Edgar Cayce met Dwight L. Moody, an itinerant evangelist, who wrote the book, *Secret Power*. His advice changed the course of Cayce's life, by suggesting, "You can serve God, wherever you go." At age 18 years, Cayce married Gertrude Evans and soon became a traveling salesman. Cayce was to test his ability to serve wherever he went and with whomever he contacted. He did heal those who he contacted in his daily life. The choice Cayce made was to serve one and to serve many. He healed himself through love of another, Ms. Evans, and he chose to move around in a job as a traveling salesman, while at the same time giving his healing readings. The choice he did NOT make was to remain stationary or all about his own needs, wants, and desires. Nor did he keep his gift of healing or his ability to love small and only for himself. Again, he became a bridge between the one and the many, separate and unified, physical and spiritual. The theme of his core life premise, to be a blessing to all with whom he came in contact became even more refined.

18-27-YEARS-OLD

From the age of 18-27 years, Cayce juggled being a husband, working, and traveling. At the age of 27-29 years, another crucial nine-year demarcation, Edgar Cayce made interesting choices. He left his first wife, married another woman, and had a son. This son, Hugh Lynn, later grew up to help establish, reinforce, and protect his father's image, wisdom, and legacy, especially after much scrutiny and controversy. It was the son that he bore during these prime demarcation years who established Edgar Cayce's longtime legacy with the Edgar Cayce Foundation, which educates and heals many to this day. Even after his passing, Edgar Cayce is responsible for healing protocols for other's healing and welfare, though he is not here in body and form.

The notoriety of Cayce and his healing abilities were spreading quickly. The decision NOT made was to be just a family man. Instead, he devoted his life to the masses and the betterment of mankind while he raised and healed his own family. He found that healing self and family was also important while healing mankind. Again he straddled both worlds, and became a bridge to both. He bridged the past and the future as a way to make sure his healing knowledge continued, through a son who formed a foundation to house the information for future generations. Cayce was a bridge to the Akashic records. Even after he passed, Cayce contributed to the betterment of humanity.

27-36-YEARS-OLD

During this time, Edgar Cayce had an article published in *The New York Times* that gave him nationwide publicity. He was working in the limelight and his public image became an issue in his life. He was learning the lessons that came with fame. Unfortunately, he also had a second child that died, and his wife became ill with Tuberculosis. His healing readings saved her life. At this time, also he was under investigation by Dr. Munsterberg of Harvard University. Cayce was fulfilling the role that others expected of him. He still was bridging the worlds between healing for his private family as well as the public and humanity. What he did NOT choose is to opt out of either family or healing because of criticism or adversity. He made decisions and gave attention to both responsibilities using his gift of healing.

36-45-YEARS-OLD

During this period, Cayce's son injured his eye while playing. Doctors wanted to remove the boy's eye. After his father's healing

CHAPTER 1: STEP 1

reading, Cayce was able to save his son's eye. His son's eyes and vision remained healthy the rest of his life. Cayce, himself, underwent an appendectomy during this period and used his own healing knowledge on himself. During this time, Cayce also had another son, Edgar Evans. His choices continued to bridge healing between the personal and the public.

45-54-YEARS-OLD

After much traveling, Cayce returned to Alabama to focus only on giving healing readings as his life's work. He then moved to Dayton, Ohio to work with Arthur Lammers, giving readings on mind and soul, as well as illness. He expanded his healing readings to include more of a spiritual connection. He gave information on reincarnation, numerology, astrology, and other subjects. His own personal healing readings suggested he move to Virginia Beach. There he built a hospital to give the treatments he prescribed. More and more people became interested in Cayce's work. Prestigious individuals, like Morton Blumenthal, aided him. Cayce was still strongly religious and firmly committed to helping others. The hospital did not succeed. Cayce was sad and disappointed at the failing of the hospital he had opened. Nevertheless, that same year he also established the A.R.E., Association for Research and Enlightenment. Today it has over 100,000 participants. At his fifty-fourth year demarcation, Cayce had to evaluate just how successful he had been thus far in the thread of his life. How consistent had he been at his core life message of being a channel of blessing in the lives of everyone he contacted? Cayce dug in and committed himself even more to his core life message. This time he took the traveling out of his life equation and settled down. He had succeeded in taking his healing gift anywhere he went. Now he decided to keep it in one place, with a consistency that had evolved over time.

54-63-YEARS-OLD

Edgar Cayce moved again to Arctic Circle, which became his permanent home for the rest of his life. His mother passed away the same year that Cayce's son Edgar Evan went to college. Cayce's father died when he turned 60-years-old. When Cayce was 62-years-old, a man named Thomas Sugrue came to live with Cayce. Even though Sugrue was ill, he wrote a biography about Edgar Cayce after living with him for two years. The book is *There is a River, 1942.* At 63-years-old, Cayce added an office to his house, which allowed him to give his healing readings in comfort. At this time Cayce's son, Hugh Lynn took over the management of A.R.E. Cayce was content to be free of the responsibility of the Association. Edgar Cayce was beginning to pass the torch of his healing writings to the Association to give them viability without direct access to Cayce himself. He started to let the personal spiritual side of him have more of a say in his life than the physical had been earlier in his life.

63-72-Years-Old

At age 65-years-old, Cayce published his series of books, *Search for God*. These books are in circulation still today. Cayce's last healing reading was September 17, 1944. His physical body was complete. He died at 67-years-old. Yet, many still feel the influence of Cayce. There is a library and a vast amount of information available that came through the instrument of one man, Edgar Cayce. His life thread, pattern, purpose, and core life message of being a channel of blessing in the lives of everyone he contacted evolved and was passed on to us in this day and time.

The Boxer Leg Theory

My Boxer Leg theory is one about choices NOT taken. It is about your 'No' decisions and their connection to your core life legacy message. It is about your non-measurable spiritual intangibles. I developed this method as a shortcut to your core life message.

As I said before, you are unique. You are a separate magnificent soul, busy experiencing your expression of yourself. I am sure you often have a hard time even contemplating that at the same time you are part of the totality of Oneness, GOD, the universe, speaking the non-measurable spiritual language. You may try. You may pray to feel it. You may meditate to feel it. You may go into nature to feel it. You may take drugs to feel it. You may use generosity, gratitude, and forgiveness to feel it. You may fall in love to feel it. You may search for it through adversity and grief when you are looking for meaning. However, the totality of Oneness is all around you. It is like Dorothy and the red slippers. You have only to click your heels together to know you are already home, already at one. The totality of Oneness makes you who you are. It is your substance.

Zeroes, Cycles, And Circles

Zero, Cycles, Circles that rotate in time and space become spirals. That symbol of zero, circles, cycles, and spirals are your original totality of Oneness. You never stop. You never start. You are all of this substance. You are all of this substance of the cycle of totality of Oneness. You are forever moving. Just like nature, you are made of verbs, prepositions, experience, and expression that are continually evolving. Just as you think you have the totality of Oneness in your grasp; it vanishes like sand in your fist, always moving. That is because you are all verbs, prepositions, and movement. It is very hard to see yourself and 'be' yourself at the same time. Yet, that is exactly what is happening.

If all there ever was were circles and zeroes then there would be no humans. There would be no you and no me. There would just be a continuous flowing totality of Oneness, just God. However, when God needs an experience of itself, man is the perfect piece; a line, a sliver, or a leg of the continuous circle of the totality of Oneness. Man, as a piece of the circle, can separate off and go out to experience itself as its unique piece of God. Man experiences, expresses, and evolves in life. At death, in the end, Man comes back to God to share his or her piece of life experience at death. God gets to experience itself this way. Man shares his or her life experience and expression of God; then again, merges back into the totality of Oneness as part of the circle, cycle, spiral, and zero while blending again into God as the totality of Oneness. In this completion, Man returns home.

Man's very nature, when separated from God itself, is to be a unique expression of God. However, you and I forget that us being separate is an artificial illusion, because really each one of us is just a separate piece of the same circle of Oneness, of God. You are really part of God. Just for the sake of God's experience, you are the illusion of a piece and separate for just a bit of time.

Each one of us is a piece of the magnificence of God. You are still part of God, even though it is not in your awareness, and your concentration is not on that truth. You are busy with your attention, energy, and actions spent on living your unique soul's piece of the life experience of God. You and I are busy doing the job we came to do. You and I experience our piece, our unique expression of ourselves in our lifetime and bring that experience back to the totality of Oneness of God at our passing.

In life, it is not the time for you to meld, blend, and become one, when you opted to actively experience being a particular unique piece of God. That is why it is not your job to blend in and pay attention only to your similarities with others and what unites you. Instead, it is your job to pay attention to what your particular different experience is within your lifetime. You are a steward over the soverneighty of your particular piece of God with all its gifts and unique magnificence. Only then, have you done your soul justice, and the rest of us justice, too, by bringing your life experience of your piece of God to fullness. You have mattered. You have contributed to the collective. You have been God and apart from God at the same time. You might be asking yourself just how do you and I go from being a complete circle of God then suddenly to a piece of God? How exactly do you go from a circle to a one and become separate from God?

One Or Separate

The explanation may seem over simplified, but let's try. Just so that you can experience your particular piece of the totality of Oneness, you separate yourself off into a number one as a piece, leg, or a part of that circle, zero. You go from being zero and infinite to a static

CHAPTER 1: STEP 1

and separated number one. Your piece becomes a number one into separateness, as a section or part breaks away from the totality. You shift out of the totality of Oneness, a zero, which moves you from being a verb and a preposition of movement. Your flowing in the totality of Oneness artificially halts and you move into the static separate nature of the number one, a noun, sliver, leg, or piece of that circle. You are not moving in the totality now. You are separate and static. You become the defined, different, and separate just so you can experience yourself away from the oneness. It may be artificial and an illusion, but it seems very real to you and me. It gives us the ability to enjoy and express our particular piece, pattern, premise, and our core life message away from the flow of the One as unified and infinite. Maybe you are a mother, father, teacher, or friend, for example, as a separate number one. However, the truth is that this is artificial and that you are always really a piece of the totality of Oneness, even though you have labeled yourself differently. If we agree that the zero (0) is the totality of Oneness (1) and is separateness or differentiation, then splitting off is artificial. We use the symbol of one (1), to show a piece of the whole of the circle, cycle, spiral, or zero of totality so we can differentiate ourselves from others and express ourselves, our way. We can find out how we are a unique piece and contribution to that Oneness and the whole of existence.

So it looks like, at any given moment in time, you are either zero (Oneness) or one (separateness) in your perception; born or dead, verb, preposition, or noun. However, if you could switch your attention in a flash, blink your eyes to a different way of seeing, like looking at the blob of an inkblot Rorschach of the kissing couple transforming instantly to the wine goblet, with just a shift of your eyes and attention, then you would know you are both. It all depends how you shift your attention back and forth from kissing couple to wine goblet. Back and forth, kiss to goblet, goblet to kiss. You are zero and one together at the same time, separate, and one both. You are the noun and the verb at the same time. To experience yourself you split off as a piece in separateness as the number one. As you move towards death, to become part of the spiraling cycle once again, you become a preposition in the spiral too.

In essence you are mentally cloning yourself, so that you can observe yourself and experience yourself at the same time both the unified and the separate, the zero and the number one, man and god. We flicker back and forth in our attention. Zero to One, One to Zero, just like a computer with many different variations.

- Attention to this, attention to that.
- Goblet to Kiss. Kiss to Goblet.
- One to Whole. Whole to one.
- Back and forth.

The even bigger epiphany comes when you can experience yourself as the totality of Oneness *and* the separateness as the number one, as a piece, *at the same time*. As you observe yourself, while at the same time experiencing an expression you made in the moment, it is a true healing.

Clara, one of my patients, was in a very abusive marriage. She came to me for her symptoms of Multiple Sclerosis, an autoimmune disease. As a Homeopath, I must include all symptoms, mental, emotional, and physical, so the abuse was one of the symptoms I had to reprioritize and include in the prescribing of her constitutional remedy. Even though my heart had angst for her struggle with beatings and emotional abuse, I could not tell her to leave him and go to a safe house. That would not by itself heal her from the pattern. I would have done that if I were her friend, but not her doctor. I was her Homeopath and my place was to match her with a life form that could help her to evolve at her own pace, time, and choice of leaving her husband. Only then, it would be a sustained healing, because it came from her.

After about three months on her remedy, Clara called me, left this message on my phone voice mail, and exclaimed, "Dr. Boxer, it happened again. I was watching myself go through the whole script of him yelling at me with rage, threatening me, and breaking something in the house. However, this time it was different. I felt the fear and wanted to run and hide just as I usually do. This time I did not say a word back to him. Instead, I just observed it all: He and I, in the house, at night, after his drinking, just as it has happened so many times before. The odd thing was, it was like a

CHAPTER 1: STEP 1

movie I had seen over and over and over again, so that I knew so well how everything would turn out. It actually became boring. Can you believe it? Boring! I just wasn't interested. It just felt like I was over this experience and it had lost its juice. I instantly remembered the friends and the fun feeling I had working on the community project I shared with my classmates at adult school. Something clicked in me. I realized I'd much rather spend my time doing something fun like that, than spending all my wasted energy on this drama. I packed my things. I am staying with my sister. It is odd to be experiencing the same old thing, and watching yourself do it at the same time. I know my remedy is working, because I never would have seen it this way. Never. Thank you."

It was after this phone call that Clara's MS symptoms started to abate. Her vision started to stabilize and become less blurry, and her muscle weakness with her legs giving out on her, became less and less frequent. Nevertheless, it was the epiphany that she came to on her own, that revealed her oneness and separateness at the same time.

Clara's core life message clues are within the choice she made to leave her abusive, alcoholic husband. Instead, she opted for a feeling of self-confidence and expression of herself by contributing her gift to the community in her adult school project. She liked herself when she made others lives' better for her having been there. Clara's core life message is held in the decision she left behind, the decision to no longer yield to the bullying, overbearing of her husband, and be the receiver and scapegoat of his unfelt feelings, thoughts, and projections as an act of love and bonding. She had been there and done that in the rotating, repetitive mouse wheel of her life. She wanted to get off the wheel and into experiencing the original essence of what she was born to experience in this lifetime: her unique separate gifts. While the experience of being in an abusive situation will also be part of her experience that she will take back to the totality of Oneness, when she finally passes on; she will also take with her the experience of the polar opposite too. By choosing her light, brilliance, and learning about her core life message from the lighter topside of life, Clara gets to experience herself exactly opposite from the experience of abuse, dark and destructive sides of life. Both of the extreme opposites will give her experience of her core life message and are effective, fast, and strong. However, learning through the underbelly of life can be deadly too.

I have seen this many times in my own healing practice when a patient calls to tell me they are experiencing their same old symptoms, but it felt to them like they were watching themselves go through it while at the same time feeling it. It is when I hear this 'being and watching self' sensation, at the same time, that I know a true healing is happening at a very deep level, through mental, emotional, and physical symptoms having taken place. It is like being the observer and the observed at the same time. It is like being nestled into nesting cubes when we are able to experience ourselves out of us and in us at the same time. Putting it into words just seems weird and does not do it justice. I would suppose some would call it enlightenment. It all happens in a blink. Once having experienced the nesting cubes of separate and one at the same time our existence never looks quite the same. We never see ourselves quite the same. I wonder if we haven't just sat on the lap of God when that happens.

You cannot both experience and observe yourself *all* of the time. These epiphanies do not happen as a daily occurrence. I'm not saying they cannot, but I have not seen us living this way in our culture where we are observing and experiencing at the same time. I can liken it to taking a photograph while at the same time enjoying and experiencing the event in the photograph itself: creating and memorializing, living in the present and living in the past. This unusual experience usually happens when there is a meeting place in your blind spot where the light of you meets your shadow side. You do not have this happen, everyday.

A correctly matched homeopathic remedy is uncovered and prescribed from this meeting place in your blind spot. This phenomenon peaks when the correct homeopathic remedy, providing energy and wisdom, matches the way a person responds in their life. I am sure that it can happen without a remedy, too. I think this simultaneous experience of being one and whole happens when there is any peak of experience: death, supreme accomplishment, falling in love, getting divorced, falling into financial ruin, and hitting bottom; the worst and best of any situation.

Remember, your job is not to be cycling in the verb of oneness while you are human. Your job is to be separate in a unique way and experience and express yourself fully so that you can bring your uniqueness home at death. You don't need to learn how to have more epiphanies at an earlier age so you can evolve faster. The whole point of being a human being is to revel in the mix of the part of God you came in with, and what you choose to do with it. Relax, be curious, and enjoy the way you respond to the wholeness of your life. There is no wrong and nothing to fix. You are doing it perfectly with choice, after choice, after choice, and your core life message. It is those nine-year increments when it all comes to fullness, and another cycle starts with a new chance for another experience of your piece of God. Enjoy the ride.

Choice Marks You Both In Body And Spirit

When you choose to both be part of the totality of Oneness as well as separating off into a piece or segment of one, your choice leaves a mark where you exit. It is a marker like boy scouts leaving ribbons on a tree while hiking in the wild to mark where they have been, and find their way home; or Hansel and Gretel leaving crumbs to lead them back home from Grandma's house; or rings on a tree; or layers on sedimentation; or wrinkles on human skin. Choices leave markers in the path of a life. You can retrace your life not by the choices you made, but by the choices, you did NOT make because those are the ribbons left on your life journey. You can see your true nature not by what you said yes to, but rather to what you said 'No'. What you are not defines you more than what you are; the complete opposite from the way most of us live and define ourselves.

You often define yourself by your resume, your job description, your place in a family, your hobbies, your medals, your gifts, your infamy, your mistakes, your achievements, your successes, and your relationships. However, the true consistent defining edges of your spirit defines you more accurately, by what you left behind, and to that which you said 'No'. A 'No' choice was a possibility that did not warrant your including it in your attention and expression. You do not give full expression to a choice with a 'No'. For instance, a simple example might be when you choose a best friend. You make a decision to spend much of your time with this friend. You choose to understand yourself through the experience of the interaction you have with your friend. You choose to be vulnerable, exposed, and give yourself permission to weather through the merging of expressions together. That choice to cast out all others from that special friendship and attention to your internal and external resources says more than even the choice of picking that particular best friend.

What was it that all the others had that did not make the grade? That choice is a direct reflection of what parts of you get to stay in the totality of Oneness rather than to be separated out in a piece for experience and expression. The cast-offs remain undifferentiated and do not gain access to expression and experience. By making that choice, no matter how big or small, you define your life. You define your premise, your pattern, and your core life message. When you go back into a high school yearbook and see all the people who were never your friend, it says more about you than those who signed your yearbook. There are faces in the yearbook that you never knew. They remain undifferentiated in the totality of Oneness with no possibility of expression in your life. They could not support your pattern, core life message, your premise, and experience of yourself apart from the totality of Oneness.

EVERYDAY CHOICES

A more complex example is the small everyday choices that leave a trail of your experience of separate and differentiation. What time do you wake? What time do you go to sleep? What do you eat to satisfy your hunger? How much attention are you giving yourself? How many details make it into one of your decisions? How deep or

CHAPTER 1: STEP 1

superficial do you think about any one subject? What you choose NOT to do defines your experience of separate more than what you DO choose. Why is that so?

What you pay attention to gives you your experience of being separate. Your attention is like clicking the select button on a computer screen. Once you click it, give attention to experiencing yourself as being different, unique and unblended, you also perceive the contrasting program default running automatically underneath, the totality of Oneness. It is like having a split screen in your minds eye. In the default of the totality of Oneness, it is where everything and everyone blends and flows, by comparison. Separate on one screen, blended on the other. Nevertheless, your spirit sees both at the same time. You are also choosing what exactly you want to take away from that totality of Oneness. You choose your piece, and give attention, while at the same time you are also choosing to ignore and leave behind things, not experienced by your spirit.

Just like the computer, it is like choosing from a drop down menu on the computer of what you will click and give attention.
- Choose or ignore.
- Experience or no experience.
- Unique or the same.

It happens second to second at each decision made and those left behind. It's second by second that defines the pattern, piece, core life message that makes you uniquely you. Just as every cell in your body uniquely carries your signature DNA, but also has another job it must do to make you survive in the physical world. Each tiny decision you make is like a fractal in the universe of YOU. But like each fractal, the piece also contains the whole. That which you separate out for experience still contains the whole of the totality of Oneness. You are God and Man at the same time. The piece contains the whole and the whole contains the piece.

You will always see yourself as part of the totality of Oneness itself, even if it is in the background of your mind, no matter how hard you try to experience yourself as different. It is how we relate to one another. It is how you connect to spirit, or Oneness, or to GOD. It is this totality of Oneness, the whole, where you come from, when you are born, and where you will return when you die. It is this connection to the totality of Oneness where your character and beliefs sit as censors to your "NO." These censors decide what experiences you will or won't have. Your censors make these decisions based on character and the non-measurable, spiritual intangibles. The totality of Oneness is the reason we all speak the same spiritual language, no matter the culture, religion, or gender. When we interact with one another in relationships, what we are really deciphering with each other is our spiritual language, and our commonalities. Do our universes have common spiritual language of character? Are we experiencing ourselves on the topside or bottom side of life? Do we need a polar opposite to experience our piece? How will you help me to evolve? How will you help me to bring experience of myself back to the totality of Oneness when I die?

I have had patients ask how I can speak so confidently about the idea of separate, and whole. The best answer I can give is that some of it is from training in holistic medicine: Chinese Medicine, Herbology, Homeopathy, Naturopathy, and Nutrition. Some of it is from my western university education and postgraduate education. Some of it is from my ability to discern correspondences and see where they overlap, relate, say the same thing in a different way, and see patterns. Some I learned by observing nature. Some of it is a sense of intuition and knowing from somewhere I don't know. Maybe some of it is from those souls on the other side who want to make sure you do know this. In addition, some of it is from my initiation into a language, and a knowing from another time and place from my mentors and shamans. Nadia K. Eagles was one of those shamans. She taught me about the Huna Tradition and their knowledge about the relationship between death and life, as well as many other different healing practices and sacred information. I felt blessed to have been in her presence and to have her as a mentor, in the oral tradition. She was a brilliant soul. I feel her around me all the time. This is a real life story I shared with her. It is the moment of her death.

CHAPTER 1: STEP 1

Huna Tradition

At death's door, Nadia K. Eagles, Shaman in HUNA Tradition spoke of a process that happens immediately as a person enters the afterlife, into the nine gates in the immediate afterlife. She said at the moment of death, we sort out our life and experiences that we lived within our lifetime, our choices, our attention, our actions, our deeds, searching for the totality of Oneness. She said that as we enter the first of the nine gates of death, we sort out our life with, "It's not this. It's not that." The soul experiences the physical dismantling of the illusion of separateness of a soul one by one, reviewing each memory and experience. The five senses are the folders, so to speak, that hold the categories of experience and expression of separate and different. We sort through the five senses and the memories that are associated with them. At death, our artificial perception of being separate or one goes back into the homogeneity of Oneness of the collective pool. When one reviews each of their five senses and experiences at death it is like admiring the fish just caught with the fishing pole and throwing it back into the ocean to swim once again. By retracing your choices and decisions NOT taken, while still alive, you too can garner the legacy of your true soul's shadow with the living. You do not need to wait until you enter death's door.

You can use this skill in life. Obviously, it will be a different experience at death, but the skill will help you to identify your core life message. Remember, it may look like it, but it is "not this, not that," because what is true is that we never really left the totality of Oneness and the collective. Usually you do not focus your attention or energy on choices NOT taken. You put all your attention and focus into the decisions that lay ahead of you. You focus on what you choose to see. However, that does not mean the choices you do not take do not exist. In fact, they exist in static time, because those decisions are not having the animation of your will, intent, and interest behind them. On the computer, you can just click the 'back' button to see again those ideas you left alone. Because they have a static nature to them, you can identify what made you choose this over that. They are the fossils of your will, your destiny, and your legacy. By contrast, you can see who you are by the pattern of choices you did NOT take as being much easier than the choices you did choose. The choices you did not take do not have movement and change that so often grab your attention. Nevertheless, clarity is so much easier looking for the NOT, or in the play on words in the title of this book, the Forget Me K-NOT.

To bring this idea home, I have created the Legacy Formula, which symbolizes and simplifies the identification of the choices you choose and those you leave behind. The Legacy Formula is a play on words: The Leg-A-See Formula. The idea is to see the legs, or the choices left behind. When you identify the legs or choices left behind you can see the pattern of your legacy, your experience, your expression, your character, spirit, premise, and your core life message.

EMBRYO

It all starts with the embryo when being formed in the womb, after formation by the fusion of the sperm and the egg chromosomes. You can find a summary on this, in an article from Wikipedia:
"As a baby, your sex is determined at the time of conception. When conceived, as a baby, either a chromosome from the sperm cell X, or Y, fuses with the X chromosome in the egg cell, determining whether you will be a female or male. The (XX) chromosome means you will be a girl, and (XY) means you will be a boy. Even though your gender is determined at conception, you as the fetus don't develop your external sexual organs until the fourth month of pregnancy—seven weeks after conception. As the fetus, you appear to be sexually indifferent, looking neither like a male nor like a female. Over the next five weeks, as the fetus, you begin producing hormones that cause your sex organs to grow into either male or female organs. This process is called sexual differentiation."

Using the biology of sexual differentiation I will attempt to explain the energetic relevance to your 'No' decisions. Once your XX reveals itself as an XY, in the fourth month of pregnancy, a leg drops off the X chromosome making it a Y, a changed legless X. A differentiation,

CHAPTER 1: STEP 1

making a spiritual choice, and everything unlike it drops away. In the case of gender identification, female drops away from male, and contrast is set in place for experience. 'No' you will not be a girl with a chromosome combination of XY. But, that tiny piece left behind that broke off from the Y, making it a legless X, that tiny piece that made it an X before it differentiated at 4 months is still there. It is there metaphorically, energetically, for the person who is to become a male. Created at the chromosome level is the polarity of opposites and the oscillation between what it means to be female or male, yin or yang. Its contrast defines what he is not. It is not a female as an XY. Oftentimes it is a lifetime of oscillating between the opposites created at the chromosomal level, which the male searches for his lost piece in the search of the feminine, the XX. Females, too, search a lifetime for the missing leg for the males in their lives. They do this because at the physical level, a 'No' on becoming the female gender leaves a ribbon/ choice or a trace back to one of the first decisions when breaking apart from the totality of Oneness.

Interestingly, human legs and arms are extensions of the sensory organs: Sight, Sound, Smell, Touch, and Taste. If you look at the human body with legs apart and arms outstretched apart, our body is in a type of X form, just like the X chromosome. In Chinese medicine, many of the main treatments for helping the body heal from disease are through the acupuncture points on the arms and legs. These acupuncture points, when stimulated, help the sense organs to perceive our experience as separate. These acupuncture points are electrically measurable in life, and up to seven days *after* death. I wonder if within these 7 days after death, that the download of experience of Man's contribution is uniquely separated for the totality of Oneness during that time. Perhaps it is one of the means Man unloads the physical experience, within the nine gates, to become purely spiritual and One with God once again.

All the extremities that extend from center trunk of your body, or 'waves in the wind' are more capable of sensation and expression, and increase the intensity of your experience of your five senses and the making of memory and experience. All moving extensions like arms, legs, hair, tongue, toes, fingers, breasts, penis, ears, nose, eyelashes etc. intensify experience of expression and separateness. The raised ridges of your fingerprints house the differentiation of your experience, as does your facial features and the wrinkles and variations on your skin. While these differences are happening on your physical body, they are also happening on your mental, emotional, and spiritual parts of you as well.

Your senses are the portals to wholeness as well as that which you experience as differentiation, separate, and unique. Your senses collect data about whether something is the same or different, whole or part. Your senses are the portal between totality of Oneness and separateness. Your senses relate to your hormones. Your hormones are often considered the messengers of GOD or Oneness. Some often feel that as your hormones diminish in aging, your attention to your physical procreation switches to a more spiritual perspective; a tendency to gradually move your attention from differentiation and separateness toward one of wholeness, oneness, and blending in with the source of all that is, back to GOD. The aging process, with the diminishing of hormones in the physical body, makes way for the attention toward the spiritual part of you and it readies you for your connection back, at death, to the totality of oneness and wholeness where you originally came from at conception. You come full circle with the help of your hormones.

The Leg-A-See Formula is a way for you to take a short cut to finding the long lost decisions and the core life message patterns that helped you to reinforce your core life message and to help you to discern the most important life decisions for which you have faced. The Leg-A-See Formula sets you right between two life choices, two polar opposites: go to this college or that college; pick this life partner over that one; live in this city or that one. You get the picture. They are usually polar opposites. That is, they are the polar opposite to your perceptions and your core life message. That is why and how you can make your important decisions as they come up. You measure them based on the criteria guided by your core life message. The stronger and clearer your two choices are, the more movement between those choices. The more movement between the two choices, the more you experience and express. The more experience of being separate you have to bring back to the totality of Oneness when you pass on to the hereafter. Again, it all comes full circle.

For example, the difference between a Democrat and Republican is their very different political points of view. When you put them together there is much bantering, posing, debating, and such. They oscillate between their polar opposites expending a lot of energy trying to stay true to their ideal. As the two interact, the two amplify their differences to create movement, energy, and change. Hopefully over time, the cycle peaks to some evolution of what they both started with in commonality. It goes full circle, back to blending and oneness. Healthy growth is like that. Two polar opposites create a lot of oscillation between them; a lot of up and down movement. There is movement to fruition where it peaks, and then it returns to emptiness from fullness. It is the reasoning behind the yin/yang symbol. Bringing something to fullness will eventually bring it to emptiness to start all over again. Therefore, the spin of the yin/yang symbols full to empty, empty to full. This is where you experience yourself: full and empty in any one experience. As a Homeopath, I know true healing has occurred when my patients have experienced both polar opposites. Think in your own life, the people who have had the most influence on you. It would have to be those who have been your heroes and later become your villains or vice versa. The best one is the one who has been your hero, turned villain, and then makes things right for you, only to again become your hero... only wait long enough...they may also become your villain again. Therefore, the yin/yang symbol turns in all of us.

THE LEG-A-SEE FORMULA

1.   2 Choices   1————2 Polar Opposites
   (i.e. Black vs. White, Night vs. Day)

2.   X   A Choice is made. The Crossroads.
   A Path is chosen.

3.   Y   Seek the "Why" of the experience.
   Search for the missing piece.

4.   Y /   A "Leg" or piece is left behind as a fossil.
   The choice is not chosen.
   The "Leg" is left behind.

5.   XXXX   In a lifetime, many XXXX crossroads.
   YYYY   Many YYYY whys.
   / / / /   Many / / / / Legs left behind.

6.   Collect the Legs and you will see your legacy.

7.   The years where the largest decisions are made are 27-29 years, 54 years, & 81 years. It is the easist place to see the largest fossils of choices left behind at these times.

I have made the Leg-A-See Formula so you could visualize it and set it up clearly in your mind. The two opposite tracks are your choices, choice A and choice B; or in this case, I made them legs or sticks. The legs cross when you make a decision or commitment to an idea, experience, or expression. (Do you remember the position of ideals taken by Democrats and Republicans?) Have you ever heard the saying, "X marks the spot"? That is where you made a choice. This choice is where you want the stamp of experience for your soul. It is interesting we use X as a way to sign our name, too, when a signature is impossible. Leaving something behind, or death, is what happens when the two legs or sticks cross. A choice untaken goes dormant, not to be experienced. As I said above, it is also where the gender changes from female to male, a legless X at the fourth month of pregnancy becoming a Y.

CHAPTER 1: STEP 1

Criss-cross. We cross many things: railroad crossings, cross our hearts, our fingers, or even Christ on the cross. It is where something always dies; a choice or leaving something behind. At this point, you have decided which of the polar opposites will recede in your life, and which will be yours to experience. You have chosen your path. When that happens, and the choice made, a piece of the 'X marks the spot', a leg drops off and remains, just as it does when you are sexually differentiating as an embryo. The piece that drops off is a choice let go or untaken. That is the point when you choose to experience your choice and move on.

Now, what looked like a criss-cross becomes a Y, which is really a legless X after you made your choice. The unchosen has become the lost leg left behind. It is the fossil or the clue to your core life message. In your lifetime, you will have many crossroads of Xs and many left behind fossil legs of Y's. Left with just the Ys you are always asking yourself that question. "Why did I do this? Why did I do that? Why does this pattern keep on happening?" It is our metaphorical and figurative 'Y' or 'why'? Nevertheless, our history has a traceable path just like the computer. It is like Hansel and Gretel finding their way back to Grandma's house by the crumbs left behind. You can find your way back by the lost legs of your crossroads; at your decision-making moments, if you collect all the dead legs of your choices and see the pattern for which they represent. This is how you can claim your core life legacy message.

In the Forget Me Knot experience, you can retrieve the lost dead legs. These are the ones that you may ask yourself your whole life, "Why?" Where the lost dead legs are located is the same place where that core part of you is discerning with your beliefs. Your conscience has come into play and you use your core life message to help make your choices. When you find the lost forgotten leg, it will be right next to your conscience. Right there will also be the criteria and perception that led you to make the choice that you did. This criterion has created a core life pattern. As you evolve in this pattern, over and over again, you experience and express your life uniquely. You bring your own life to fullness and then into the empty void of death. Therefore, your own life spins the yin yang symbol, birth to fullness, fullness to emptiness, and back to the totality of Oneness once again.

Now that you have stretched your brain to understand just how you differentiate your spirit from the totality of Oneness, you probably want a rest with something simple you can understand now and use today. You probably want to know how you can use this information to retrieve your simple one-liner of a core life message. The easiest places to find the lost legs that reveal your core life message are at the ages of 27, 54, and 81-years-old. At these ages, it is a time of you coming to fullness: youth to power at 27 years; power to wisdom at 54 years; and wisdom to spirit at 81 years. At your fullness, where there is a lot of your energy from oscillation and attention, it is easiest to see your pattern. At these ages fullness is just ready to change to emptiness and the spin of the yin yang symbol is the clearest place to discover your lost legs of 'No' that make you so unique.

I use this method all the time when trying to retrace a symptom in prescribing a homeopathic remedy for a patient. A mental, emotional symptom is just another expression of a pattern just like the physical symptom. They house the same theme. For example, a patient who has the tendency to make cysts and tumors on their physical body also has the need to separate, consolidate, organize, and categorize his/her life into little understandable, workable compartments. The body is reflecting the same pattern on all three levels: mentally, emotionally, and physically. The tendency to quarantine is on all three levels: mental, emotional, and physical, so I can see the lost legs on all levels. The pattern shows up everywhere. If I can see it, you can too, by using the Leg-A-See Formula.

In summarizing the concepts above, as a reminder, the general meaning of the nine-year life segments where emptiness oscillates to fullness and then oscillates to emptiness again are:
1. BIRTH in bringing oneself into Existence
    0-9 YEARS
2. GROWTH in Being Original, Independent, Dominant
    9-18 YEARS

3. RIPENING in Adaptability, Cautiousness, Following
    18-27 YEARS
4. TRANSITION in Creativity, Communication, Sociability
    27-36 YEARS
5. TRANSITION in Stability, Work, Discipline
    36-45 YEARS
6. TRANSITION in Freedom, Adventure, Change
    45-54 YEARS
7. HARVEST in Family, Love, Social Responsibility, Healing
    54-63 YEARS
8. HARVEST in Philosophy, Intuition, Inspiration
    63-72 YEARS
9. HARVEST in Power, Recognition, Responsibility
    72-81 YEARS
10. STORAGE in Love, Compassion, Selflessness, Universality
    81-99+ YEARS

At the shifting of these nine-year life segments, you can collect the legs of choices you left behind. First, gather the choices that you made at each of the nine-year segments. Recall the big changes that happened around that time. Remember what choices you faced when making that choice. What did your conscience or censor reveal by using your non-measurable spiritual intangibles? What did you leave behind? Was it a relationship? An ideal? A fantasy? A belief? Was it a way of doing things? Was it toward or was it away from the way things were? In identifying the two choices, remember it is not the choices which mattered. Reverse your attention from what you created or denied, the noun based polar opposites of one and two. Instead, place your attention at the censors, the criteria, or your conscience, by which you made the decision to choose one or two. That is where the lost legs are and where lies the crumbs back to Grandma's house, or the pattern of your core life message. Those are the legs left behind. They are the fossils of your character. It is what makes you different from me. Those choices will lead you back to your core life message, your premise, which makes you tick. This core life message is what you will bequeath to your loved ones.

The truth of you comes from the hidden 'NOT' of you, even more so than the 'you' that everyone sees. Now try using the blank template at the end of this book to plot your nine-year segments. Use your memories. Plot your two choices at the nine-year segments. Then discipline yourself to put the objects of the choices themselves on the back burner of your mind. Instead, pay attention to the censors of preference and aversion, those based in character, and listen to the language of your own spiritual language, the totality of Oneness. Ask yourself, "What criteria did I use to make that choice?" Retrieve your process of selection so you can use it to make a core life legacy message for those you love. You will leave it behind in physical form. Leave your spiritual language behind for them as well, so they can find their way back to your heart and feel your love for them. They will recognize you even when you are only in spirit in the totality of Oneness, having passed on to the hereafter. Your core life legacy message will help them find their own pattern in themselves in their own life. They, too, will feel the sensation of the totality of Oneness while they are still in physical form, because of you. They will start to be fluent in our common spiritual language, and their life will be more meaningful for it.

As you read this *Forget Me Knot* guide and are nowhere near your end, but rather at the middle of your life, you have already passed some of the nine-year segments where you made choices and left behind bits of you. You may have regrets that you made the wrong choice, especially when viewing your choice from another's conscience and core life message. Regrets happen when you forget the core life message that created the standard you used to measure that decision. It is for this very reason the Leg-A-See Formula is so valuable, because it lets you retrieve not only the leg that you left behind, but also the precious reason you did so. With that precious reason it all makes sense and your choice was sound. Then, you are at peace. It makes sense to you and your being. You can let the 'why' of it all rest with the choice not taken.

You can use the Leg-A-See Formula to find your core life message, right now, and with confidence live from that place from heretofore.

CHAPTER 1: STEP 1

Your core life legacy message is the current running underneath all that you do and all that directs you in your life. Share it proudly with color, spice, and with your unique nature, so there is no question what makes you tick to your loved ones, once you pass on.

I remember a patient whose father died suddenly. He had to sell his house and put all of his father's affairs in order. The house was in Newport Beach, a very expensive part of Orange County, California. He sold his father's house in a depressed real estate market. He regrets not only selling it for too little money, but for selling it at all. The home is worth at least four times what he sold it for after his father's passing, not to mention the prestige of the address. Nevertheless, for the choice taken, it was correct to his core life message. Honesty and fairness were paramount to both him and his father. They both liked to do things in a speedy manner. In fact, his father had a habit of collecting the mail from his mailbox and ripping though it, eliminating all his 'throw away mail' as he walked towards the trash can, so it was all ready to trash by the time he arrived at his trash can. My patient felt he was honoring his father's wishes and not including himself in the decisions by selling the house promptly. He acted as if he was responsible just like his father. He was trying to fill his father's shoes at a time when his father's death was still a shock and life felt unreal. For that moment, his conscience matched his actions and his choices. He spoke his father's spiritual language. Afterwards, when he took a broader more physical view that included him, the market, and other factors, he became regretful. He was using other events, people, and perspective to evaluate his choices. Nevertheless, the core life legacy message of honesty and fairness decided his fate. The speaking and acting from spiritual language isn't measured in money. It often isn't measurable at all. However, it is worth the most and feels the best.

You may have also wondered if the choice you left behind would have been better to lead you to a better experience and expression, or even a better life. The leg not taken would have given you a different choice, certainly, but not one better matched with your core life message. You are very true to that perception and core life message whether it is on your radar or not. You cannot help but make those same choices over and over again. If I had your same core life perception as you and the same choices as you, I also would make the same choice. It is from this point that I, as a Homeopath, can prescribe because of the patterns of your choices keep on showing up everywhere in your life. Those choices you made that are not exactly true to your soul's purpose will find their way back for you to choose again. You cannot escape it.

I knew from a child that I would be in medicine, but I took a turn in a decision to teach, though I remained in biology and health. I took a turn in business, which still had a place in health and medicine. I ended up in the place my choices and my soul took me. It was a fine-tuning at every one of the nine-year demarcations. You have those places, too, just like me. If you think you live from regret, I encourage you to retrace your choices to 'X marks the spot' to find the 'why' of that choice and surprise yourself on just how in line you have been to your being and to your unique expression of your life. Remember, even learning from the underbelly of life or the polar opposite has the same lesson in it that the sunny side of life has, too.

[1] Nadia K. Eagles, 1989, Shaman of the Huna Tradition

STEP 1 LIFE CYCLE SEGMENTS

After reading this chapter you can identify WHAT in your life is most important to you. This is the first step in tracing your own fingerprint mark on life. You are now able to identify the one thread that runs throughout all the important choices that you have made at each of the nine-year segments of your life. This thread is less about your story and more about the values and beliefs from which you discern and develop your character. You use these values and beliefs each time you have to respond to life challenges and adversities. Your ONE core life message is housed in your values and beliefs. The skills you have learned from this chapter will help you to identify the area you can dig deep for your ONE core life legacy message that raises itself above all the rest.

WHAT YOU'VE GOT:
- When you approach 81-years-old you will have at least nine main life choices.
- The nine main life choices show a pattern of where you spent attention and energy.
- You understand the Boxer Leg-A-See Formula as a way to retrieve your core life legacy message.

WHAT YOU CAN DO WITH IT:
- Listen to what you hear yourself saying.
- Look at what interests you today.
- See the same pattern of interests through and into your present life.

Rain beats on a leopard's skin but does not wash out the spots.

CHAPTER 2: STEP 2

THE CHINE OR KNICK POINTS OF LIFE

There are three points in your life where you face yourself and how your life is going compared to your dreams. These points are 27, 54, and 81-years-old. These three points I call 'The Chine' or 'The Knick Point'. A Chine usually starts at a waterfall at the cliff's edge. It initiates rapid erosion and deepening of a streambed into a gully leading down toward the sea. The Chine is also the sharp angle that cuts the human's umbilical cord of breath to life as part of the Grim Reaper's scythe. The three main decision making years of life, 27, 54, and 81-years-old are the Knick Points of your life when it is at its peak and will determine the direction of your life as it heads back to the sea of Oneness from where it came, where birth and death meet.

As a Homeopath, we call the Knick Points or Chines to be the time when a patient says, "I have not been well since...." It is the point at which we go to search for the reason that the health took a turn. Therein usually lays a good example of the pattern we need to prescribe the correct remedy match. We hear things like, "I've not been well since I took that joy ride in that convertible Cadillac." Or, I have not been well... "since my husband died," or "since I had that panic attack." These points are Chines to us. That is where we dig for clues. Another area we Homeopaths often look for clues at the Chine or the Knick Point is when a patient uses the words, "As if." It might sound like this, "My head feels like it is being beaten against my skull, *as if* my brain was loose." Or "I feel *as if* some horrible calamity is impending, even though I have no reason for it." We know the place where we will get the most information about what remedy to prescribe will be under these words when we hear them.

Even your untrained ear can use these two statements. "Not been ____ since" or "As if" as places where there is a Chine or a Knick Point you can look for your core life message. It is under these words, decisions, and choices let go. What is interesting is that I have noticed that many Knick Points happen for many people at the crucial decision making years of life: 27, 54, and 81-years-old. Your tendency to look where you got married, or started a brand new job, or birthed your first child are obvious, but look also to other Chines in your life. See if those decisions don't coincide with your key decision making years.

Can you imagine your life demarcations as literally and metaphorically the backbone of your life? This concept of 'Chine' is not too different from the human backbone or spine with the cervical vertebra, thoracic, vertebra, lumbar, and sacral vertebra. Each vertebra has different functions, different shapes, and different relationships to bone, muscle, and organs. Your life is like a backbone, with the Chine, or sharp angle cutting a different path, with different functions just like the vertebrae of your own body. The ages of 27, 54, and 81-years-old are the sharp angles, the Chine, the Knick Point of a spiritual life: birth, youth, power, and wisdom just like the cervical, thoracic, lumbar, and sacral vertebrae of the spine. Your largest decisions will be decided based on your values, beliefs, and character at these Knick Points. If you were to do an emotional autopsy or even an emotional MRI, you could see just how different life was for you as you evolved in knowledge, emotion, and spirit after your Knick Points.

These Knick Points relate to three important phases of your life: youth, power, and wisdom. The decisions you make at these times are important in determining the direction of your life. When you make the decision to have your life a certain way, you do so by self-evaluation at these Knick Points. When your choices are successful to you in your self-evaluation, then the next stage of your evolution in youth, power, or wisdom enriches your peace within. You like yourself and your life. On the other hand, if you did not achieve your positive evaluation, then the next stage you take on is to evolve trying again, with your same character of expression. The difference is that you must experience it again within the confines of the next stage. Each one of the three Knick Point years is a time of personal spiritual reckoning. Let me summarize just what each one of these Chines or Knick Points of your life means to you.

YOUTH 0-27 YEARS: YOU ARE FORMED, CONDITIONED, AND EXPANDED

Your mind and your character form from the time your soul enters your body, at birth. Your mental and spiritual expansion takes place during this time. Your body is the base for your mind expanding. As we all know, during this period, your body grows very fast. Youth discovers his/herself in body, mind, and spirit, the world he/she lives in, and how to survive on his/her own. Youth also discovers how to belong. The young absorb habits, opinions, and beliefs during this time, selecting out which ones will serve his/her spirit and help him/her to survive. They determine how he/she is the same as his/her family and how he/she is unique from his/her family. Youth absorbs more and more information, feelings, and actions around him/herself, as time passes. Trial and error is the order of the day.

During this time, risk taking is at the highest because the fire and energy in the spirit of youth is also strong. Youth checks under every one of the mental rocks: who, what, when, where, how, what, if. Youth collects, stores, and chooses. The choices Youth makes expands him/herself right up until the Chine Point at 27-29-years-old. This is where the height of testing, absorbing, and melding with all in his/her life comes to fullness and empties into individuality. 27-29-years-old is the Chine or Knick Point of youth. You may know this point of fullness by a time you might have decided on marriage, job, home, or family. At 27-years-old, you will begin to think about your roots rather than the gathering of your flowers and leaves. You might ask yourself where you want to plant yourself in your life, your work, your relationships, and your family. You might ask those questions of yourself at this crucial time. You might ask, "What happens to my soul at this crucial time?"

POWER 27-54 YEARS: OPERATES AS A SINGLE INDEPENDENT ENTITY IN THE WORLD

You gain your own soul at approximately age 28-years-old, the Chine or Knick Point of your life. You might get married, have a baby, or decide to move across country. You differentiate yourself from your environment. You create structure, form and crystallize your thoughts, ideas, and dreams as uniquely yours during this time. Now, the rubber meets the road and you try to survive on your own with all the information, feelings, actions, and lessons, from trial and error that you collected from Youth. It is when your soul mixes with the fire of your spirit; very similar to what happened when your soul first entered your body at birth. It is at this age the fire can burn and destroy you, or you can transmute your fire for your spirit to use. This is a time of reckoning at 27-29-years-old. It can be painful for you if you are bound to past conditioning, and cannot let go of habits, opinions, and beliefs that restrict and encase you in the past. On the other hand, you can use the experiences and learning from the past as a firm structure upon which to build your future. When this happens, the flame in your spirit inspires you to follow your true path of your destiny.

If you have observed the experiences of people between these important ages, you can see how the fire can either burn and destroy, or rekindle and transmute their life. It is true for all of us. When Youth makes it through the Chine of their fullness they make it to the Power portion of their lives between 27-54-years-old. This period is all about the material plane and manifestation. Material gain and comforts are what Power strives for with job positions, salaries, housing, and personal possessions. The quest is to put to use the ideas, feelings, and actions acquired at Youth and to see how they work for him/her. This power period tests survival skills.

CHAPTER 2: STEP 2

At this time, 27-29-years-old is a place where your mind rules your choices, you are free of the psychological restrictions, and childhood conditioning that encompassed your Youth. When you are in the Power portion of your life, you are free to determine which way you want your life to go. It is during this time you individualize yourself. How you think directly influences your life. During this period, you build your life in a material way achieving financial freedom, raising a family, maintaining a home, and involving yourself in community. Another Chine to fullness comes at the age of 54-years-old, just as it did at 27-years-old. What happens to your soul at this crucial time?

WISDOM 54-81 YEARS: ANALYZE AND ASSIMILATE FOR YOUR SOUL'S GROWTH

At 54-years-old, you self evaluate your true inner self. At this Chine or Knick Point, you might evaluate that you were a terrible husband who cheated on his marriage partner; or that you have been overly responsible and need some space and freedom if your spirit will survive. Again, at this point you may look like you are going through a 'mid-life' crisis because you have evaluated your Power years and maybe you did not like what your evaluation turned out to be. If you express approval of your past efforts and reward yourself with the fruits of your labor, you are happy. Instead, if you see dried dead fruit scorched by destruction you will decide to do something different. Whatever you reaped you now get to see what you have sown. Balance brings justice because of your past actions. If you have not chosen wisely this is the time in which you can easily make the decision to change your direction to create a different kind of future.

At 81-years-old, this period of wisdom holds for you much introspection. You reflect on the past failures and accomplishments and the present station of life you find yourself. You start to consider such issues as death and the immortality of the soul. At this time, your mind must now turn from the material world and build a bridge between the physical and the spiritual worlds, by synthesizing the results of your life.

During this time, you become more philosophical, introspective, and your analyzing skills are peaked. You are beginning to put more emphasis on your spiritual discovery and opinions about the intangible ideas and feelings that link you to God or spirit. If you live to the age of 81-years-old, there are three choices for you to make at this Chine and point of fullness: 1. Leave your body and die; 2. Stay in your body, and depending on the seeds that you have sown to this point, either become dependent and childlike, eventually to become senile and cared for like an infant; or 3. Be revered and honored because your very presence blesses those near. Your touch is healing and your words light the way for the weary heart.

You change from stage to stage-youth, power, and wisdom-by bringing your experience and expression to fullness and then beginning again the next stage on empty. It is the spinning of the Yin/Yang symbol: empty to full, full to empty, and empty to full again, repeatedly up until death. You are in the natural course of living.

These transitions are sacred to healers and shamans throughout time. Many initiations and embarkations happen at transition points of human life. Many cultures have their own sacred teachings about these vulnerable and sacred transitions of life.

THE NARROWS

In the Egyptian Huna Tradition, belief is that when you make your Knick Point choices you must go through "The Narrows." In hieroglyphics, you often see a canoe with a person alone rowing through The Narrows, the stream of the collective consciousness. The Narrows is one place where you must go by yourself. It is yours alone. There is no room in the canoe for anyone else. To be in The Narrows is to be floating in a stream or on a river of thought. The canoe you ride is floating on the collective river of all human thought, from all time, that flows through The Hall of Records. The mythical Sun God 'Ra' took the first thought or word as a ray from the sun. This first thought was the original one in the Hall

CHAPTER 2: STEP 2

of Records. The collective stream of consciousness contains every thought from every mind that ever lived. It is this stream of collective thought and consciousness from where you evaluate your choices. When you are at your Chine, you must make your choices in The Narrows, all by yourself.

The Chinese named many of the acupuncture points of the neck after sacred points that relate to the Hall of Records, where The Narrows lead, metaphorically. The neck leads to the brain, where we 'know' things. Imagine yourself on a canoe that you row right into the enormous Hall of Records. You see the pillars, the rows and rows of names and dates of souls and all their experiences, expressions and choices, placed in this hall. Everything recorded is in this hall before, during, and after the construct of time, as we know it.

Some of the names of the acupuncture points of the neck are *Heaven's Window, Man's Welcome, Heaven's Contents,* and *Heaven's Pillar*. Even the sages who created the acupuncture point system were aware of these sacred portals of the body. Warnings given to Acupuncturists are never to needle these sacred points on the neck. We Acupuncturists believed it was for safety because of the sensitive physical structures beneath the points like the carotid artery, which is true. We did not want to cause harm in the name of seeking health and flow. However, the other reason is that the area of the neck is your narrows. It is both your birth and your death canal or tunnel. It is the bridge between your head and your heart. The other side of The Narrows always holds light, truth, and loving in the spiritual realm. This is important for you to know so you take hold of the importance of your will and intention in choosing life at every choice, but especially at the Knick Points of your life and most importantly at death.

Remember, it is your will and willingness to experience your individual expression and experience of your soul, whether through the light or the dark, upside or the underbelly of life, both polar opposites will provide you with the core life message inscribed in the Hall of Records in all of time. Your decisions matter to you, to us, to

God. Every one of your choices does matter. With each decision you act like God acts, deciding which thought will live and which will die and recede into the background undifferentiated. It is through this recording of the Hall of Records you can have your memories. You can use your memories to retrace your steps to the site where you left one of the legs of a choice you let go. Again, aligned right next to that difficult decision is your precious core life message that helped to guide your life.

For you to tie yourself to your loved one, it does not matter what decision you made as much as the conscience and intangible reasoning that led you to make that choice. Your core life legacy message springs from that intangible reasoning. There is no wrong choice. There are an unlimited number of choices from each choice made. Each choice leaves a pattern and a trail. The obstruction that happens along this trail happens more often than making a perceived 'wrong choice'. It happens when there is indecisiveness, and therefore no choice made. On the face of it, it looks like you are treading water, and biding time when you are indecisive. However, in reality that is not what is happening. Something, an ideal, a non-measurable spiritual intangible is left dormant unused, and is in fact dying. With indecision, you are not the one who is choosing which one choice will die. You are not acting like God.

In a way, indecisiveness creates obstruction of flow, even disease, to the life you want to live. Make a choice. Be willing to 'be wrong'. Be willing to choose again. There is no last train coming down the track. You choose all day, everyday, as long as you are in this body up until death. As you enter death, where the marshland of freshwater of life meets the marshland of the infinite seawater of death, a different type of sorting process goes on that is not about decisions. There are questions, fears, and curiosity at death, yes, but they have a different quality. As you enter death, the introspection turns to questions like, "Is this love?" "Is that compassion?" "Is that loyalty?" "What experiences and expressions am I returning home with as I go to God, in completeness and Oneness?" When you arrive at death, you will start the process of stating to yourself, "It's not this. It's not that."

CHAPTER 2: STEP 2

IT IS NOT THIS, NOT THAT

As I explained in Chapter One when I explained Huna Shaman Nadia Eagles' teachings about 'Not this, Not that', we can use this concept in identifying in life our core life message. I will explain the concept in more depth. At death, often times, there is mortal reckoning where you lay in your deathbed and review your life, your memories and experiences one last time with a mortal perception. This mortal perception is from a unique, individuated human point of view, just before entering back into Oneness. It is a review of everything you have been though, from your first breath to your last. Within Oneness, none of these human questions has any relevance at all. They just don't matter. At that point, there is a new way of being that has no place for being separate and discerning. Being separate takes your intention and your will. Being human is courageous and miraculous. Every one of us should pat ourselves on the back that we have come to life with our soul to accumulate our individual experience and expression of God. To stay in the Oneness is bliss and effortless. One wonders how hard it must be to leave such a state of flow and belonging before we are born into this world.

It has often been said by those who have "crossed over into the light" only by some miracle to return to life and breathe again, that they had to review every hurtful thing they had done to another and feel the visceral pain that they had caused to another. It may be true. That I do not know.

However, I do know there is a revisiting of human experience, expression, and choice. What I also know is this review is not for karma or making even. No, it is because there is a search by the dying to find out just what is up ahead. How else does their soul take the next step? Inquiring souls want to know. Your soul will want to know what exactly is Oneness, and what it is not? Further, you will want to know how to recognize what is the wholeness of home. Where is the way home to God's Oneness? It is a "Where's Waldo" of a different kind. Instead of Waldo, it is God we are looking for, as we have perceived God to be from a human point of view, maybe religious point of view, but certainly a separate point of view. Where is God/Oneness in the scheme of things? Therefore, your soul skims and searches every nook and cranny of your life experience in your mind and heart. Where is God? How will I know if I am recognizing God/Oneness?

One by one, with each memory you say to yourself internally, "It is not this. It is not that. Not this. Not that. Not. Not. Not." You are not asking, "Is this it?" No, you are instead only identifying what it is not. Is this me or not? Is this God or not? Is this separate or not? Is this one or not? Is this patience or not? Is this abuse or not? Is this hate or not? "It's not this, it's not that." Maybe we do it this way in the form NOT rather than the IS form because everything is all Oneness. Oneness is not nameable in one thought or one word. One word or thought is just too confining. It just is. Perhaps that is why Jewish people use the dash in writing the word G-D, because it is unnamable, and unconfined by humanity.

The sorting by NOT is the last act of trying to separate into opposites. Separating into opposites is impossible after death. There are no opposites. There is only Oneness. What is left is for you to disengage from the perception of opposites that you placed on your soul while you were in human form. It is your birth crowning. Just like when a baby is born into the light from the womb, but instead it is your coming into the light of the hereafter into Oneness. You birth into the totality of Oneness again.

There are no opposites when you cross over into Oneness again. There is only one, no polar opposites. However, at death, you 'flicker' hottest in your heat, just like a candle, just before your flame goes out at the moment of death. At the same time, you speed up your sorting process of what made you different and unique. You try to consolidate your experience, expression, and choice into Oneness so you can take it home. You are, in essence, packing up your uniqueness and going to throw it back into the grand sea of Oneness from whence you came, like throwing the metaphorical individuated fish back into the sea of Oneness at death.

CHAPTER 2: STEP 2

Again, no way can any human know the verb/noun of Oneness in mortality until they have passed through the portal of passing. At that point, there is no need to know. The one IS all that was, is, and ever will be. You are fused into the fabric of beings, as is also all your experience, expression, and sensation. Oneness experiences itself as its pieces, like you and me, in human form, within its whole. You are just one of God's experiences of being a separate unique fingerprint in life. At death you are absorbed back, digested, and blended into the One of wholeness again.

When you tick off each memory with, "It's not this, it's not that," what *is* left is the silhouettes of 'Nots'. You might be saying to yourself, "That's not love, and neither is that or that or that; that's not compassion and neither is that or that or that; that's not cruelty, that's not brotherhood, that's not fair, that's not sympathy, etc." Just like a dot-to-dot, fill in the form numbered pictures; these 'Nots' are really the illusion of the form of who you think you are. The 'Nots' outline a pattern, a shape, a distinct form, if you connect the dots. They shape themselves into a closely held belief. You prove that belief your whole life. It is that belief that can become your core life message or 'ism', too. It is hard to imagine, but your core life message becomes the mantra and motto of your life and comes from your 'Nots.'

I remember when I was first learning homeopathy. As most students, I tried to use my newfound knowledge to find the homeopathic remedy that was just right for my health and me. Foolishly, I tried to heal myself. I remember one day in class where I just wanted to cry. In my naïveté and ignorance, I was doing what many of my patients do as well. I said, "I think I am the remedy Sepia (Sepia is a remedy that comes from the ink of the Cuttle Fish). I hate that remedy. It is a sad, pathetic, overworked, and overburdened state. That makes me sad and pathetic. I don't want to be Sepia." Well, I was not in a Sepia state. Moreover, even if I had been, I was not the Cuttle Fish or her ink. Had I been in the same state as the Cuttle Fish, I would have just used the wisdom of the Cuttle Fish's survival skills and experience it's energy in the medicine. The energy of the homeopathic medicine was the energetic source that would have alleviated the overwork and overwhelm, not the Cuttle Fish herself; and not her ink, had it actually been the correct remedy match. The healing match is in that which is unnamable. It is in the verb, the 'Not' of what this magnificent life form, the Cuttle Fish contributes to humanity for healing. It is not in the name of who she is but in *how* she does it. If it were the correct match, the medicine of her speaks my same energetic, spiritual language, and my body, mind, and heart systems learn *how* she knows. I survive better by piggybacking on her wisdom, her healing energy.

I think all of us are walking talking remedy states, not just the remedies in my pharmacy. We are medicine for each other. By identifying our core life message, we are identifying the name and state from which we heal our loved ones that we leave behind. Our core life messages then become their healing remedy. We do this even though we have no presence or body to share that wisdom. Our core life message is a type of spiritual healing homeopathic remedy that holds the wisdom of our life's experience here on earth.

Just as I was doing, naming myself with the nouns of the world, know that they are never big enough to contain the expression or experience of my soul or my spirit. I suppose each of us should have a dash in our names once we return to the totality of Oneness at death. Perhaps that is why we have dashes between our birth and our death dates on our tombstones. Would my name look like A-A? What would your name look like? After all, we are all pieces of G-D.

It is no different from people thinking they know you just because they know your name. Your name does not even begin to give the essence of who you are at your core. Many people think it makes sense to know your name is to know your fingerprint, your contribution, and value. People think they know you because you are a jazz singer, or make beautiful quilts, or love to raise Corgi dogs. They think they know you because you have a doctorate and have published articles. They think they know you because you have raised six children. They think they know you because you are a liberal or a conservative, or that you are a big supporter of the Green Global Movement. However, if they knew the reasons you let go of all the other interests and opportunities they would begin to know what really makes you tick. If they knew why you chose to give attention to those interests, then they would know your core life legacy message and a deeper part of you. They could connect with you there through your 'No's and Nots'.

The 'Nots' at death's door are the illusions you have clung to in defining yourself apart from the whole of Oneness. All the 'Nots' are artificial illusions. The 'Nots' also serve another purpose. They form the outline to the space and void around your unique piece for all that "Is" you. You cannot touch, feel, or identify what 'Is'. We never know what 'Is' is until we return home to it after death. Is it God? Is it love? Is it compassion? Is it gratitude? Is it understanding? Is it the feeling of belonging? No one knows. You can only know, while you are in human form, what IS in Oneness of the whole, by the shape that it is not; by the outline of 'Nots', the void, the indescribable, the truly intangible, and non-material. There is no word for 'It', as long as we are separate and human. Perhaps it is God. Perhaps it is love. It is too big and expansive to confine to one word, thought, or idea. I do not know. I do not even try to pretend I could make a noun out of a verb like God. It is the light left in the outline of the dark, the edges of our blind spot. Maybe it is that small dark or the light dot inside the yin/yang symbol. It may sound convoluted, but the void's outline of your miraculous spirit, its edges, leaves the mark of your unique contribution. It outlines your core life message and you by its edges, not filled in by the substance of the illusion of whom you think you were in life.

Therefore, when you knit together this pattern of, "It's not this, it's not that," you glimpse only at the possibility of what Oneness could be. It is a hint. It is not 'it'. It is the fossil of Oneness. This idea of being a 'hint' is similar to the story my mother used to tell me about the philtrum; the physical mark on your body between your nose and lips-the little canal below your nose and above your upper lip is what I was told is the 'mark of remembering'. It is about remembering what was, is, and always will be. I suppose it is remembering what it was like to be in the totality of Oneness with God before being a soul inhabiting a body.

SHHHHHHHH, DON'T TELL

My mother, Rita Marie, told all of her six children a story when we were very small children. I remember this story and can relate it to the philtrum, above the lip, mentioned above. The story went like this:

"Babies wait in heaven for God to send them to a kind, good family on Earth below. Before they are born, God knows that the babies know all things, just like God. The babies have no hardship. They know love. They know all that has been, all that is and all that will be, just like God. In heaven, babies swim in goodness, love, and all that is the best in the Universe. But, when it is time for babies to be born to a family on Earth, just before God has the baby take its first breath and howl its first cry, God presses his index finger across the two lips, like this, (and my mother pressed her finger across our lips) and says, "Shhh, don't tell what is in heaven." When God lifts his finger, he leaves a mark right above the upper lip to remind the baby to keep the secret. That little canal is called the philtrum. Sometimes, young babies remember what is in heaven. They may not be able to speak yet, but they still know. When they smile and laugh, they know. If adults listen very carefully to very young children, they will hear some of the secrets dribble out of the mouth of these babies as they begin to talk. The older the babies get, the more they forget what was in heaven, because the further away from heaven, they are as they grow, they forget. Sometimes adults will remember very faintly, what was in heaven. Even then, it is very, very fuzzy. Then as time passes, as the old men and women get close to death, they get small and their skin gets softer and see-through, just like babies. The elderly then start to remember what is in heaven again just before they get there."

My Mother's lesson to her children was that the totality of Oneness is unknowable to us humans while we live. Just like the story that my mother passed onto her children; every family, culture, and community passes on its lessons, core life messages, experience, expression, and choices through stories. While my mother had told me this story of the philtrum when I was a young child, I saw another point of view about the philtrum when I learned Chinese medicine. Though it is a different story, it still speaks of the sacredness of that point on the philtrum. My mother knew it one way. The Chinese know it another way. Still other cultures like the ancient Greeks connected the philtrum with love, charm, or a kiss. They considered this one of the most arousing places on the body.

The story is more important than the name philtrum. Your story, based on your belief, experience, and expression, will define your choosing in your core life message. My adding to the knowledge of the philtrum from my childhood with a Chinese perception changed my point of view of the philtrum being a sacred place that closes at birth, to a portal that goes both ways and affecting man himself, not just God. My experience changed my expression.

THE PHILTRUM

In Chinese medicine the acupuncture point that sits in the philtrum is one that we needle or press when someone drowns, or faints, in a coma, or needs immediate revival from life threatening shock, seizures, hysteria, psychosis, motion sickness, and acute low back strains. We use it to clear the senses, cool heat, calm the spirit, and help the lumbar spine. It is a powerful point where three channels of energy cross. It is the point where the most male and the most female acupuncture channels also meet. It is a point that connects the male channel and the female channel together, and the criss cross of the original choice of gender for the fetus. It is a powerful point. In an emergency I have needled a drowned unconscious boy to breathe again by needling this point. All meeting points are powerful. In addition, it is said by the ancient Chinese medical face readers that if there is a scar line cutting across, or wrinkle across the philtrum the woman has had a miscarriage, abortion, or stillbirth. It shows some ailment at the point of conception. Western studies have found that a flatter philtrum is often a sign due to fetal alcohol syndrome. The philtrum is a sacred area. No wonder it sits right above your kisses, your words, and is the riverbed for your tears of grief that run out of your nose.

SILHOUETTES

You will never know anything as it really is, because it is always moving, shifting, and changing. However, you will know what it is *Not*. You live in a world of *Not* with a glint of an experience and sensation of what *Is*. Your experience and sensation does cross the portal of passing along with you. You take it home. It does make it over the hearth. It returns to the One of wholeness upon your death. However, it does so with a spiritual perspective not a physical, earthly one.

When looking for spiritual truth, look to the silhouettes, the shadows. It seems that silhouettes are where the verb of you meets the noun of you, on the edges. It is where the moving meets the stagnant and the still. Look to the NOTS. When I say *Nots*, I mean look at the decisions you made when you were abandoned, betrayed, dishonored, disappointed, sick, near death, lost a loved one to death, stolen from, violated, beaten, ignored, dismissed, etc. If you look at what is left after these events of adversity, where there is destruction, you will see the edges of the silhouette of what IS as well. They sit right next to each other. You will see it in your response to adversity, disease, and death. If you cannot see it in your own life, or it is too close to your vulnerable places, or in your blind spot; then look to the outside edges of yourself and follow the villains, the outcasts, the lepers, the maggots, vultures, and the predators in life. They lurk on your edges. Many people project their unwanted feelings, thoughts, and actions onto these people in the world. You can use them as surrogates for what you are unwilling or unable to observe or transform within yourself. These outcasts will leave the stain of what *Is*, by comparison, as well. They help to define your polar opposites and the edges of the territory of your core life message.

CHAPTER 2: STEP 2

The Language Of Opposites

The language of opposites is the language of the intangibles, of character and conscience. You cannot feel it, touch it, or see it, if it is an intangible, but it has value. For instance, Truth and Honesty are intangibles and have value. You know they exist by comparing them to Lies and Cheating. In addition, Love and Attention are both intangibles and have value. You know them by comparing them to Hatred and Apathy. Patience and Focus are also intangibles and have value. You know them by comparing them to Impatience and Scattered. There are many intangibles, many character traits. You cannot measure most intangibles. Very often, they are not valued as much as material concrete objects. Nevertheless, their value is infinite. If we measured our wealth by our use of the intangibles, we would love ourselves so much more. Since you cannot measure intangibles you know intangibles by their opposite, by comparing them to what they are not. It is common to overlook the intangibles and take them for granted, while their counterparts get all the attention. The intangibles are what remind us of our connection to the wholeness of the totality of Oneness. The intangibles are also our character traits. These character traits will tie you to them in the Forget Me Knot experience. Other ways are not common ways that you can see what makes you tick. Modifiers are one of the uncommon ways to define your core life message.

Modifiers Define Us, Too

Besides your intangibles and character, the modifiers you use everyday also give you value. When your soul self defines itself as it enters your human body, you choose your modifiers. The soul chooses things like pace, intensity, timing, flow. Pace, for instance, is the speed at which you move, speak, process thoughts, ideas, and feelings. Intensity might be just how much energy you put into your interactions.

One patient said, "We don't cry in my family. We yell and talk loud enough for anyone in the room to hear us." Another patient claimed when stressed, he joked and used humor so as not to feel the tension and pressure. He said, "If I don't laugh, then I'll cry." When his mother died, he joked about the environment with his brother and sisters being one that was a cross between *The Jerry Springer Show* and the movie, *Birdcage*. In one of his descriptions, he said his sisters were hitting each other while crouched over his mother's stiff cold body. The devoted gay caregiver to his mother was waving his hands in the air wildly, and screaming with a lisp, "I've never seen anything like this!" It was funny the way he told the story, but there was something also odd and sad about the timing. This was his modifier of intensity in full bloom.

Timing might be your staccato, pulse, or beat of how you are in the world. Are you a person who gives your all at the beginning and peters out at the end? You would have a different mark on the world than another who starts slow and gains momentum to a grand finale in the end in everything he or she does.

I had another patient who was a Dreamer who felt that life was organic and no one should live from some artificial time clock. She felt things had natural closure and that things do not always end promptly just because another appointment is waiting. While it wasn't by more than five to ten minutes at the most, her family and friends branded her with 'always being late'. When asked why she was late to her own wedding ceremony, her answer was, "The time on the invitation is when the guests have to be in their seats, not when I, the bride, walk down the aisle. After all, I have to give space for the latecomers so they don't miss the ceremony! It was only a ten minute difference!" Timing is one common modifier.

Another modifier is flow. The flow of your life is the starts, stops, pauses, and gushes, in your life. Another one of my patients felt you were late unless you were a half an hour early to any appointment. He left many a doctor's office when the doctor was fifteen minutes late, no matter the reason or the emergency. He felt his time was just as important as the doctor's time and he should not have to pay the consequences for their "double booking." He felt that the doctor should leave more time between patients for the unplanned.

CHAPTER 2: STEP 2

This patient was a person who moved fast, talked fast, and finished things fast. His flow was fast. He finished my sentences before I completed them even though it was not what I was going to say at all. He assumed a lot so he could move and flow onto the next. He was irritated and impatient when the flow stopped. He told me of a golf tournament in which he was winning by a large margin. However, when the play ahead of him became slow and the holes backed up because the players were slowly observing their putts, he said his game fell apart from the break in his tempo, flow, and pace.

Modifiers qualify the movement of your soul in your human body. Your modifiers temper your experience and expression. Modifiers are your spice in life. They are powerful and as important in observing your pattern, as are your intangibles. The presence of your modifiers helps to make your fingerprint of your unique soul.

Take the background of your life out of the shadows of your perception so you can see your own pattern. Bring it to the foreground. The background holds all the gems of secrets that get you closer to housing both your separate piece with your sense of Oneness in a full perception. Your modifiers also help you to find your core life message.

Here is the sequence of finding the edges of your own personal silhouette. In so doing, remember to review your decisions in the nine-year demarcations of your life, paying close attention to the three crucial years, 27, 54, and 81-years-old.

When you made the choice you did, at those crucial years, ask yourself these questions:
1. What was the choice I made?
2. What was the choice I let go?
3. What was the reason I let that choice go that corresponds to a character trait that I hold dear and have repeated often in my life? What did my conscience tell me?
4. When I made that choice, what were the modifiers: pace, flow, intensity, and timing?
5. What are the 'Nots', the disowned parts of my choices and my life?

You will begin to see the outline of the silhouette of your core life message. It will also make it easier for you to see your own character and learn to speak your own spiritual language more fluently. In so doing, you will see where you are housing both being separate and one, noun and verb, in a silhouette. In the Forget Me Knot experience, you will also see that you gain an agility, resilience, and easy movement in your life. You will do so without attachment to the typical definition of yourself, or your 'stats'. It will be clear as to who you are, and who or to what you have attached yourself, your psyche, and your emotions. You are so much more. You are precious.

Another area that hints of the edges of your authentic nature and your core life message is in your use of negative words. Negative words are red flags to where you are playing your own game in life, and where you will find your core life message.

EVERYDAY WORDS OF DESTRUCTION

Listen to yourself saying these words in your daily conversation: Not, can't, won't, isn't, never, and always. These words point to your truth. Pay attention. They are the words of destruction. That which you cast away with the words not, can't, won't, isn't, never, and always are the red flags and markers of where you placed your polar opposites. These negative words or words of destruction you often like to project onto another, and cast far away from yourself. It is not important for you to feel embarrassed about using these words or try to extinguish these words out of your vocabulary. They are just markers that determine where you are going to play. Put no effort to change the way you speak. Instead, just notice you say these words, and when you say them. The words of destruction are fabulous clues to your own core life message. As Homeopaths, we use them all the time, to help us to find the correct match for a remedy state.

I remember learning about my own red flags of destruction. It was when my special needs child was a baby, and in and out of the hospital in life threatening situations on a weekly basis. I remember condemning other mothers who gave their keys to their teething

CHAPTER 2: STEP 2

babies to pacify them so they would not cry. I remember exclaiming, "Why would any sane mother allow their baby to put those filthy keys in his/her mouth, when those same keys have been laid down on God knows what surface, with germs, drugs, disease, pollution, or poison?"

I was sure I would NEVER put my child in harm's way with such a careless act. That was true until one day; harried and frazzled at the closing time at the bank, when I needed cash for a prescription for my sick baby's health I did just that. When the baby fussed, while I was speaking to the bank teller, I automatically reached into my purse and handed my keys to my special needs child to quiet her so I could think and get what I needed done. I glanced down to look at my quieted child with her eyes wide open chomping and drooling all over my keys and key ring. My "never" decision was right between two polar opposites: mothers don't harm their babies. Mothers do harm their babies, even when they don't mean to. Red Flags. It was where I was playing my game in my early years. Health and harm. Safe and dangerous. Responsible and irresponsible. These are polar opposites. After all, I had just given birth to a baby who was in a very unsafe place in regards to her health. I suppose one of the core life messages of my life at the time would have been from the Hippocratic Oath, "First, do no harm," or "Prevention is preferable to cure."

The words of destruction are really the rules you play by in your own life. Those words are your referees. Everything you perceive you judge by your rules, so you must keep constant attention to those rules. That means that if, for example, integrity is one of the character traits that are most important to your life, and anything unlike it must go in your subconscious rulebook. Therefore, as the referee, you must discern constantly what is true and what isn't, or who is honest and who isn't. After a while, you know intimately who the cheats are and why they cheat. You garner that information because it helps the referee in you to keep the rules going that you play by in your life. Actually, you need the cheats because they help you to understand honesty by what honest is not. Honesty is an intangible and not measurable by money or numbers. Without these cheats, you would never really know what the intangible quality of honesty is all about. However, because of the cheats, you know what honesty is.

You need your polar opposites. They are the guides to your life decisions and clarify your knowing exactly where you are between these two polar opposites by their contrast. Enjoy them, and notice where you make your absolute negative statements. It is where your censor and discerning parts of yourself reside and are part of the magnet of the compass of your life journey. It helps you create your core life message you will share with your loved ones before you pass.

Sometimes when you work so closely with the 'Nots', 'Nevers', and 'Always' in your life you become just like that which you have cast out. For instance, one of the first tele-evangelists, Jim Bakker, married to Tammy Faye exemplifies the effect of the words of destruction. Remember, Tammy Faye, the woman with the spider lashes? Their Christian evangelical TV congregation loved Jim and Tammy. Jim and Tammy talked strongly about sin of all kinds and the need to NEVER sin and to stay true to God's scripture. Jim took such a strong stand about prosperity and the acceptance of peoples of all color, creed, and gender identification.

As time passed, with a guilty verdict for fraud and embezzlement charges, Jim faced prison as an embezzler of parishioner donations, accused of rape, and called a sexual deviant. It showed him as a hypocrite of the scripture he espoused and brought his and Tammy's conspicuous consumption to a high pitch level. Yet he became very close to the 'Nots' in his own life. We all do this in some way, shape, or form in our own lives. Maybe in an odd way it is 'The Stockholm Syndrome' where the victim aligns with her captors. We align with that which we abhor because we have spent so much of our attention on it.

Another example of this is the founder of Mothers Against Drunk Drivers (MADD), Candy Lightner. Candy had three children. Each child was in a separate accident, permanently disabled, one killed, all by drunk drivers who got off scot-free. Before the creation of MADD, no one took drunk drivers seriously. Candy took the dismal statistics and reminded people that each of these numbers was a person; many were children, who were maimed or killed. MADD made a very big impact on the reduction in driving under the influence car crashes and deaths. Candy made this her life purpose as she struggled with her own personal grief of the disabling and loss of her children.

Then MADD organization took a different turn. Instead of driving drunk, it started to espouse abstinence. This is not the message Candy wanted for her mission. She felt her movement had lost direction. She stepped down from leading her crusade. Later, they arrested Candy herself for drinking and driving. It is not about right and wrong. It is about how we find ourselves getting so close to that which we cast off. These cast offs, your villains, are also your teachers. Your cast offs destroy, but they also give you life by comparison. By comparison, these everyday destructive words, the cast offs and referees of your own rulebook, give you answers about light and the totality of Oneness. These light answers are all around the carcass of these every day destructive words: Not, Can't, Isn't, Won't, Never, Always.

For instance, when someone says, "I never lie," they probably do lie. The truth surrounds these words. Shakespeare said it nicely, "Thou dost protest too much!" He recognized the red flags. They may lie to themselves or use white lies or fibs. The flags are up. The polar opposites of truth and lies erected, and the person has placed themselves between the two. In order to know truth, this person also has to know when truth stops being truth and becomes a lie. He/she studies it closely. It is his/her game in life. The rules are clear. No lies, only truth. However, you and I know that it is impossible to have only truth without lies as a comparison. How would this person know truth if there wasn't lying to compare it with? Remember, "It's not this, it's not that." We do that all day every day. Sometimes you play with your destructive words just to know the polar opposite better. Candy Lightner did with alcohol. I did with my keys.

Your everyday destructive words are just clues as where to look for your core life message. Do not disturb them. Keep them right where they are. The core life message is right by their side.

Life And Renewal Next To Death And Destruction

If you can forgo the luxury of judgment of the polar opposites of good versus bad, you can possibly experience something more about the pattern of the totality of Oneness. Your own personal spiritual language will be clearer to you. That would mean you would have to be a little uncomfortable, and more curious than judging or discerning. Sometimes it is the leftover bones that tell you more about yourself, than your immediate disgust or discernment. Even the vultures and the maggots leave the bones for Archeologists to find in the future. Even disintegrated remains leave fossils of shapes and forms of what was. If you are curious enough, then put fear and judgment in your pocket for later use. Instead, dig through the remains of the shadows, the intangibles, and the modifiers as well as the leftovers or the words of destruction. Be courageous and willing to take your perception past fear, revulsion, dirty, forbidden, taboo, and wrong, which stop you in your tracks and make you look the other way. Bits of light, like bits of gold, are there in the shadows, for the pickings, when you courageously look to see with a different eye and another perception. Surprisingly, if you get adept at this, you may find you can peek past the portal of passing at death, a bit, without having crossed over with your soul, just like me.

The Portal Of Passage

When you peek past the portal, maybe when you are present with someone at hospice, just before he or she is passing over, you will hold the responsibility of that secret, just like me. Moreover, you will want to tell someone. Not just anyone, you will want to tell the secret to someone who will take it further and wake others up to their knowing of the totality of Oneness. You may want to go through any of the well-known methods like prayer, meditation, sensation, nature, forgiveness, adversity, etc. Then there might be more of us waking up others to their spiritual language. If that happens, it will be more common for others to speak their spiritual language. Remember spiritual language, the language of character, more directly links us to the totality of Oneness while we are happily experiencing our soul's individual separate piece in life's adventure while we are still alive.

You can be happy with your experience of marriage as well as divorce; happy when you are stable in your home or restless because you need to travel; satisfied with your ample finances or even when you must repay financial obligations; exhilarated in your working two jobs at once or in even in job hunting while unemployed; peaceful in your vibrant health or weakness in ill health, etc.

Your experiences, responses and expressions that come from those situations can be bad or good, peaceful or stressful. They let you feel confident that you did it wabi-sabi in your unique special way so you have honored your soul as a separate human being.

Moreover, it feels good. You will be agile to move from perception to perception, separate to one, and back again. Fluid. Easy. Flipping your perception. Zero. One. One. Zero. The two perceptions will be simultaneous. When you finally die, you will easily recognize the reuniting. It will seem familiar to you because you have fluently spoken spiritual language all your life.

In my dream, I imagine a group of souls like you and me. We will have evolved the experience of God/Oneness as just separate pieces, experiencing our fingerprint of separateness in the world. At the same time, you and I will be part of a clump of souls in unison, experiencing the moving in and out of separate and the totality of Oneness together, noun and verb, oscillating in and out. The experience of the God/One will have our attention when we move in and out, separate and together, rather than each one of us as individuals doing our own thing, experiencing our separateness alone, like children playing in the same sandbox, separate but together in parallel play. It will be more like an orchestra playing the song of God. Our agility in flipping from Zero to One, whole and separate will allow the evolution and growth of the totality of One, in its entirety. Spiritual Language, the language of character and the intangibles will be a much more common language. We will all be able to hum the tune of God's wholeness. We will not be just separate pieces of God, doing our own thing. We will be individuals, but at the same time aware of our connection to the wholeness of the fabric from whence we came.

When you and I are aware that we are both individual and connected at the same time, there will be a consolidation of light, of force and all mortals will evolve at once in light. Therefore, it behooves us on an individual basis to be agile with both perceptions of zero and one and the movement between them. First, you and I must allow ourselves to be willing to look and experience what we have been unwilling to do or see. We must look to the destroyers, the shadows, the intangibles, and the modifiers, and to that which surrounds them.

You and I must put aside, for a while, our judgment and repulsion and desire to project the unwanted into others so we can, for the moment, be free of their weight within ourselves. You and I must allow them to backpack on our dreaded, taboo, uncomfortable, rejected, and abhorred thoughts. We must get dirty and look through the ugly and abandoned parts of humanity, and ourselves and to reclaim our own light and agility, as well as the cast off parts of ourselves, intertwined with our sense of the totality of Oneness and God. You and I need these puzzle pieces. We cannot evolve without them. Go now. Courageously look to your shadows. Reclaim them and take them with you. It is easier than you think.

Take the first step. When you think you are a victim to someone else's cruelty, ask yourself, what part of yourself is being cruel? When you judge another for abandoning their duty, ask yourself, what part of your duty have you abandoned? When you judge yourself for not completing a task, ask yourself, what part of you needs it to stay incomplete for you to remain whole? Be willing to shift your attention. Give equal time to the voice of the polar opposite that has remained unspoken. Give it a voice. Let it come home. Tag anything, word, action, or person, that has the 'NOT THIS' attached to it. Therein lays the unpolished gems.

The steps you can take to bring home the cast off parts of yourself is to:
1. Collect your absolutes and your destructive words. When and where do you say them? It is one side of the two polar opposite of your life game. Where is the exact opposite red flag planted?
2. Look to the places that are taboo to even think, never mind act, in your life. What is the worst thing about them? It is one side of the red flag of opposites. What is the exact opposite?
3. What parts of yourself do you hate and would like to get rid of if you could, physically, emotionally, or mentally? Red flag. What are the opposites?
4. What are the worst actions and people in humanity, which you believe should not live on this earth? Think again what quality is it that you find abhorrent because it is one side of your red flag. The other one is its exact opposite.
5. What is it that you fear and dread the most? Red flag. What is the exact opposite?
6. What idea, emotion, or substance is it that you cannot digest? Red flag. What is its exact opposite?
7. What idea, emotion, or action hounds you so that you can think of nothing else? Red flag. What is the exact opposite?

When you collect the two opposite red flags, know that you place yourself somewhere between these two polar opposites. You have staked your territory of where you will be separate or different. They are your rules now. This is where you will find your core life message, as well.

Commonly you do not like to look, think, or feel in the extremes. However, when you are retrieving parts of yourself for your core life message it takes courage for you to do so. It is where you must dig. It is where the gems of your precious self exist.

There are other ways to find the places where you have lost bits of yourself. You can find these lost little bits in your daily indecisions, wavering, second-guesses, as well as when you sit and don't stand, or when you mean one thing but say another. When you do this, a small bit of you is dying every single day.

In life, you make decisions all day long. You have mini loses all day long; good choices left behind. These choices left behind are the markers of your journey. Like Hansel and Gretel who left a path of crumbs, you too leave the choices untaken on your life's journey toward the finality of death.

Indecision Does Not Buy Us Time

This concept describes the toll that indecisiveness takes. So often, you think that indecision makes you feel like you are treading water or biding time. It is an illusion. Since change is always happening, something lives and something dies, always. When you are indecisive, something is dying, but you have left it to chance as to what dies. Often you are surprised and disappointed when you have the consequences of what dies from indecision 'dropped in your lap'. However, your indecision was a decision to let chance make the decision, instead of you. If you in fact do make a decision, but it is a wrong decision, you can make another one to change or rebuild it. Therefore, indecision is death of what you will not know until perhaps it is too late.

Once you have your five senses trigger, your one-liner, and symbol of your one-liner that opens up your legacy, you will be able to leave a trail and a path for your loved ones to reach out across the portal of passing at death and shake the bond of loving between both of you. You will let them feel your presence, in an instant, and feel comforted, directed, and loved by you. You will have tied yourself to them.

In this way, your life becomes a culmination through your core life legacy message that you will leave for the generations that come after you. They will know more than your name. He or she will have the

CHAPTER 2: STEP 2

code to know that there is a loving bond to speak spiritual language with you through his or her heart, even though you have no body or form. You will have tied yourself to them.

This is where you can identify the moral or premise of your life story, your proverb, quote, and mantra. It is the spine of your life, and your influence on other's lives too.

Once found, you can consolidate the core life message or premise into a one or two liner that captures the essence of the most important mantra that you lived by in your life. It is your thought or idea that, over all others, was your teacher when all else failed. It is a simple process.

Death is a measuring spot, and life edges right up against it, so the contrast is large and easy to see. With that said, know too, that the concepts of this book are ideas that you can use today, in your life, to live more fully and to make the most of the experience you are having here on earth now. With the skills and perception you learn in this *Forget Me Knot* book, you will learn the skill of observing the processes of your life, as well as the content of your life. By knowing about the process as well as the content of your life, or the decisions you have made, you can make your soul and spirit experiences much richer here on earth. In addition to feeling awake and confident about what makes you tick, the Forget Me Knot experience will make you feel even more authentic, deeper thinking, more introspective, and more purposeful. A Forget Me Knot experience will feel like you have been privy to 'a secret'. With that secret, you can make even more of a difference in your present life, as you are living it, from your core life message. You can feel unapologetic, freer, more creative, less attached to the inconsequential, more facile with change, and more resilient with adversity, as it comes your way. Most importantly, you will be aware, of the swirling, shocking, immobilizing, vitality-siphoning funnel of grief coming your way. This poem is about life as it relates to death. It reinforces in an elegant way, how both birth and death relate to one another.

Birth is a beginning.
And Death a destination.

And life is a journey:
From childhood to maturity
And youth to age;

From innocence to knowing:
From foolishness to discretion
And then, perhaps, to wisdom;

From health to sickness
And back, we pray, to health again;

From offense to forgiveness,
From loneliness to love,
From joy to gratitude,

From pain to compassion and grief to understanding-
From faith to faith;
Until, looking backward or ahead,
We see that victory lies
Not at some high place along the way,
But in having made the journey,
Stage by stage,
A sacred pilgrimage.

Birth is a beginning
And death a destination.
And life is a journey,
A sacred pilgrimage-
To life everlasting.

-Neilah Service for Yom Kippur
Stephen Wise Temple, Los Angeles, California

There are many misconceptions about death. I would like to bring to the surface what subtly bubbles below each one of us when we entertain the idea of death. These misconceptions are some of the reasons that no one wants to think about death, grief, or any topic that is close to our extinction. When you read these misconceptions, notice how you go blank almost immediately, just like a deer in the car headlights. It is almost instinctual and automatic. Thinking these thoughts brings the animal instinct in you alive and it even affects your brain chemistry. Do it anyway. Override your tendency to want to look away. See which one of these misperceptions has a resonance with you.

12 Misconceptions About Death

1. Death is Final.
2. Death is the opposite of Birth.
3. Indecision buys more time.
4. Imminent Death is a stable passive moment.
5. At the very moment of Death, we all experience death the very same way.
6. Death is the ultimate failure.
7. Life is only for the living.
8. Our Life is defined by our choices.
9. Funerals/Memorials are the occasion to pay our last respects.
10. It is up to the living to keep the Dead alive in memory.
11. Death leaves an unfulfilled void.
12. Death's end belongs to the dying and is not my responsibility.

Where Can You Use Your Core Life Message?

Besides dropping your 'ism' everywhere and anywhere while you are alive and healthy, a nine-minute eulogy is a place to state your core life message, whether you are planning it in advance for yourself, or you are making a eulogy for someone else. Supporting that core life message or premise with three or more examples in a eulogy reinforces just how your core life message was expressed and reinforced in the three major life decisions in your life. Another place to express your core life message or premise is the individual nine-year decisions, segment by segment, showing the evolving story of your core life premise. A timeline from birth to death, shown in a multimedia expression in a Life-o-graphic™ (as discussed in Step 5 of the Forget Me Knot experience), is a wonderful way to express your core life message. A Life-o-graphic™ is a multimedia snapshot of the most important snippets of the nine-year demarcations of choices, time, energy, and attention in your life.

Most timelines are a linear graph of your years from birth to death. What makes the Forget Me Knot timeline different is the placement of nine-year segments. Completion of a cycle happens after each nine years. As the cycle culminates a shift is noticeable.

The most important shifts in your life timeline happen at the three most important times in your life: 27, 54, and 81-years old. A Forget Me Knot timeline plots the decisions and changes in your timeline at the nine-year marks. These major shifts are the easiest places to identify the core life meaning in your life. The nine-year chunked timeline repeats a pattern, over and over, revealing the core life meaning at each of the nine-year shifts in varied forms. Your life meaning is usually identifiable in the language of character by the choices you make and don't make at each of these transition points. At each of the transition points at the nine-year chunks of time, especially at year 27, 54, and 81-years-old you can gather:
1. The core life meaning,
2. The way you express the core life meaning,
3. The senses you used to best express that core live meaning.

The responses you make at those key decision-making shifts that happen at your nine-year transitions also show the way you experience and express change. In your core life message or premise, you want to capture the way you respond to change and shifts, because it is one of the best ways to define your perspective and response in your life.

CHAPTER 2: STEP 2

LIFE CYCLE SEGMENTS
(BITING EDEN'S APPLE)

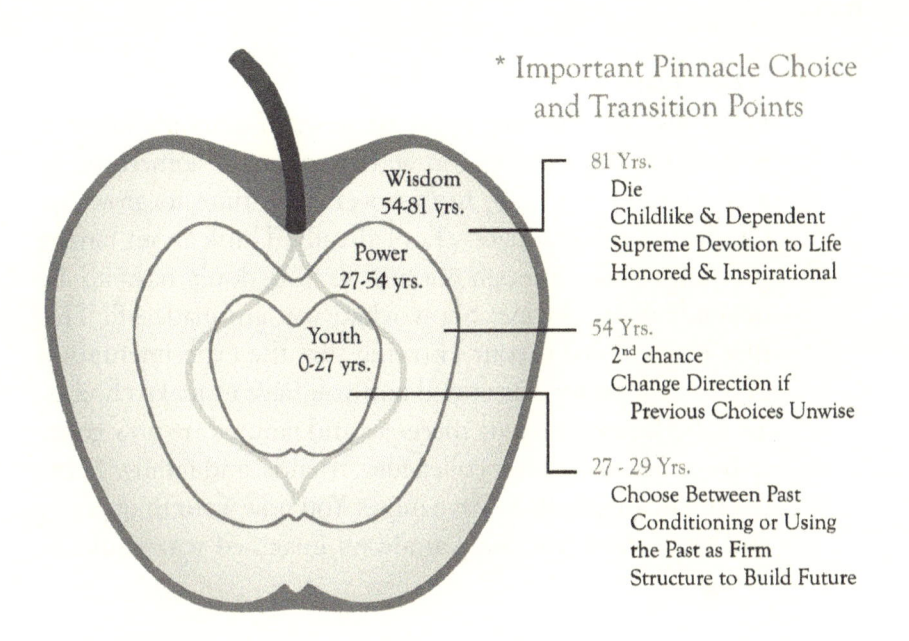

* Important Pinnacle Choice and Transition Points

Wisdom 54-81 yrs.
Power 27-54 yrs.
Youth 0-27 yrs.

81 Yrs.
- Die
- Childlike & Dependent
- Supreme Devotion to Life
- Honored & Inspirational

54 Yrs.
- 2nd chance
- Change Direction if Previous Choices Unwise

27 - 29 Yrs.
- Choose Between Past Conditioning or Using the Past as Firm Structure to Build Future

Youth 0-27 Yrs.   *27 - 29 Yrs.
  Formed
  Conditioned
  Expanded
  Mind & Character Formed

Power 27-54 Yrs.   *54 Yrs.
  Operating in the Material World
  Independent Entity
  Choose Positive or Negative

Wisdom 81 Yrs.   *81 Yrs
  Reflection on Reason, Order, Logic, Understanding
  Introspection - Innermost
  Reap What You've Sown
  Bridge Physical & Spiritual Worlds

NINE-YEAR TRANSITIONS

The three major shifts or transitions in your life usually require life-changing decision-making in which way the course of your life will take. The stakes and trade offs are usually high around these time frames:

1. **27-29 Years:**

    From just an ordinary point of view, 27-year-olds know it is time to stop playing and start working at something in a committed way. The fun is over. It is time to grow up. Graduate from graduate school already. Think about having a family. Make enough money so you don't have to be dependent on anyone. Show what 'you are made of'. This first Knick Point is your knowing that the experimentation period of your life has ended and you have to make choices. You also know that your successes and failures are now going to be compared to your colleagues, friends, and family. There is a fire in your belly to have more. You now want to quantify and truly create the life you always imagined you would be living.

    What is happening behind the scenes is that at 27-years-old, your soul encounters the fire of your spirit for the first time. There is awareness that youth is lost when your soul enters your body between 27-29-years-old. You gain your soul at 28-years-old. Between the ages of 27-29-years-old things are precarious. The fire of destruction can burn you or the fires of your spirit transmute you. It can be painful to you if you are bound to the past and past conditioning. If you cannot release those habits, opinions, and beliefs that encase you and restrict you from the past, it can be a prison of your own making. On the other hand, if you use your experiences and learning from the past as a firm structure upon which to build your future, it is then that you are touched by the fiery flame of your spirit, which reaches into your life and inspires you to follow your true path to your destiny. Fire can burn

CHAPTER 2: STEP 2

and destroy, or rekindle and transmute. That decision is at hand for you at this most decisive turning point.

2. **54 Years**:
    From the ordinary point of view, at 54-years-old, you evaluate your success as a breadwinner, family builder, homemaker, and your involvement in the community. You take a strong look at how much money you make; the kind of home and possessions you own; what kind of parent you have been; and if you like yourself. You evaluate just how responsible you were and how you measured up to the ideal you have carried with you, as to the life you always wanted to lead. You ask yourself if it matches. If it doesn't, you know you have some time to make it match the way you always wanted your life to look before it is too late.

    This is the second time in your life you encounter your own true inner self. Your inner self will express approval of your past efforts and reward you with the fruits of your labor, or you will evaluate that your will has handed you dried dead fruit scorched by your burning fire of destruction. You reap what you have sown. The universal law of justice comes into play. If you have sown wisely in the past, at this point you can easily change your direction. The future is yours to create.

3. **81 Years**:
    At 81-years-old you know that whatever you could have, or would have done, should have been done. You know death is up ahead and you can hear it whispering every time you get notice of the death of someone you know. It seems closer and closer. Your energy is less. You have to be more discerning as to where you spend your time. You might feel you have plenty yet to express and exude before it is time to leave this earth but the physical energy just doesn't support it. You think about how you mattered and just how you can influence those who will live on long after you are gone. You evaluate just how much you want to live or die. This is your

karmic choice. Your three choices are, to die, to experience senility and dependence, or to experience reverence and honor. Whatever the path, it is based on your merit of your previous choices.

It is sobering isn't it, the short impermanence of your life? The first instinct is for you to look the other way or not to think of the bookends of your life at all. What will that get you? Now that you know, you cannot un-know what you have just learned. Inherently you do not want to be wasteful or inefficient with this blessed God given piece of sacred Oneness that you have sovereignty over in this lifetime. You want to make it count. You want it all to matter. Nevertheless, your life is finite whether you are conscious about it or not. We all face the same evolutionary oscillations and knick points. At least try to look now and see where you are in your own lifetime.

RESPONSE AS A CLUE TO YOUR CORE LIFE MESSAGE

One of the ways you are different from the man sitting next to you, your sister or brother, or even your twin, is by the way you respond. While classifications can be dangerous labels and confine a person by their very definition, we can loosely use one of the principles of response that we Homeopaths use to find the correct remedy state. We are not so concerned with your story. We all will have similar stories in the end. We are more concerned, as Homeopaths, on your response to the story. Your response to life is what sets you apart from any other. In Homeopathy, we group remedy states into plant, animal, and mineral. For our end of life purposes, we will group your end of life responses into Thinker, Feeler, Doer, and Dreamer. To classify your responses this way, it will be easier for you to dig deep for your core life message.

I use the Thinker-Feeler-Doer-Dreamer throughout this *Forget Me Knot* Book, so I will describe what I mean by a response as a Thinker-Feeler-Doer-Dreamer.

Types Of Responders

Thinker

You might recognize yourself as a Thinker if you like structure, organization, or are an observer first. You might hate a break in organization, structure, or failure in relationships or performance. You probably would be highly systematic and organized. It may be very important to you to defend your thought or position. Symmetry would be important to you, as would exactness, written points, and percentages. You probably like to take things slow and ponder on just how and where things fit. You might speak uniformly and to the point. Your work is very possibly very important to you and you hate losing things. You trust repetition. You have a desire to fix things and keep them steady, similar, and unvarying.

If you are a Thinker, you might be an accountant, computer technician, manager, house builder, engineer, or even a performer of some kind. You talk a lot about your relationships, home, family, bank balance, performance, joints, skin, and nerves.

Feeler

You might recognize yourself as a Feeler if you are very sensitive to changes in the external environment. You feel it is necessary to be able to change, adjust, and adapt as things shift in your world. You like nature, even flowers. You appreciate the irregular patterns in nature and adore the irregular, rounded, wandering, and disorganized. Things may seem random, scattered, incomplete, and not ordered, but you are fine with that. Things may seem abrupt, and fast changing and you find yourself responding. You may get 'hurt feelings' easily sometimes to the point that you cannot bear it. You have variable mood changes, and affected by nature, music, and art. Others can easily influence you, and you have a quick reaction. Things come on quick to you and you often feel hurt, shocked, or strained. You can be soft, yielding, sensitive, emotional, or irritated, hurt, and in pain.

If you are a Feeler, you might be an artist, psychotherapist, nurse, or teacher. You talk a lot about random things but find it hard to complete a thought and often find yourself intermingling yourself with others problems.

DOER

Doers often have a conflict with two different sides of themselves. They are concerned with survival, competition, attracting attention with their behavior, and appearance. Doers can also be aggressive, malicious, deceitful, and have self-contempt. Doers often have mixed feelings about themselves, wondering if they are good enough. Doers also concern themselves with disappointment in love, and performance, and worry about poor views or attacks from peers. Doers are animated, warm, alert, and charming. They give eye contact easily and achieve a type of chemistry with others. They give and get rejection, neglect, are aggressive, and attacking. Doers worry about defending themselves and failing in love. It is important for them to relate and be a better person so they feel good enough. They like vividness, color, being amorous, and getting attention. They are alert and quick to react. Doers are restless, curious, jealous, expressive, and communicative. They worry about being isolated. Doers are multi-faceted, abrupt, and unsteady.

If you are Doer, you might be in advertising, athletics, acting, fashion, or competing in some way.

DREAMER

Dreamers are often all about expansiveness, the universe, and the unlimited nature of life. They are concerned with existence and expanding one's boundaries. Things often feel floating, out of space and time and unguided for a dreamer. It is important for a dreamer to connect to the spiritual and the non-duality of spirit. Dreamers are often concerned with immortality, having no roots, no identity. Dreamers sometimes feel isolated and separated from other human beings. They understand void and emptiness. Personal

Identity is evasive to a dreamer. Dreamers often have fantastic spiritual experiences and have no fear of losing their ego or identity. Dreamers like music and rhythm.

If you are a Dreamer, you might be a visionary, evangelist, psychologist, philosopher, professor, architect, CEO, recreational drug user, or writer.

Once you have identified the way you respond in the world, it will be much easier to not only find your core life message, but also to choose a symbol that best anchors and triggers that life message.

The way you respond is one aspect of your core life message. Another aspect of your core life message is the reason *why* you might have to respond and react to a problem in life. By knowing the way you respond as a Thinker-Feeler-Doer-Dreamer, you can identify just how best you will express your core life message. Your perception of reality and the reason to react at all to any problem will be where you find the content of your core life message and what is most important to you.

Below are the ten most common perceptions and reactions that Thinkers-Feelers-Doers-Dreamers use to justify their reaction in their lives. When you find which one of the perceptions you might use to make your world as you want it, you will also find the area you most likely will find your core life message. When you know how you respond and to what you respond to, it is like finding where the cross hairs intersect and you can dig underneath that spot quite successfully coming up with your core life message.

PERCEPTIONS OF REALITY AND REACTIONS

As a Homeopath, the reasons for a response are much different from the way a person responds. When we Homeopaths dig deeply, we find there are general reasons and reactions that Thinkers-Feelers-Doers-Dreamers as responders use to make their world okay. They are:

1. **Panic:** Escape as soon as possible. Life is in danger.
2. **Crisis:** Intense effort to solve a problem quickly.
3. **Possibility:** Optimistic because you can solve a problem by breaking it down.
4. **Persecution:** Solving the problem is doubtful, give up, and then try again.
5. **Doubtful:** Nothing can help. Find another way.
6. **Fixed:** Problem is harassing and persecuting. I am unfortunate.
7. **Chaotic:** Problem has to go away, whatever it takes; my life depends on it.
8. **Claustrophobic:** Limited time to solve this problem. Race against time.
9. **Isolated:** Dangerous and hard to solve problem. Many reasons impossible.
10. **Impossibility:** Problem is hopeless, and always makes me angry and frustrated.

Once you find yourself on the above list, you can find a problem that you solved in your own life. Each problem solved this way reinforces why the landscape of your life looks like it does. You have now identified how you respond to your life and what motivates you to do so. Below, I have described some examples of where the two crosshairs intersect; Responders and their perceptions that motivate them.

Examples Of Responders And Reactions

Imagine a young man who is forlorn and disappointed because his girlfriend has left him for another man. Depending on whether he is a Thinker, a Feeler, a Doer, or a Dreamer, he will perceive this differently:

Thinker

If the young man were a Thinker, he might consider the situation a terrible loss. He viewed his girlfriend as support that he could trust and depend on and for whom he could lean. She gave structure and substance to his world. Now he is lost and empty, all alone. He wonders how he will get the emotional support he needs. If only he was stronger inside himself, she would have not looked elsewhere. If only he was stronger, he could get through this.

Feeler

Another man might see the situation as a shock, something that just came out of the blue and completely unexpected. He is hurt, shocked, saddened, and confused. He reacts to the shock with numbness and paralysis.

Doer

Still another man could perceive the situation as one of competition, where he compares himself to the other man. He wonders if this man is better than he is and is contemplating revenge. He has rage and feelings of strong jealousy and the urge to "show him" who has the upper hand and more going for him. He feels victimized, betrayed, and rejected.

Dreamer

The last man might interpret the situation as the universe looking after him. A grander plan is in order and if he bides his time, it will reveal itself why this situation happened in the first place. Life is perfect, even when it doesn't look like it, and only time passing will make it clear. This man responds to the loss with the quote from Kahlil Gibran, "If you love somebody, set them free. If they return, they were always yours. If they don't, they never were."

In addition to the way in which the man responds, you would want to look at the reason or perception for the response:
1. **Panic**: "I feel like I can't breathe with my heart racing. I feel completely exposed and in danger. I will die because of her."
2. **Crisis**: "I have to solve this quickly. I know there is something I can do to get her back. But I have to move quickly or lose her forever."

3. **Possibility**: "I know this can be solved. We can go to counseling and work this out. We can break it down to see what went wrong. We can do this together."
4. **Persecution**: "Why even try? She has cheated, so I can never look at her the same way. I could try, but I am not sure it will work."
5. **Doubtful**: "Counseling won't work. Our relationship has been on a thread for a while. It would take a miracle to make it what it was."
6. **Fixed:** "This isn't the first time I have felt this way with women. I am such a loser. I always pick the cheaters. Something is wrong with me."
7. **Chaotic**: "I have got to find a way to get her back, even if I have to go into hock with my house to do it. I will just shower her with everything she wishes. Whatever it takes to get her back, I will sell my soul."
8. **Claustrophobic**: "If I don't act right this minute, the window of opportunity will have passed and she will have moved in with this dude. No time left."
9. **Isolated**: "I guess I just have to get used to being alone. It is my lot in life. I am just a leper. No one could ever really love me anyway, I am sure."
10. **Impossibility**: "I hate her. I hate me. I hate relationships. It is an illusion they really work. It is all a lie; a phony lie that I bought. There is no such thing as love. People lie. She lied. I hate her. I hate me for thinking there was a chance."

As you can see when you identify the way you respond with the reason you respond, you come up with an area that may house your core life message. The reason for the reaction you choose is where your choice comes from. That reason is the area where your most important core life message will light up and jump out at you.

MAKING A FORGET ME KNOT TIMELINE

As with most timelines, you graph a straight line for your years from birth to death. What makes the Forget Me Knot timeline different

CHAPTER 2: STEP 2

are the nine-year segments. A cycle is complete after nine years. After each nine years, a shift is noticeable.

After you have chosen the segment of life that best expresses the part of your life that speaks of your core life message to tie you to your loved ones, and the legacy to leave to the living in their everyday lives, you can also plot the evolution of your core life message into your own Life-o-graphic™.

1. First, draw nine horizontal lines one for each of the nine-year segments.
- On the first line mark 0 on the left and 9 years on the right of the line.
- On the second line mark 10 on the left and 18 years on the right of the line.
- On the third line mark 19 on the left and 27 years* on the right of the life.
- On the fourth line mark 28 on the left and 36 years on the right of the line.
- On the fifth line mark 37 on the left and 45 years on the right of the line.
- On the sixth line mark 46 on the left and 54 years* on the right of the line.
- On the seventh line mark 55 on the left and 64 years on the right of the line.
- On the eighth line mark 65 on the left and 72 years on the right of the line.
- On the ninth line mark 73 on the left and 81 years* on the right of the line.

2. Put an asterisk (*) at 27, 54, and 81 years. They are the key decision making years.

0_____9 yrs

10_____18 yrs

19_____27 yrs*

28_____36 yrs

37_____45 yrs

46_____54 yrs*

55_____64 yrs

65_____72 yrs

73_____81 yrs*

3. Plot *above* each of the lines the major decisions made. Plot *below* each of the lines the decisions let go at the 9-year culmination points.

For example:
18__Move to the East Coast to get married.__27 years*
Move away from my family and all that I have known my whole life.

4. Next to the right hand 9-year culmination year, state the character driven discerning criteria that was the deciding factor in letting go a life choice.

For example:
18__27 years* – To be independent. Avoid being abandoned. Avoid being compared to my own original 'perfect' family. Avoid feeling guilty that I did my original family wrong because I did things differently, my way. I avoided judgment and feeling abandoned.

5. Find the thread or pattern used for the core life message.

For example:
Abandon others first so I don't have to feel abandoned. Belonging is what is most important to me.

CHAPTER 2: STEP 2

6. Pick a life segment. Plot the years on each of the lines:
   1. BIRTH   0-9 YEARS
   2. GROWTH   9-18 YEARS
   3. RIPENING   18-27 YEARS
   4. TRANSITION   27-36 YEARS
   5. TRANSITION   36-45 YEARS
   6. TRANSITION   45-54 YEARS
   7. HARVEST   54-63 YEARS
   8. HARVEST   63-72 YEARS
   9. HARVEST   72-81 YEARS
   10. STORAGE   81-99+ YEARS

Double Star (**) the line that seems like it is the segment of life that contains the clearest example of your core life message. They may all have a piece of your core life message, but one will stand out on its own. Typically you will find the most important decisions at the knick point years 27, 54, and 81-years-old, as in the example above.

CAN YOU GIVE ME AN EXAMPLE?

For example, this is Sherrie's timeline. She has a stand out, life defining segment of her life.

Sherrie explained her defining segment this way:

Ripening 18-27yrs:
"My most important changes happened at 28-years-old: I was engaged to be married. I decided to make a family unit of my own, separate, and apart from my parents. I moved across the country. I decided to make my own community from scratch where no one knew me, and I could get to know myself on my own terms, with my own will, desires, dreams, and aspirations. I wanted to be a big fish in a small pond, and move to a small town from a big city. The more different I think I am evolving from my own family line the more I see, in reality, it is much the same in character and depth, with my own particular twist of interpretation and expression. Still, it has the same bones as the original family that I left. I miss my original family

and all the ritual and tradition that went with them. I try to create it on my own where I now live. It is not the same. I feel isolated and alone much of the time, except for my husband."

Chosen Ripening: 18-27 years
    "Doing" Physical Changes:
    Moved out into my own apartment with a roommate.
    Got my Drivers license. Got my first car.
    Went away to college.
    Graduated College.
    Moved back home after college.
    Found an apartment with a difficult roommate.
    Moved across country for first full time job.
    Quit my job.
    Moved to another state to online boyfriend's home.
    Lived in basement in online boyfriend's parents' home.
    Moved into an apartment with boyfriend.
    Bought and moved into our own home together with our dogs.

"Thinking" Mental Changes:
    Got my first bank account.
    Got my first job.
    Had part time job to contribute to his parent's household.
    Started a small home business together with boyfriend.
    Bought two dogs.
    Bought small home together.
    "Feeling" Emotional Changes:
    Got my first boyfriend.
    Got my first Fail at college, almost thrown out of college.
    Could not find a full time job. Money worries.
    Difficulty in relationship with my parents.
    Wanted freedom. Broke up with first boyfriend.
    Homesick but still wanting my freedom and money.
    Found friendship online, against my parent's wishes.
    Fell in love with man online and left all I knew for him.
    Got married to online boyfriend I love.

CHAPTER 2: STEP 2

"Dreaming" Spiritual Changes:
>I wanted a family of my own.
>I wanted to know that I could be proud of what I have achieved.
>I wanted to be different from my family, and recognized for it.
>Went to Friday Night Services at College five times.
>Went on two birthright trips to Israel.
>Went to High Holy Days every year before moving.
>Left home on the Day of High Holy Days
>Went to High Holy Days when living with online love.
>Got married to online boyfriend by a Rabbi under the Chuppah.
>Felt connection to my family via the Temple.
>Reflection on how my life is different/same at High Holy Days.

The core life message for Sherrie is:

Family: I take my family everywhere I go, because they are part of me. I am not abandoned, and I cannot abandon them, because they are in me always.

The second step in a Forget Me Knot core life message is choosing the perspective and favorite way you respond to the world. Choose one section of your entire life timeline that best represents your fingerprint of your soul.

For Sherrie, she decided the defining decision of her life was at her wedding at age 28 yrs, where the two generations crossed and she found her preferences and values were very much like her own families. Her wedding was non-traditional, outside in nature, with a spiritual theme at the core. It looked very much like her mother and father's wedding, except for the inclusion of her dogs.

Sherrie's core life message was:
"Margaret Mead once said, 'No matter how many communes anybody invents, the family always creeps back.'"

Her symbol or take home giveaway for her loved ones is a little tiny barrel with a red cross symbol, the kind a Saint Bernard Dog would wear around his neck to save someone who was seriously ill in the snow. Sherrie volunteered for animal hospice with her therapy dogs. Therefore, this symbol was perfect for her core life message.

In summary, knowing your life cycle will lead you to the theme, symbol, and essence of your life and your core life message. As you live through the three major phases of the life cycles, it becomes clear as to what is your theme in your life. It can also be clear when you choose only one segment of your life cycle. Each part of your life holds the whole of its meaning. You build on your previous choices. There are patterns within all of us, and they repeat themselves every 9 years. You can squeeze more out of your own knick points if you ask yourself these questions:

The Knick Point Transition Points of Choice are at three points of one's life:
1. **27-29 yrs***: Where you choose whether past conditioning is carried forward as a limitation or used as a firm structure to build your future: "What values beliefs, experiences and morals do I keep to build my structure and which ones do I let go?"
2. **54 yrs***: A second chance for you to choose again is to change direction if your previous choices were not wise: "Did I accomplish what I wanted in the physical world without giving up my own wants and needs along the way?"
3. **81 yrs***: To die; or choose childlike dependence in either some kind of dementia or helplessness; or to choose to be an inspiration and to be honored and receive supreme devotion in life while lifting others in their lives. "How much do I want to live? What do I want to experience with this free space on life's bingo card? What do I want my death to look like?"

THESE ARE THE FEELINGS YOU MIGHT HAVE IN THIS EXPERIENCE

1. "I don't know if the important choices that I made at the Knick Points of my life were deep enough to do justice to my spirit or soul."
2. "I am not sure what choices I let go. They were so hard to make at the time. I don't know if I put that much thought into them."
3. "I am not sure of the reasons I let go of the choices I left behind. Maybe I had no choice and life just happened and made the choice for me."
4. "What did my choices and the reasons for choosing/not choosing them have in common? What is my pattern? They look like separate unrelated choices that have nothing to do with each other. I can see no pattern or relationship."
5. "What direction did I lead? I just showed up and did what had to be done. I see no direction, or that I was leading it. I felt like a follower."
6. "What did I say yes to and to what did I say no to? It all just happened so fast, I wasn't aware that I was saying 'no' to anything. It just felt like I had the option to say 'yes' otherwise it was not my choice."

If you are finding this hard to do, it is because you are just looking at the facts and the core content of your life. At the same time, while you are making content with the nouns and structure in your life, ask yourself what also are the verbs and movement of your life as the process by which you live? You are trained to look at the nouns, because that is how we look at our lives: the structures, the endpoints, the polar opposites, and in contrasting black and white. You are looking at your life like a map in the mall: "You are here" and you want to be there. *Forget Me Knot* is not a mall map. It is not about the path. It is about *the way* you get from here to there. Do you skip? Do you run? Do you cartwheel? Do you go piggyback? We all have similar stories, adversities, delights, and interests. Nevertheless, what differentiates us are our verbs: the movement and process of our lives. It is there you get to see the best of you and your uniqueness. The few key questions that will help you through the Forget Me Knot experience are when you ask yourself, "What made me move in my life?" "When I did it, how did it make me feel?" and "What was I so hungry to express?"

STEP 2 LIFE DECISIONS CHOSEN AND UNCHOSEN

After reading this chapter you can identify your specific ONE core life message. Your ONE core life message is the premise that guides the pattern of your life. It is especially evident at the three turning point years in your life: 27-years, 54-years, and 81-years-old. You can identify the premise, principle, or point extracted from these key turning point years in your life. These three important times are when your decisions are the most significant in determining the direction of your life. Because of the seriousness of these decisions, there is clarity as to what values and beliefs make up your moral compass and guide your life. They help you to judge what you keep and work with in your life and what does not fit your core life message. The best way to clarify your ONE core life message is NOT by what you've chosen at the three forks in your life's road, but rather by the REASON you had to leave behind those other choices. Your core life message is embodied in your 'one-liner'. This is the snappy saying that guides and weaves throughout your life.

WHAT YOU'VE GOT:
- You have identified your core life legacy message.
- Your core life legacy message is based on life decisions made at your three knick point years.
- You can also include the shadow side of yourself in retrieving your core life message.

WHAT YOU CAN DO WITH IT:
- Reinforce your core life message with your loved ones as early as possible with your advice, stories, and modeling.
- You can notice your core life message premise in all the decisions you make day-to-day and when you communicate with your loved ones.

Writing on the memory can never be erased.

CHAPTER 3: STEP 3

Expressions/Responses

In this chapter, I discuss another way that you mark your character, beliefs, and values onto your life; to separate you from another through the way you respond and express yourself. Two people can have a value of integrity, but it is the way you express it that personalizes your ties to those you love most. Most people don't even recognize the way they respond in their lives. They have no idea if they are a Thinker, Feeler, Doer, or Dreamer. Most people are too busy experiencing their lives even to notice why and how they express themselves. Responses and expressions are the underpinnings running automatically under all that you do. They hold the clues to who you are. After reading this chapter, you will be curious and interested in the nuances that make you unique in the world. You will find that when you are with people who communicate in the same way you respond, that communication is easy. For those in different response styles, it becomes a struggle to try to translate your meaning to their own perception and style.

Expressions and responses are in the color palette you use to mark yourself on the world outside. It is not just for artists, musicians, or writers. It is for all of us, all day every day. You have a style and a unique way of taking up space and making yourself known in the world. It stems from your inner intentions, perceptions, aversions, and preferences. While these expressions and responses are infinite,

I have categorized expressions and responses into four groups. The reason I have done this is, from my experience as a Chinese Medical Doctor and Homeopathic Doctor, I have seen these patterns of response in the healing arena and in life.

Expressions show your favorite way to respond to the world. Expressions are your perspective or spectacles that you view and respond to in the world. In computer terms, expressions are the operating system in your hard drive. Responses carve and weather your spirit as you meet the challenge of adversity, disease, growth, relationships, travel, power, money, loss, betrayal, peace, etc. Response is your personal 'magic eye' that includes some things for your attention and leaves out others for a deeper more spiritual journey. Response with expression is your method to mark your personal imprint on life, and makes your small piece of God your contribution to the experience of the totality of Oneness.

The importance of identifying the way you respond in life is not only to have your one-line core life message that captures your pattern, premise, or motto, but also to authenticate that it came from you, your way, and from your perspective. The challenges you faced over time honed your perspective as you developed in the nine-year segments. Your perspective comes from your pattern of response and includes the spiritual language of your life: your character, beliefs, values, and the information you have garnered with your responses. By identifying the way you respond to life, you bring a way to see the pattern of your mark on your communications and your core life message. If you never include your response, your one-liner would just be a nice generic quote for future generations to read. It would not have you intertwined in it so it is rich with what makes you tick. Intertwining your response with your words brings to life your core life message by subconsciously engaging with others, in your own personal way, beyond their conscious thinking and discerning.

While your character and your spiritual language may change, your method of expression and response to your character will remain constant.

CHAPTER 3: STEP 3

The way you respond to the world falls into four categories. I introduced this in the previous chapter, and now we will explore the four major ways people respond: Thinking, Feeling, Doing, and Dreaming.

For instance, the person who maps out the terrain of the whole mountain and strategizes the best way to get to the top is a Thinker. The person who writes a love letter with their picture to tuck in the pocket of the climber is a Feeler. The person who climbs Mount Everest is a Doer. The person who reaches the highest peak of Mount Everest, plants the flag of freedom, and shouts their voice, in victory, at the top, with its echo into the caverns, is the Dreamer. In your life, you predominantly use one way of responding over all others.

Thinkers are very structured, organized individuals who have a sense of make/break, performance, or defending. They need relationships, have to form relationships, struggle with relationships, and worry about rejection and collapse of relationships. The thinkers know it is their own strengths and weaknesses that determine their survival in the world. The answers to the problems they face are all inside themselves.

A Forget Me Knot core life message from a Thinker might come from quotes, poems, proverbs, jokes, oxymorons, memories, endearments, repeated words, phrases, trite sayings, stories, suggestions, and 'isms' of the deceased. Thinkers love to rename things to make them interesting and identifiable. Thinkers like proof in structure and replication. You might be a thinker if you have to measure everything. You might be a thinker if you must check the sources of all statements and the authority must have inscrutable reliability and reputation. You might be a thinker if you need double blind reproducible results. You might be a thinker if you feel you have to defend yourself and watch your back all the time even when you have achieved great success. You may be a thinker if you take on most of the responsibility for problems and feel, if they are unsolvable then it is because of some weakness *inside* you.

Feelers are very sensitive to the world. They adjust and adapt. They feel rooted and unable to move in a dangerous, uncertain *outside* world. Feelers have to weather or reframe the problems that come their way. Oftentimes they are artists or healers because they receive stimuli so easily and make something better with their expression. They are flowery, flowing, and have irregular patterns, and aesthetic tastes. Their feelings are important. They are soft and emotional. They fear being hurt. Anger, joy/sorrow, worry/grief, and fears move them.

A Forget Me Knot Feeler likes to cry, laugh, nod, have ah-ha creative moments or secrets, or have unusual choices. You might be a feeler if you wear your heart on your sleeve and can anticipate how another feels just by listening to their voice. You might be a feeler if you feel you are super sensitive and get your feelings hurt easily. You might be a feeler if you are often getting in the shoes of another, and wonder if the world would just be a little bit gentler if everyone would just get along. Feelers are very emotional and start with their hearts before their heads.

Doers have conflicts within themselves. They wonder if they are attractive and good enough. They concern themselves with attraction, attention, competition, aggression, sexuality/sensuality, falling in love, and the animal side of themselves. Sometimes they are deceitful and malicious, jealous, dominating, or submissive. They like to learn through doing and touch.

A Forget Me Knot Doer likes to use gestures, props, symbols, pictures, rituals, colors, quirks, and eccentricities for their core life message. They like to charm. You might be a Doer if you like to wear animal prints; or like to be the center of attention at a party; or like to win any game that you play. You might be a Doer if you like to be on top and dominate in any relationship. Doers like to make sure they will win. They are competitive. Doers want proof of their prowess.

Dreamers would have all structures dissolve if they had their way. They care about the completeness of existence, to exist or not to exist. They want escape. They hate feeling pressured and feel content to be separate and expansive. They are impulsive, hate constraints and feeling obligated, and yearn to break free if confined. They might say, "Run in Feet, Dream in Miles."

A Forget Me Knot Dreamer talks about the global effect and universal principles. They are character driven, concerned about commonality versus separateness, and love to float and expand. They often concern themselves with causes, charities, dreams, misunderstandings, gratitude, their favorites, their hobbies, and their pet peeves. They speak about groups. They often are linking the physical with the spiritual, bridging the ethereal and non-material to the material world. You might be a dreamer if people just don't get you, or often consider you 'way out there'. You might be a dreamer if you have been told you are before your time. You might be a dreamer if you always think up odd solutions to problems that no one has thought of yet. You may be a dreamer if you feel you have to feel an expanse and be in nature because you feel zapped when stuck inside a building. You might be a dreamer if you feel you have a vision that no one else has yet that will benefit mankind.

When you identify yourself as a Thinker, Feeler, Doer, Dreamer, you can then use those qualities proudly when you state your core life message. Using the qualities that make you unique gives authenticity and depth to your signature one-liner, a core life message of your own life.

Some examples of the occupations of Thinkers might be Accountants, Computer Technology, House Builders, or Engineers. Possible occupations for Feelers might be Artists, Musicians, Nurses, or Psychologists. Doers might be Athletes, Advertisers, Veterinarians, Actors, or Politicians. Dreamers might be Writers, Speakers, Visionaries, Clergy, or Inventors.

You will find that you tend to find an occupation that best allows you to express yourself in the way that fits, so you can express your gifts comfortably. You will tend to feel comfortable in communities of like-mindedness in the way that you respond. You can more easily feel understood and accepted when you share with people who respond to life the same way as you do.

To get an idea if you are a Thinker, Feeler, Doer, or Dreamer, look at the following chart and see where you might feel most comfortable. We all have some of the qualities in each one of the columns, but there is an affinity when you see many of the qualities that you either prefer or would rather avoid.

THINKER-FEELER-DOER-DREAMER CHART

THINKERS	FEELERS	DOERS	DREAMERS
Structure	Sensitive	Competition	Expansive
Pattern	Flowery	Animals	Inadequate
Checks	Irregular Patterns	Attention Seeking	Isolated
Symmetry	Wandering	Warmth	Lonely
Organized	Descriptive	Alertness	Exaggerated
Percentages	Adjusting	Eye Contact	Perceptions
Systematic	Random	Attractiveness	Brighter
Exactness	Worry About Others	Love	Sweeter
Points	Influenced Easily	Human Interaction	Better
Numbers	Quick Reaction	Being Good Enough	Impressed
Chronic Problems	Rapid Onset	Felling Split Up	Fascinated
Slow Onset	Emotional	Human Cruelty	Impresions
Slow Progress	Hurt	Being Beaten	Heightened
Break in Relationships	Shocked	Animated	Bored
Failure in Performance	Strained	Charming	Addictive
Home/Family	Begins Suddenly	Affectionate	Fear World
Bank Balances	Mood Swings	Playful	Deserted
Health	Varied	Amorous	Forsaken
Performances	Disorganized	Mischievous	Theorizes
To the Point	Soft	Aggressive	Laughs
Uniform	Adaptive	Restless	Whole of Existence
Strong	Irritable	Deceitful	Without Boundaries
Calculative	Nature Interests	Curious	Spiritual
Losing Something	Irritable	Malicious	Merge Surroundings
Repetative	Greenery	Jealousy	No Roots
Fixed/Unvarying	Plants	Expressive	No Identity
Steady	Music	Vivid	Separate
Similar in Situations		Communicative	Void
		Fears Being Attacked	Empty
		Fears Being Rejected	Spiritual Identity
		Fears Being Neglected	Space
		Changeable	Imortality
		Unsteady	Flight From Reality
		Abrupt Changes	

CHAPTER 3: STEP 3

There are other nuances that make you different from any one else. These nuances, when brought into the light of your attention, are useful to fine-tune your core life message. In this Forget Me Knot experience, my intention is to take out of the shadows the inner workings of you that make you unique from anyone else. One of the areas that make you different is how you use tone, pace, volume, and intensity, in your life.

TONE, PACE, VOLUME, AND INTENSITY

Your signature of tone, pace, volume, and intensity helps to make your Forget Me Knot core life message match the words in your one-liner. It is usually the things unsaid, not described and unidentified that often makes your core life message unique or memorable. Imagine someone saying, "Come up, and see me sometime." If Opie on the nostalgic TV series *Andy of Mayberry* said it, rather than old time sensual film actress, May West, it would have a very different connotation and effect. On the other hand, if it was, "Come home." It would be very different if it was Auntie Em calling to Dorothy in *The Wizard of Oz*; or the little boy Elliott calling to the alien in *E.T.* The words have a different effect when we put our own pace, volume, and intensity in its meaning.

My father used to say, "It is the spaces between the words that make the sentence make sense." When writing the core life message or motto, use tone, pace, volume, and intensity by deciding the slowness of speech, the loudness of the voice, the intonation, and accent of the words. Try to match at least your key repeated words so your loved ones can identify your core life message with you because they heard your words, your way, repeatedly. I remember my father repeating such phrases as, "Always put it in writing." Or, "Life is not fair." Also, "Always pet the fur the right way." When I hear those words in my head, I can hear his pace, intensity, and volume. I am sure anyone who also heard him speak those words hears something similar in their own heads and hearts.

Have you ever noticed how high the tone of your voice is raised when you speak to your pet, or a small baby? Why do you do this? Is it so

105

the baby or the pet recognizes that you are speaking only to them? Though we do this subconsciously when talking to babies or pets, you also do this when you speak to others. Have you ever noticed your tone change when you feel victimized, chastised, or helpless? How about a tone change when you are an authority in charge of a large group? We all have a tone that is uniquely ours.

In the Chinese language, tone changes the meaning of a word spelled the same way. An inflection of any word will change its meaning. Most very young children do not know about tone. Sometimes they say the most profound statements, but because they have no idea about tone, what they say can be lost and undervalued. Make sure you listen to very young children. They often carry very spiritual messages that you will miss if you depend on tone to hear if it is important or not. In the 1960s, host Art Linkletter built a television show around that very topic with, *Kids Say the Darndest Things*.

How you express your tone, pace, volume, and intensity are easier to see once you identify yourself as a Thinker, Feeler, Doer, or Dreamer.

EXAMPLES OF EXPRESSIONS AND RESPONSES

Here are some examples from some of my patients who represent the different types of expressions and responses to loss, grief, and death for the various responders: Thinkers, Feelers, Doers, and Dreamers. I have chosen what perspective each one of these responders might have after just losing a loved one. Below is an example of what each of the different responders might say to their loss:

Thinkers: "I lost my support system when I lost Nick. He did everything for me from writing checks, to fixing the house, to planning our trips. I don't know if I can cope. I need support, a shield, an anchor, and some protection, and now he is gone. I feel incapable to go on by myself. I should have died first. I do not have the capacity to fend for myself. If only I had taken more responsibility, I might have been less overwhelmed. However, I am just not as smart, strategic, strong, and methodical as he was."

CHAPTER 3: STEP 3

Nick was a hard, yet anti-authority type policeman who felt superior and proud of his ability to protect and defend the community. His colleagues considered him a 'cowboy' because of his driven nature, disdain for mindless red tape, and his strong need to fight for others to protect them from wrongs and the antisocial elements. He had a strong sense of duty but at the same time, was also intolerant of contradiction, though he himself was always saying no, and correcting others. Nick believed we should all be vigilant and fight against thieves and wrongdoers.

Nick's core life message might be a quote from Delores Ibarruri, "It is better to die on your feet than to live on your knees."

Nick's symbol of his life message, for his loved ones might be a small nickel star the size of a dime, to tuck into a wallet. It would signify each of our personal duty to protect the victim and fight for the weak in the land of the free.

Nick's wife was a Thinker, too. Thinkers can be the ones creating the structure and protection as well as needing the structure and protection. The red flags of polarity between which the two of them played their game of life was support and protection. Nick gave it, and his wife needed it. It was just like a lock and key. The two of them bonded within this core life message, Nick was on his feet, and his wife was on her knees.

Feelers: "I feel numb and sensitive at the same time. I don't know what is coming next. I am hurting so much I cannot bear it. Why did he leave me? I am so angry that he never considered what my life would be like if something ever happened to him. I still feel he will walk through the door and everything will be back to normal. Everything seems chaotic, unorganized, and unsteady. I am so emotional and easily influenced because I have no compass and direction now. He brought the world to me in a colorful, creative ever-changing Technicolor movie. Now, my world will be still, boring, and black and white."

Emotionally sensitive, Remi, who emigrated from India, came from a noble family. Prior to Pakistan's taking over the territory that was once owned by India, his family had a very respectful position of wealth and stature in society. Remi's family had to flee the area, leaving all their wealth, stature, and dignity after the Pakistanis took over their land. His family had to survive, working from the bottom up, in an oppressed state, for the very people that took their home, while maintaining their own dignity and honor. Having lived through the ridicule and humiliation of the Pakistani control, Remi believed strongly that one should hold their head up high no matter how oppressed or insulted they are. He felt a sense of self-control and rigid persistence in morality and class. It was his belief that dignity was something that no one could take from you unless you allow it.

His core life message might have been a Gandhi quote, "I will not let anyone walk through my mind with their dirty feet."

Remi's symbol of his core life message, for his loved ones, might be a small bar of soap to remind them to keep their mind and heart clean for themselves and others.

Remi's sister is a Feeler, just as Remi was a Feeler. They were both affected by what went on around them in their environment. For Remi, he had indignation, and self-pride, as his response to the dramatic changes he and his family lived through when their family's station in life was 'stolen by another culture.' His sister, too, felt that with Remi's passing her environment changed from being colorful and creative to being stark, confined, and sterile. Both Remi and his sister are feelers that are at effect to what happens in the outside world.

Doers: "I have mixed feelings. Part of me feels relieved that she is gone while at the same time relieved and restless. I felt trapped by my care-giving duties as her mother. It is time for me to live my own life and start mixing with other people again. I miss the vibrant fun I used to have in my life, before she became ill. Illness drains the life out of everyone. The other part of me feels rejected and isolated from her passing. How could she leave me so suddenly without warning? A place in my heart that she occupied is empty. I wonder how I will survive when I look in the mirror and immediately think of her and our mother-daughter bond? She looked so much like me, and my side of the family. She was my family. We bonded so, that losing her is like losing a limb."

One of my patients, Patricia, a beautiful model, and a Doer, had herself arrested when she pushed a security guard into the swimming pool once she noticed him staring at her in her bikini and swimming in the pool on her honeymoon. This was a defining moment of her core life message. She was attracted to and repelled by people looking at her, yet she was a magazine model by occupation.

Her core life message might be what Shirley Lord said, "Believing in yourself and liking yourself is all part of good looks." Or even what Joan Rivers said, "The psychic scars caused by believing that you are ugly leave a permanent mark on your personality."

Patricia's symbol or relic for her core life message might be a small 'evil eye' bead for her loved ones to carry with them in their wallet to remind them of beauty and to keep away anything that does not adore beauty or spirit, and may have intention to harm.

Both Patricia and her mother are Doers. Being attractive, included in a group, and adored are important to Doers, just like them. The red flags of opposites for the two of them lie between people looking at them for beauty because they are safe or people looking at them for beauty because the intention of others is to exploit and harm. Others looking at them or looking at oneself in a safe way are the keys to the core life message of these two beauties, mother, and daughter.

Dreamers: "I feel like all boundaries have expanded and I cannot get my bearings. I just want to run away, not think about the permanence of it all. I am sure that she is complete wherever she is now where there is no pain and she is free to be whatever she wants to be. I want to remember her at her best. Therefore, I am glad I did not visit her at her deathbed. I did not want to see her in her decline. I don't think she would have wanted that. I want her image of wellness to be etched into my thoughts of her, not her illness, weakness, and death. I know she lives forever and will be around me at all times. Even though she is not in a body, she is everywhere in nature. I know where to find her. "

Mindy was a new age healer seeker who was curious about all the newest healing techniques or tools that came onto the market. She would share the new healing concepts with her family and friends and tout its benefits, until the next new tool came onto the market. She loved her apartment because it had many solar tubes and three fourths of her apartment wall space was glass windows, with a view of a forest of green trees. Mindy was a homebody and thought the outside world was harsh and sometimes cruel. She said she felt safe within the confines of her 'glass cage'. Her family worried that she was agoraphobic because of the extended amount of time she spent being homebound. Nevertheless, Mindy felt that viewing things from home made life less risky. In her home, she could expand her world through her mind meshing with nature and the great outdoors. At times, she felt isolated, forsaken, and bored. However, the outside world terrified her and the insides of her home sometimes bored her.

Mindy's core life message might be a line from Jonathan Swift: "Vision is the art of seeing things invisible." The symbol of her core life message might be a small crystal prism that reflected light and beauty in all directions to remind her loved ones to look for truth and beauty in the spaces and void.

Mindy was creative and safe inside the 'glass cage' of her apartment. She had found a mediocre way of having both. She wanted to expand into nature but the world just wasn't safe to her. She could only look to nature from afar through glass. For Mindy, the red flags of opposites were between expanse into nature and safety in staying confined. Mindy had found a reasonable compensation by pretending she expanded in nature through the glass, even though it wasn't so. For Mindy, being with nature through glass is as close as she could get to feel unlimited. At the same time, she felt safe. Mindy was a Dreamer who wanted to feel expanded, but wanted to make the expanded and unlimited come into her four walls. She chose the two polar opposites: unlimited and limited, expanded and confined. She found herself somewhere within the two polar opposites. Her twin sister who grieved for Mindy was a Dreamer, too.

By this time and at this point, you have decided on your most important character trait and core life message that you want to leave for your loved ones. You have decided just what perspective you want them to take when they apply it to their life. You have also discovered how you want your core life message delivered. Further, you have identified just how you respond to life, whether you are a Thinker, Feeler, Doer, or Dreamer. You can now match your message to how you want to communicate your message.

If you haven't yet decided if you are a Doer, Feeler, Thinker, or Dreamer, then look at the chart to decide just where you fit. This is where you are and this is where you are going to be able to tie your core life message to them. Now that you have your core life message and the way you express it in the world, you will now find out just how to anchor and embed your core life message into your loves one's attention. By doing so, your core life message or motto will be triggered into their everyday lives by the use of the five senses. You will also know which of your senses is your lead sense of all your five senses. It is that lead sense that sends and receives information and expression. You will embed your core life message or motto by using your five senses. The five senses will also be your tool to imprint your tone, pace, and intensity.

In addition, you will assign an everyday symbol, that best exemplifies and matches your core life message as an anchor to trigger your core life message in them. In this way, your loved ones will feel you are around them every time one of those every day symbols appears and triggers your core life message in their memory, especially when you have passed on.

One area it is useful to know if you are a Thinker, Feeler, Doer, or Dreamer is when you are crafting your Life-o-graphic™ or when you are choosing the symbol that triggers your core life message. The more congruent and consistent the core life message is with the way you respond and express yourself, the more authentic, deep, and reproducible your core life message will be when tying you to them. Furthermore, your core life message will make certain to your loved ones that it is you, and you alone, that is making that message come alive in their life, even though you have passed on. That is because it is you and you alone who would have said or done things just that way.

PREPOSITIONS

You naturally think of yourself as a noun: a static person, place, or thing. You know and identify nouns easily. Since you are an animal, you are constantly deciphering if the noun you sense will kill you or not. Therefore, you are more interested in nouns than any other word. When you speed read, you concentrate on nouns so you can get a gist of the story line. Next, you look at the verbs, just how something is moving so you know how you must survive. Therefore, the parts of your mind that get the most attention are the nouns and the verbs. However, the part of your world that gets very little attention, but holds the most power in making the core signature of you is the prepositions in your language and in your life. A preposition shows your relationship to another word, person, place, or thing. A few examples of prepositions are up, down, around, through, in, out, about, between, beyond, near, or within, for example. Prepositions are much better at differentiating you from another by how you use the prepositions of your life. My patient, Jack, can help you to understand the importance of the prepositions in your life.

Jack was 'The Untouchable'. He did not want anyone to touch him, not even his own wife's embrace. He had a hard shell around him; refused hugs and any demonstrative example of feelings. If you overrode his wishes, it was like hugging a stiff board. He even gave handshakes as little as possible in his business dealings. Jack was not a touchy-feely type. He was a Thinker. He used logic and structure. There was not a place in his life that didn't make sense. The prepositions, or lack thereof, defined Jack and his core life message. He liked to control what he thought and what he experienced and expressed. Making the world predictable and safe was his life mission. He was the opposite of The Cat In The Hat, a spontaneous fun loving sort.

When Jack would talk, especially when he was angry, his hand gestures would make a fist and pound the air downward. His gaze, when he was speaking to me, was downward cast. Even his handwriting was mostly basic bold printed capital letters, with such a heavy downward pressure that the papers below the one he was writing on were imprinted with the same; just as readable even without the ink. He wanted certainty in the world and walked among men as the Jolly Green Giant, with each step clomp, clomp, clomp. His mark on this world was solid, certain, and predictable. He was a walking anchor to all who knew him. He grounded the people he loved with common sense, loyalty, and responsibility. He selected out of conversations and life what did not make any sense and seemed to him unpredictable and erratic. Jack was very comfortable with the preposition of "down."

Imagination, feelings, and issues just gave Jack too much anxiety. He needed the sense of feeling grounded. The prepositions in Jack's life determined him more than his job as a computer programmer, or his love of old time radio programs that he would listen to in his spare time. The fact that he would let few people or new ideas in his world said more about Jack's inability to handle chaos and change. Jack needed predictability and certainty. Therefore, it was no surprise that Jack had collected pictures of boat anchors, and was writing a book about the history and shapes of boat anchors.

Jack's preposition is mainly down, grounded, and predictable. His love of anchors is one more example of the down of him, the anchor being the rooting and planting of him safe and predictable. His wife probably had to have the preposition "around" to be with him and be in his world as lock and key. You see, if we just looked at the Thinker part of Jack we would miss the part that makes him different from other Thinkers. Prepositions make it much easier to observe just how you are making your mark on the world.

When you are determining how best to make your core life message to your loved ones, and put your authentic signature on it, make sure you include your own prepositions or your direction and meaning in relationship to other people and other ideas. What determines your fingerprints on your literal physical fingers are the swirls and spaces between the raised lines. They move this way and that, unique to you. Additionally, your metaphorical fingertips of the prepositions of your life determine your stamp on this world, the way you swirl this way or that. So make sure you include how you relate to other people, the prepositions in your life and your ideas when determining just how you will communicate your core life message.

At this point, you have one more skill to discover and fine-tune your search for your core life message. You can identify your polar opposites. You can identify the destructive words in your speaking. You are able to identify the outcast, judged, and despised parts of your life. Now you can see how you move with those you love and care about by the use of your living preposition. Jack's energy goes downward. His wife's energy probably goes around. My own personal preposition is probably from a gopher's eye view, looking at things from their upside down and maybe inside out. What is your personal preposition?

All these methods of processes I am presenting to you are very different from the usual content or story of your life. You are not used to paying attention to these parts of you. Commonly, you are not observing the 'how' you do your life. You are too busy just living your life. I am giving you the skills to do both: live it and observe how you live it by selecting out the things you most likely will not be looking for. Since you have never thought of yourself as a preposition, or realized that the 'Nevers' of your life have anything to do with you, it will now be a little easier for you to actually see into your blind spot. Without any experience in this area, you also have no preconceptions, so you can see the purity of yourself as you enter into your blind spot, and discover this way of perceiving yourself and your core life message. As you try it, you will be curious and intrigued by what you find. As a Homeopath, I am always in awe at not only what I find in any human being, but that it is so beautiful and hypnotizing. Alice must have felt like this when she fell down the rabbit hole.

I have written just how you find two polar opposite ideas and plant yourself somewhere between these two ideas. I have explained how you move and oscillate, use the prepositions of your expressions, your destructive words, your senses, and use your outcasts to reinforce your core life message by *how* you live your life. This is on the mental/emotional plane of your life. The same expression that happens on your mental and emotional levels can be seen with the physical plane the same way. Your body has two matching, bilateral organs, created so they can feed information off each other and get you your bearings on a physical level. You need two organs to get information on how to respond and live your life.

YOUR PAIRED ORGANS

Paired organs set up a way to have polar opposites within the physical body just as you do in the mental and emotional constructs you create. As you have seen, polar opposites allow you to find an emotional or mental place between two opposing ideas to experience and express yourself your own way. Placing yourself between the two red flags of opposites in the game of your life allows you to oscillate, move, and evolve your spirit in expression and experience. The physical body does the same thing. It sets up two identical but opposite organs: two eyes, two ears, two types of the same teeth, two lungs, two nostrils, two kidneys, two ovaries, two testicles, etc. When you have two organs, they set up a type of communication system where energetic information transfers between the two. It is just like two telephone poles with electrical wires between them, or even in the child's game of "Telephone" with two cans held together by a string between them, so you can hear the conversation on the other end.

Having paired organs allows the communication and information between your organs to oscillate, evolve, move, and transfer biologic processes to create homeostatic balance, energy, and life. It also helps your physical body to function in a peak way, and for you to know your next step to take so you can function at your best, survive, and efficiently use what energies you have, so you live longer.

I bring this up to you so you can see all the same principles and patterns that are examples on all four levels: your mental, emotional, physical, and spiritual levels. Each of the levels holds the same pattern of you.

In Chinese medicine, we know that every organ has an external exit and entrance in the body. The lungs external doors or openings are the nostrils and the pores of the skin. The external doors or openings to the lobes of the liver are the ears. The external doors or openings of the stomach are the mouth, etc. These external doors from our organs are what we call our five senses. Your five senses give information about you and your connection with the world around you. They also link you to your paired internal organs. These paired internal organs have their own oscillation and information that is expressed throughout the five senses. Therefore, you can see how all the mental, emotional, and physical levels connect and relate to one another because each has a similar system of pairing, oscillating, and evolving. All the levels: mental, emotional, physical, and spiritual provide the same pattern for your core life message. It is for that reason a Homeopathic doctor does not have to look under every rock in a person's life to match the correct remedy. The pattern leaves its mark all over your life, so it is there for the pickings. I can't miss it.

What does the pairing of organs have to do with your core life message? As you look to all areas of your life, the information is showing a pattern of what is important to you. It is in your body, your organs, your gestures, your hobbies, your job choices, the foods you eat, and the way you relate to the people that you are closest to in relationship. When you look to the physical body to give you confirmatory clues as to your core life message, you can be sure they are accurate, because the body does not lie. It holds the fossils of

CHAPTER 3: STEP 3

your choices, preferences, and aversions and the consequences of those choices.

As Homeopaths, we care very much, what your daily preferences and aversions are in your life because we know they will help us to find the correct remedy match for you in treating your illness. We care if you don't like ice in your drinks, or on the other hand, if you like to chew ice cubes. We care whether you like spicy hot food but hate slimy foods, like oysters. This information all points to this interlinked communication system that is mirroring itself on the inside and outside of you on the mental, emotional, physical, and spiritual levels.

Yes, even the spiritual levels. There is a concept in Chinese medicine, "So above, so below." What it means is that whatever you find in the upper realm is also in the lower realm. If it is in heaven, it can be found in man and vice versa. One metaphor I can illustrate this idea is with the tree. The roots of the tree that spread and move in the ground are searching for water and minerals. The roots are also just like the branches reaching up into the sky searching for oxygen and sunshine. Branches look very much like the underground roots. This metaphor is also in the body. The arms are the branches and the feet are the roots. When I use acupuncture points to treat disease I can use the same principal, "So above, so below." When I want to treat a pain on the upper body, I can often treat the pain better and more effectively by needling the lower body in an inverted mirror image. We can treat your left elbow with tendonitis by needling your right knee. Many times I get better, quicker results than if I used the traditional Chinese medical method of treating an elbow for tendonitis.

I mention this in this paired organ systems section because I want you to know that the gathering of the same information is on all levels all the time. You cannot miss the pattern of your core life message. It is everywhere. You cannot be wrong because your core life message and all your nuances are blatant and repetitive. Find a truth in one system and you will find it in all systems.

It is for this reason I am not as concerned about double blind reproducible studies. I look to nature for how it processes energy. If I can find the same truths in the patterns in nature, then I can count on it to work in our physical system as well. Nature is tried and true, surviving long before man could think, so I can have good certainty that when I find principles in nature, they probably are true for man too.

I looked to nature when I wondered why I have a matching pair of major organs and corresponding orifices. You, too, might have thought your paired organs were to have a spare, just in case one did not work. This may be true for the sake of your survival, but it is more the case that the two orifices that lead to the bilateral twin organs are that the organ needs the information from both sides of the body to gain enough information from the outside world to know what to do next. Each orifice bounces and feeds off information from the other. The two nostrils are an example to know what you smell. Your nostrils lead internally to your nose, which smells. This leads to your lungs that breathe, which oxygenate the blood that feeds your tissues so you can carry on the work of your own body. Having information from each nostril gives your body location, pace, distance, intensity, and more. This information found in your intangible world, is just as vital to your survival. It helps your body to function automatically without your thought. Your paired organs give you information about yourself and the world around you. You can also use your paired organs to confirm information about your core life message, the way you respond to your life, and the five senses you use to gather information.

For example, the gas company puts a sweet smell in natural gas so we can detect a leak and either leave the situation or turn off the deadly gas. You smell that sweet smell from both nostrils to locate not only where the leak is coming from, but how severe is the threat of explosion. Each nostril bounces and feeds off the other to give information that is more specific. The sense of smell is one of the five senses that can give you information about who you are and what is your core life message. Scientists say that you 'smell' fear before you are sure you are being threatened. Animals can smell your fear and attack the weakest one in your group who exhibits the scent and movement of fear.

LIES, MISPERCEPTIONS, AND FANTASY

When I am in a homeopathic consultation to find the constitutional remedy for a patient, I often tell them that when they don't know the answer to what I am asking they can make it up, lie, or guess. There is no wrong for them. What I have found is the pattern of how a patient responds, and the key to the correct selection of the homeopathic remedy found in what my patients cast off, pretend, and even misperceive. You can see what makes you tick, and what your core life message is by what you cast off, hate, and pretend. Just like the orifices in your body that pick up location, intensity and pace, you define what makes you tick, or makes you unique in the entire world by the bouncing off your polar opposites. In other words, you choose your polar opposites, your angels and devils, heroes and villains. They bounce off one another, give you information about you, how you want to define, and carve out your own unique life. By choosing the players, words, truths and lies, or preferences and aversions, you are also, at the same time, defining where your soul will play in your life, and what core life message you will mark on this world.

To make this idea more concrete, pretend you are in a toy store in the game section. When you choose Lincoln Logs over Monopoly, you are defining your pattern by both Lincoln Logs AND Monopoly. Maybe you chose Lincoln Logs because you are a Thinker and like predictable building structures, and to rely on yourself for the control. Maybe you cast off Monopoly because of the erratic, unpredictability, and emotional interaction of the game as well as the people you have to play with to enjoy it. On the other hand, maybe you choose Monopoly because you like strategy and competing to win all the property and money because you are a Doer and like to compete to be the best. You love the hunt of the game and need the others to reinforce your prowess.

When you decide the game you play in life, you do so by deciding who will stay to play and who will be outcast, unable to play. Either way, when you look at whom you keep and whom you do not keep in your world, you are determining what makes you unique in the entire world. From this information, you can identify your mark on the world and your core life message, and what truly unique difference you wanted to make in this world. Your lies tell me what are your truths. Your absolute truths tell me your lies. I care not what your lies are or your truths are, per se, to agree or disagree, or to judge you in any way. I care that the process and perceptions you are using to play your own game of life. The process you use to play your own game of life is where your core life message is and the best essence of your expression and experience found. So look to anywhere there are extremes, like lies and fantasy, love and hate, yearning and avoidance. You can find its opposite and find yourself smack dab between the two, experiencing your life, expressing yourself, evolving your spirit, and growing your uniqueness.

Another area you can find the pattern and clarity of your core life message is where you are trying to make your square self fit into a round peg to force yourself to fit into a round hole. The trouble is if you are a square peg, then there is no way you will be able to fit yourself into a round hole, no matter how you try, pretend, or force yourself. The fact that you are trying to force yourself to fit into a round hole, at all, tells me it is a good place for you to find the pattern of your core life message and the essence of you. There is heat, attention, and energy where you have force. It is a good place to look for your core life message.

NO FORCE TO FIT

For example, when I ask a patient the foods he/she prefers and the foods he/she hates, I often get a "good" diet list. This list of foods is what he/she 'should' eat to be healthy. This is his/her round hole. Many of my patients are very disciplined about their diet, too. However, the best information I receive about the pattern of a patient is when I ask them to throw out all the "rules" about good eating. I ask, "If everything you ate made you healthy and vibrant, then what foods would you love and what foods would you hate?" These patients smile, light up, and their voices get animated and loud. Now, they are talking the truth of their being. At that point, I am letting them reveal that they are a square peg and would love to be in a square comfortable hole. When asked this, I get the heroes and villains in the pattern of their food world. In addition, what makes them different and unique in the way they respond to their world.

I give this example of true food preferences and aversions because when you try to force yourself into any pattern expected of you, by society, parents, or family name, it may influence, but not determine what truly makes you unique in the world and your authentic core life message. When you try to force a square peg into a round hole, you get resistance. When you try to make yourself heal faster than you are capable because it is not your pace, you get resistance. When you try to force yourself to relax when you have inner tension because you are anxious and frightened that you will not survive, you get resistance. Resistance wastes your energy and your life source.

If your efficient body is continuously spending its resources at a place that will not reap the rewards you are seeking, and it looks like you are wasting your resources, then there must be another reward on another level that is more important. That level is where your core life message is clear. The reward may be the tug-of-war going on between your two opposite polarities and you are oscillating and gaining experience, expression, and evolution; but not where you are expecting it. You may be getting it with the process of your life rather than the actual content where you are looking. Experiencing yourself through *how* you process your life, rather than the things you achieve can be so joyful and elevating. It is so much easier to connect with others through the *how* than the *what* of life.

No amount of mind over matter can obliterate your true essence no matter how hard you try. It is impossible. It is a waste of your life force and energy to try to fit yourself into any round hole if you are a square peg. The sooner you understand this, the easier and more effective your life will seem to you. Suppression, or forcing yourself to fit and consolidating all the energy to compensate your being to make your life work by an outsider's definition, will just be a waste of the God given oneness you have been given. Your job again is not to become one and blended while you are in human form. That will come soon enough at death. Your job is to be a unique expression and experience of God so you have something wonderful to bring back to the whole of Oneness when you die. This is not the time to force you to fit. Nevertheless, if you find you cannot stop trying to be a square peg attempting desperately to fit yourself into a round hole, then you are evolving something else. It is usually the *how* or verb of your character where you are gaining benefit, other than where you are looking for your evolution.

The resistance you create is also an easy place to see the imprint of what makes you unique and what is your core life message. Resistance creates a mold of where you fit and where you do not fit. Your resistance shows your pattern of your being, kind of like a silhouette. It does it in reverse, like a negative in a photo.

So those of you who are rebels in the world, it is a perfect place to look for your core life message in that which you are rebelling against, your villain, or fitting in. Oftentimes, what you are rebelling against and the tension between the two is where your core life message and unique mark is for you in this world.

Forcing yourself to fit, or doing the exact opposite, not fitting on purpose so you are not forced, are still heated places where you are experiencing and expressing your essence and core life message. You now have one more place to look for your core life message. There are still other areas you can find the fossils of your being and your core life message. Your point of view on what should 'always' be right or wrong, and what should 'never' be right or wrong are also good places to look for your core life message.

CHAPTER 3: STEP 3

ALWAYS AND NEVER

Another area that is a good place to find your core life message is with your speaking the words, "Always" and "Never." These categorical words reflect where you are certain in what you keep and what you cast away. In so doing, you determine the polar opposites as well as the way you play the game of your life. Remember, wherever there is certainty, there is uncertainty at the same time. These are the fossils or the legs in the Leg-A-See Formula covered in Step 1.

When you are searching for your core life message, you want to look where you have had the most heat, the most attention, the most expression, and the most experience. Therein lays your core life message over and over and over again in the pattern and expression of your unique signature in your life.

An example of the use of extreme words as a clue to your core life message is with this patient, Kristin.

MR. PERFECT

A single dentist, Kristin, in her 20s was lamenting how she was looking for the perfect mate with an online dating website. She said that there are no more 'perfect' mates out there and that her search had come up empty. She also stated she knew this was true because when she and her other single girlfriends got together, they shared their lists of 'Mr. Perfect'. They all said the same thing. They came up empty. As it turned out, all their lists were the same as Kristin's with similar character traits on their preference list: honest, faithful, hard working, funny, etc. They, too, were not having any luck. She sighed and said, "I guess in a way, my girlfriends are my competitors because we are all looking for the same guy."

It was then I told Kristin what would make her unique mate come alive for her is when she also stated not only what she wants in a perfect mate, but also what she doesn't want; not who she is but who she is not. The non-negotiable, 'not and don't' list will not match any of her girlfriends lists. Each one of her girlfriends will attract a different type of guy by their 'Not' list.

When Kristen identifies what does and doesn't make her tick, she will know herself better and attract a better match for a like-minded mate. When you call home the quiet but heated parts of yourself, recognize them, and welcome them, your life will feel more authentic, and more comfortable to you. When you welcome home your 'No's', 'Nots', and 'Nevers', you can fall in love with what makes you unique from others. It is one way to identify her red flags of polar opposites that Kristen could use to weed out and fine-tune her definition of her perfect match, by refining her sense of self-first.

As you collect the information about yourself that makes you unique for your core life message, you will also be clearer, on whom you are as you live your life from this point forward. Kristen's experience with online dating made me ponder about the perception of our expression of our core life message on the Internet in our online personas.

We are all unique. In the social media platforms, we are congregating by what we have in common. However, where we match one-on-one uniquely is not by what we have in common, but rather by who we are not. Our acceptance of our 'Nots' is where we will feel even more comfortable with ourselves. Imagine a social media site that sorts us by our aversions as well as our preferences. Only then, we have found the community that really understands us and loves us for our flaws and all, will we feel a sense of true belonging.

Now is the time for you to identify the sense organ and sense that has been the most important way you respond to people and events in your life. After reading below, choose your lead sense so you can include it into the anchoring of your core life message into the everyday lives of your loved one.

CHAPTER 3: STEP 3

THE FIVE SENSES AND THEIR CORRESPONDENCES

The five senses are more than what you think they are. Most of us think the five senses are just sight, sound, taste, touch, and smell. However, the five senses are so much more than that. The five senses are portals to information coming in and information going out. The five senses have correspondences to the five elements, five seasons, five directions, five emotions, five colors, five tastes, and five life cycles.

When there is a correspondence to more than one of the five elements, seasons, directions, emotions, colors, tastes, or life cycles you can layer these correspondences to create a type of clear imprint of yourself on the world. Imagine a combination lock with five slots. When you line up all the correspondences, the lock opens easily. Human beings are no different. We are like combination locks. When everything lines up, we are more trusting and we open ourselves up to experience. Something subconscious in us trusts. We pick up congruence intuitively. It is the same type of congruence we get when we are in nature, or when we view anything that has the Fibonacci number ratio in its proportions, like the beauty in the painting, *The Mona Lisa*. We trust. We open ourselves up to the experience and let it all flow in or out. You want that open receptivity when you are anchoring your core life message with your loved ones so it can spontaneously open into their everyday lives.

When you use the five senses and layer the correspondences you can easily imprint yourself and your core life message on your loved ones so they know it is you next to them, if not in body or form, then in spirit, even when you are gone. By learning how to imprint yourself on your loved ones, using the five senses while you are alive, you are planting yourself in their consciousness to link with you when you pass on.

By now, from your work in Step 3, you have all the pieces you need to construct a Forget Me Knot core life message or motto, but you need the method to make the memory of you and your core life message stick to the hearts and minds of your loved ones forevermore. The five senses are the glue to make the core life message stay in the heart and minds of the living left behind.

THE FIVE SENSES AS ANCHORS

Use the five senses to anchor your core life message. Once anchored and bonded, the five senses can also trigger your core life message to be carried on to another generation, piggy back style on simple life triggers that open up your presence instantly, in 3-D, to your loved ones left behind. For instance, you can remember listening to a romantic song from your teenage years that stimulates a memory of one of your young loves. You can almost smell the scent of summer and the warm breeze brushing across your cheek, with the feeling of attraction welling up inside you, as if in that instant you came back to life for just a moment. The song ends, and you are left feeling a little bit more alive, even a little melancholy for those times. The five senses are what anchored that response in you. Sound, touch, smell, and sight are all alive in your imagination as the romantic summer love song plays on. However, once it stops, your attention shifts and you only feel a warm bonded glow.

In the Forget Me Knot method, imagine that that same person who stole your heart in your first summer love intentionally layered the correspondences of the five senses. Imagine that your first summer love had a ritual of collecting small black pebbles on the beach, with the sound of the seagulls, the scent of salty seaweed, and the grit of sand between your toes, every time you were together that summer. Suppose she or he used to count the black pebbles with you, play a game with you of guessing what shaped animal the pebble might be, even giving the pebbles names and a story to go with the shape. Imagine he or she holding the little black pebble wedged between both of your hands book ending the pebble so you could feel the smooth surface, and shiny wetness on both your palms. Along with that, imagine his or her deep, close, eye-to-eye soulful stare of love and warm breath next to your face just before you kissed. Imagine your heart fluttering and opening to a spark of loving and bonded

CHAPTER 3: STEP 3

connection. Imagine he/she says, "I love you. Your love makes me see love in everything in the world, in myself, in you, and even this small black pebble." Imagine your first kiss, dropping the bonding hormone oxytocin, just from your first love imprinting an experience and expression within your memories. All five senses coded that bonding moment, including a core life message.

Decades later, that same core life message is able to trigger any of the five correspondences: smell, sound, touch, taste, and sight. These senses are keepers of the special memory. Each of the five senses become emissaries for this one memory, triggering and retrieving immediately the other senses in your memory to come forward on command. The sound of the seagulls could bring up that memory. The gritty feel of sand between your toes could bring up that memory. A warm summer breeze with the scent of salted seaweed could trigger the first love memory. When that memory is triggered, all that went into that memory will come up for you at the same moment in time, as if the senses linked together with a welding iron.

Imagine 40 years later, that you stub your toe on a small black pebble, on the beach while you are staying at your sister's beach house, after going through a very acrimonious divorce. It is winter and raining and there is no summer breeze. Nevertheless, you would never know it. Because one instant look at the little black pebble triggers the core message in you, along with the summer breeze, and the smell of salty seaweed and gritty sand between your toes. Then, instantly, his/her words floats through your mind and you hear the words in your head, "Opening up to true love makes everything look like love, even this small black pebble." With that trigger, a wave of vulnerability about what loving means comes over you. A healing salve to your heart happens in that moment. In that moment, it is as if he/she has come to remind you that the end of one loving relationship does not mean that love closed off to you forevermore. In addition, her/his core life message comes to your mind at just the right time, in just the right way that it is healing to your soul. A Forget Me Knot core life message does the same thing for the loved ones left behind.

The five senses imprint themselves easily with small everyday symbolic objects. One sense layers and links with another, so when one of the five senses surfaces, all the rest of the senses, simultaneously embedded, also surface in that moment. All of the bound senses contribute to the memory that imprinted on your mind, including the core life message. For this reason, it is important to use the five senses when you share your core life message with your loved ones while you are still alive. You can take your message, enrich and layer it with the senses so you will be remembered even by the future generations who have never met you. They will have your core life message at just the right moment when they most need it.

In a tying you to them in the next chapter of this book *Forget Me Knot* Step 4, you will learn how to anchor your core life message with everyday objects, words, gestures, smells, textures, tastes, and sounds that will automatically bring up your core life message, subconsciously, within your loved ones' minds and hearts, whether they like it or not.

THE ASHTRAY

For me, even mentioning the five senses brings up the trigger of the shape of a five-fingered hand in my memory. You see, for me the hand that comes to mind is a table high, freestanding silver-plated ashtray that my mother used when she smoked her Benson and Hedges cigarettes. This ashtray, her ashtray, stood like a vertical pedestal and looked like a raised hand that held multiple cigarettes at the same time. This five-fingered ashtray was anchored into my imagination along with my mother and how she relaxed from all the responsibility of raising six young children. I can see her now seated next to that silver plated, freestanding five-fingered ashtray. I did not ask to have that whole image triggered in my mind. It just does. I can almost smell the cigarettes. I can see the long red-flamed ash that hung between the black stained ash residue on the silver fingers of the ashtray, because my mother often forgot to pick up her cigarettes once they had been perched between the silver plated fingers. I remember the smoke, the lighter, and the sooty taste in my mouth when I sat too close. Automatically the layering of my senses

CHAPTER 3: STEP 3

retrieved the image of my mother when I think of an image of my own hand outstretched to signify the five senses.

This is exactly how you bond your core life message to your loved ones in a Forget Me Knot moment, through the embedding and layering of the five senses.

In a Forget Me Knot anchor/trigger, our objective is to use as many senses as possible to layer triggers, like minefields, into the minds and hearts of your loved ones left behind so they become the worker bees that pollinate your core life message into others as they live their everyday lives.

Once you establish the leading sense for yourself, as the one you use predominantly to receive and express the best outward expression of yourself, you can then infuse your core life message with your leading sense right into them. The more senses, the deeper the anchor and the more frequent the reception of your core life message trigger symbol.

Your loved ones look for commonality and congruence with you, and welcome your core life message to mix with their own personal experience. They are looking for repetition and subconscious congruence that binds and bonds you to their own experience. They have no idea that you are layering automatic triggers so they will carry forth your core life message. It is up to you to do the work, but they have an open door to your core life message because of the love and the bond they have for you.

The result of an anchored/triggered core life message is your loved ones will heal more quickly after you pass by way of their five senses and a trigger symbol. They will also have a sense that you are around them in spirit because they feel a sense of connection and spiritual presence. The reinforcement of your core life message will ground their experience and give them purpose like a lightning rod does to lightning. Secured to them in this way, your core life message is bound beyond the physical bonds in time to forevermore.

To make it easier to think and understand the use of the five senses and their correspondences, I have put together a grid that I have included in this book to help you to form, layer, and include your usual pattern of responses that you learned here in Step 3, so you can use it in the last Step 5. This will help you to identify more easily, which of the five senses is your predominant sense, and most likely leads your incoming and outgoing of experience and expression.

5 SENSES AND 4 RESPONDERS GRID

	YOUTH		POWER		WISDOM	
	Growth	Ripening		Transition	Harvest	Storage
	0-27 yrs		27-54 yrs		54-81 yrs	
	Sight Dominant	Taste Dominant	Touch Dominant	Smell Dominant	Sound Dominant
THINKERS	Idea	Actions	Manifesting	Communicating	Reflection
FEELERS	Anger	Joy & Meditation	Meditation & Sympathy	Grief, Worry & Melancholy	Fright & Fear
FEELERS	Green	Red	Yellow	White	Black
DOERS	Sour	Bitter	Sweet	Pungent	Salty
	Shouting	Laughing	Singing	Weeping	Groaning
RESPONDERS	Doers	Feelers	Feelers	Thinkers	Dreamers

THE FIVE SENSES GRID

The grid I've included incorporates the life cycle segments in Step 2, the pattern of response in Step 3, and the senses that usually match those segments and responses for your next Step 4, in a particular life cycle.

Look at the grid. Horizontally on the top of the grid, you can see the three main developmental life segments mentioned in Step 2: Youth, Power, and Wisdom.
- Just below Youth, between 1-27-years-old, the sense organ that often leads to that development is seeing or vision as one grows.

CHAPTER 3: STEP 3

- Below Power, between the ages of 27-54-years-old, there are two developmental stages: ripening, which relates to the sense of taste, and transition, corresponding to the sense of touch.
- Then we develop Wisdom, between the ages of 54-81-years-old, with our development being a time of harvesting and storing where the sense of hearing predominates. At this last stretch of life, our senses, the sense of smell, or the sense of hearing still lead the way to life completion.

The grid also highlights which areas you are most likely to: Think, Feel, Do, or Dream. The correspondences to these developmental stages you will find on the grid for each one of your senses. This grid is invaluable when creating a layered effect on your senses to embed your core life message automatically. Think of this chart as a tool, much like a technician who is layering images for 3-D movies so the movie pops out at you. The five senses grid is a tool to help you use the correspondences of your five senses, embedding your core life message into your loved ones effortlessly. They will not even know you are making sure of connecting the two of you in the hereafter.

This 'tying you to them' is also true with your loved ones who have already passed, and you must subjectively decide for them what their core life message was. Even though the core life message for them is not coming from them, you can make one for them anyway, as you assume they would have said it. It will be through the lenses of your own perception, but it will be a translation of them, for which something is better than nothing. A weak link is better than no link at all. You can also anchor their core life message with a carefully thought out symbol so it can trigger the thoughts and ideas about your loved one in another's everyday life.

KIIKO

Take Kiiko, an elderly 82-year-old Japanese woman. Kiiko was hard of hearing and a quiet homebody who liked to listen to books on tape, watch her favorite Judge show on television, and sew quilts.

She wore mostly black, loved the salt in soy sauce, and fresh sushi. Without even noticing it, she would groan whenever she had to get up and walk with her cane due to her arthritic knee. She was a clever woman who was a thinker, a worrier, but also thought long and hard in reflecting on her family and life around her. She had come to forgive the flaws of her children and relatives. She also had come to forgive the United States of America for confiscating her parent's farmland and putting her in a concentration camp for the Japanese during WWII. Nevertheless, her standards for herself were never relaxed because the idea of her final moment of passage lurked very close. She feared she might not be ready for what might be in the hereafter. As much as she wanted to join her husband who had already died, death was still a scary thought. Kiiko was not interested in any core life message because she just didn't even like saying the word, "death." However, her children did want to feel her presence when she would be gone. They all knew that time was closer than they wanted to admit. This is what I told the children:

If we look at the grid, we can see that Kiiko falls within the Wisdom developmental phase of her life. She is in the harvesting and storage phase of her life. She is introspective at this point; reflecting and thinking. She has fear and fright about death at the edges of her attention. Kiiko's senses move toward absorption with the color black, the love of salt, and her subconscious groaning on movement. Can you see the correspondences on the grid for Kiiko? She is in the storage portion of the wisdom phase of her life.

In leaving a core life message for Kiiko's children, I would want to use the correspondences on the grid to embed her life message. Kiiko would want her core life message to be more conventional, more observing on the part of her loved ones, just like her. Kiiko is a thinker, a worrier, and a planner. It was her thinking nature that gave her the strength to survive the concentration camps and the ability to flourish with no support or help from anyone. She would want her loved ones to think rather than feel, because she was a thinker. Kiiko had also evolved because, at this spiritual phase of her life, she had compassion that included all of humanity. After all, she is in the wisdom years of her life. She would want to layer the senses of her loved ones and to embed her core life message by using the color black and use the sense of taste to trigger her core life message in her loved ones. She wanted them to experience her by eating something salty, even fishy. She wanted the sense of sound to describe her best, because hearing had been one of her strengths. Repeated words and a slower pace for the memories of Kiiko would leave her loved ones with a sense of congruence. Remember, by layering the senses you leave a more vivid, all encompassing anchor that has many more chances of triggering your core life message in their daily lives. Layering Kiiko's sense of survival with the temporary but stable, nature of the straight pin, as the symbolic trigger of her core life message, that she used in making her quilts, represents not only keeping cloth together, but, just maybe, keeping people together too in the midst of chaos and uprooting.

The color black/blue of the deep blue sea, which is the sea of all humanity and nourishes, rejuvenates, and cleanses life, might be another layered sense expressed under the sense of sight. Her warm, safe, quilts, which sew together family when there is nothing but a quilt to keep them close during the Japanese quarantine, falls under the sense of touch. The taste and smell of salty and fishy in the large sea of humanity layering the sense of taste and smell reinforces the ability of salt to break down the rocks of resentment, bitterness, and retribution so the fish can then swim freely in schools of safety and belonging. Lastly, with the sense of hearing, to listen to the core life message for Kiiko to be repeated over and over again.

Because her core life message is that of a Thinker and a survivor, the core life message of Kiiko might be a short Japanese proverb like:

"Don't make a pin into a pickaxe."

This message represents her ability to forgive humanity. It has the straight pin symbol for her sewing quilts, and the need to keep family close when adversity hits. It eases the inflamed heart that holds revenge and retribution, sadness and anger.

The symbol of Kiiko's core life meaning might be a straight pin for loved ones so they never forget not to let an angry response turn into a lifelong grudge. The straight pin is the trigger to anchor her core life message. When Kiiko embeds her core life message in an everyday symbol, then every time her loved ones see a straight pin, not only her message will surface at just the right time in just the right way, but also will the memory and warmth of one of her quilts. Her loved ones will be yearning for sushi while curling up to watch reruns of the judge shows on TV.

We see the five senses as layered, bonded, and sealed together. You can use this type of layering in your own embedding and enriching of your own core life message.

THE GRID

The grid incorporates the three life cycles and the five senses along with the Thinkers, Feelers, Doers, and Dreamers.

Thinkers use the sense of smell as strength. As a thinker you obviously love to communicate thoughts and ideas. Your head leads the way. Feelers move and transform feelings, but Thinkers move thoughts for their core life message. You move ideas to action, action to manifestation, manifestation to communication, and communication to reflection. The core life message of thinkers can also have grief, worry, and melancholy. The Thinker can obsess and loop their ideas and thoughts. The congruent environment for the core life message is white and black, and the taste of food is pungent. Thinkers will often weep to move your ideas forward. The correspondences for Thinkers are:

>Idea moves to action, moves to manifestation, moves to communication
>Colors are white and black
>Emotions are grief, worry, melancholy, and weeping

Feelers favor feelings, but feelings that move and transform. As a feeler, you also may have anger but you might transform it to joy or sorrow, and then further transform it again to that of meditation or sympathy in your core life message. Often feelers have the "Spielberg effect." Spielberg, the famous movie director, was able to garner a tear, a smile, and a nod very quickly in all of his movies. Feelers are all about ripening and transition so, if you are a feeler, you love taste and touch. Feelers are artists, musicians, and the creative sort. You might like color and light, or contrast and dark. In the environment of the Forget Me Knot experience, you might find the colors red or yellow suitable to tie your core life message to your loved ones. The taste for the food you might have would be the extremes of bitter/sweet. You will hear laughing and singing with your core life message because often times, feelers are artists, always translating, transforming, and adapting to the world around them. The correspondences for Feelers are:

> Anger moves to joy or sorrow, moves to meditation or sympathy
> Colors are red or yellow
> Taste is bitter or sweet
> Sound is laughing or singing

Doers favor the sense of sight. When you incorporate an idea with the passion of anger, the color green, the taste of sour, and you shout that idea to the heavens, it just feels right. You will have the most impact on your loved ones, and your core life message will feel congruent if your core life message has some of the correspondences on the grid under Youth or Growth. Doers often have the energy of youth to do things and to see what grows in life from your doing. As a doer, you like to experience life. Using these types of correspondences on the grid in the Forget Me Knot method would be perfect, say for the unfortunate death of a child who was a doer in life. The message would encompass the core life message, idea, and perhaps bring you to anger at the snuffing out of a life that had bubbling hope. The environment could be heavy with the color green, not only representing the beginning and movement, but also for healing as well. The taste of some food that the doer preferred would be sour, and shouting would be the emotion that would move the grief and sorrow up and out in a very physical way.

The correspondences for Doers are:
- New Ideas
- Color is Green
- Taste is sour
- Emotion is anger and shouting

Dreamers use the sense of hearing. As a dreamer, you reflect on the universality within yourself, and your commonalities with the universe outside of yourself. You wrestle with the fears and fright that binds you, so releasing to the great expanse is possible. The environment that is congruent to your core life message is black, infinite, and all receiving, just like the womb or the outer limits of space. The food for a dreamer will be salty, and the sound a dreamer hears and expresses is a groan that sounds from their depths. The correspondences for Dreamers are:
- Reflection
- Color is black
- Taste is salty
- Emotion is fear or fright
- Sound is groaning

THE CAT IN THE HAT

Another example on the use of the grid can be applied to The Cat In The Hat, the childhood first reader book by Dr. Seuss. Say for example, your core life message, like that of The Cat In The Hat book, was about imagination and the fun of reading books. The Cat, with his red bow tie and red and white-striped top hat, was a doer, always on the move, learning from trial and error, and the use of his imagination in rhyme. Nothing was ever dull and life was always topsy-turvy with The Cat, through his words and his actions. The Cat liked to use his imagination to mess things up and see what happened. The core life message of The Cat was to use books and words to spark imagination and have fun, because imagination crosses all cultures, bias, fears, ignorance, and perceptions.

The core life message of The Cat might read, "Today was good. Today was fun. Tomorrow is another one." or "The more you read, the more you'll know. The more you learn, the more places you'll go."

Either way, the core life message would be about imagination and books. A simple picture book with simple funny thoughts that rhyme, just like The Cat would have liked, would be an appropriate core life trigger for our five senses to recall the wisdom of The Cat.

On the Five Senses Grid, you can see that The Cat falls under Youth and Growth. The key sense organ is sight, as in reading books that stimulate the imagination. Under that same column is an idea: You can stimulate imagination and fun by reading a book. The Cat always came up with new, crazy and unusual ideas. He charmed and played with words, and objects in his environment.

Sometimes others would get angry at his crazy ideas. It would make them sour, and they would shout at him. Remember when the family's goldfish told The Cat to go away, and insisted they do not want to play? He said, "He should not be here. He should not be about. He should not be here while your mother is out!" The Cat would bring out the most intense feelings, thoughts and tastes in others, especially those whose imaginations had gone flat and dormant. Remember when The Cat introduced Thing 1 and Thing 2 saying, "Have no fear, little fish. These Things are good Things. They are tame. Oh, so tame! They have come here to play. They will give you some fun on this wet, wet, wet day."

When we think of The Cat, we think of pink cake frosting, juggling many objects, messes, smiles, good clean fun, simple catchy rhymes, red bow ties, and a red and white tall top hat. The Cat sparked the imaginative flame in the naysayer and the person who held back. Everything about The Cat In The Hat triggered the core life message of The Cat. On the Five Senses Grid, The Cat falls under the categories: Youth, Sight, Ideas, Angry, Sour, and Shout. If we use those correspondences with the core life message of The Cat, his core life message becomes congruent and iconic, as it already has.

When I think of The Cat, and his core life message, I instantly want to eat a cupcake with lots of extra pink frosting. I want to put my fingers into the frosting and lick my fingers clean. I want to rhyme my words in short choppy sentences. I think of a small goldfish in a fishbowl and I want to get a small goldfish and throw him back in a large pond with other goldfish to give him freedom to move. I want to read, sing, play, and twirl around in space with my arms waving and skipping to a song I hum. I want to use my imagination and my mind through reading simple books where I can let my mind travel, especially when I can't be there in time and space. I want to be a child again. I want to feel that youthful feeling where everything is curious to me and all things seem infinitely possible. With my imagination leading the way, the world looks like a fascinating place that needs exploration to find out just where are the best surprises and delights. The Cat's core life message makes me want to have fun and be a kid again in my life.

Because the book's message is so universal, The Cat In The Hat has lived on for over 50 years, leaving the core life message about reading, imagination, and fun.

When you use your five senses, you can make a congruent core life message with the words you use with your loved ones, in an environment that matches your core life message. In so doing, you experience and anchor your core life message. Your loved ones will heal on several levels when all of their five senses are involved.

When you combine more than one of the five senses by layering them with color, sound, taste, touch, smell, sight, pace, tone, and intensity, you are using Synaesthesia to embed your core life message even after you have passed on into the hereafter. Synaesthesia is the method of how you are going to layer, embed, and cement the best of you into the five senses of your loved ones making your core life message iron clad.

SYNAESTHESIA

Synaesthesia is the uniting and compressing of the five senses into one memory. A word coined in 1912, by Wassily Kandinsky, an artist who loved to provoke the five senses with angry reds, placid blues, anxious textures, loud shapes, quiet lines, or cold greens. He and his peers wanted to engage the viewer. Notice how he used an emotion to help you conjure up a color, and almost feel like you sense a texture or a shape? That is because emotion brings energy to words, ideas, and visuals. Artists, musicians, authors, and filmmakers bond you to their piece of work by the usage of Synaesthesia. They know just how to manipulate you by their skill with Synaesthesia. Politicians, government propaganda, and advertising companies use Synaesthesia as well. This idea called Synaesthesia is created by combining the senses together, layering and embedding the experience as they go, bonding you to their artwork as time passes. The result is that you co-create with the artist, musician, or author, from their point of view.

So, why do New York Best-Selling legacy-driven biographies sit on bookshelves after a while, dusty, with no one even caring to read them? Why do treasured photograph albums of your family remain tucked in cupboards until no one knows the names of those in the pictures? Why is it that the heart pounding stories that even sound too good to be true find themselves passé, and soon forgotten? Why is history considered 'nice to know' and not a 'need to know', perceived as something archaic that many people couldn't relate to in their own present day lives? There is such a static quality to the past that the emotion and energy needed to keep it alive ends up just fizzling out after a while to a faded forgotten lifeless memory.

A Forget Me Knot core life message uses Synaesthesia as the glue to set the rechargeable battery inside the minds and hearts of the living loved ones. Synaesthesia uses the bonding hormone oxytocin or vasopressin to draw out a memory to your present day consciousness.

The definition of the word Synaesthesia is from the preface, 'Syn', which means 'at the same time' or 'considered together', and the suffix, 'Aesthesia' meaning mind and emotion. Synaesthesia therefore is a memory and emotional response considered together. In Synaesthesia, a memory will elicit an emotional response, or vice versa, an emotional response will elicit a memory. When you use Synaesthesia, you are layering and weaving a type of hormonally bonded 'daisy chain' of a memory woven together with an emotion, and one or more of your senses. You weave your daisy chain of memory by the use of your five senses as the emissaries necessary to dredge up and trigger memory in your loved ones. Taste, touch, sight, sound, and smell stimulate the brain's hypothalamus to send a hormone to your loved ones to feel something and thus remember a memory at the same time. Bound together, the senses are 'glued' to a memory. The more senses you have layered and 'glued' to a memory, the more often the memory will come up in their every day lives. Artists know how to use Synaesthesia by using the medium of art, film, plays, or music to get the viewer to feel something about their work. The same is true in a Forget Me Knot core life message. The difference is that the core life message is a one-liner sentence with a symbol instead of a ninety-minute film, a three-minute song, a two-hour play, or a framed art piece in a museum. All the above examples use Synaesthesia, or the layering of the stimulated five senses with a memory and a feeling to communicate their message. The more senses used, the more bound and anchored they are to the experience of your core life message; so it automatically triggers their memory and response of you. Voila! You will feel right there next to them, even when you are gone.

If your sense is triggered, say for instance by the smell of freshly baked chocolate chip cookies right out of the oven, you are using Synaesthesia. The freshly baked chocolate chip cookies catch you in the net of your experience along with all the other senses. You might recall the hot lava melt on your tongue with the chocolate chunks on the first bite, almost burning your tongue; the crunch of the crispy browned outside edges; the sight of your grandmother in an apron with thick oven mitts on her hands removing the cookies from the hot oven. The sense of a warm, nourishing treat waves across your memory and the entire feeling of bonded love reels you into feeling your grandmother right next to you. This entire layered memory of an experience is rich even though you had only one of your senses triggered, the sense of smell. All of this happens instantly and automatically. All the senses are woven together so one sense brings up the rest. The sense of smelling hot out-of-the-oven chocolate chip cookies triggers taste, touch, sound, and sight with sweet, crunchy, hot, and the shape of a cookie, glued together in the memory.

The commercial industry, like Mrs. Field's Cookies in many of the shopping malls across America, relies on Synaesthesia, using the scent of freshly baked chocolate chip cookies to ride on your own fond memories of home, bringing you right into the front of a Mrs. Field's Cookies concession in the shopping mall to buy cookies. You not only want the sweet part, but you want the memory and experience that goes with it too.

You buy the cookies not only for the taste. You buy the cookies for the want of reliving the memory, experience, and sensation of a memory already embedded. With each sense triggered, you remember. So when you are using Synaesthesia to embed your core life message, the more senses you use, the more frequently you will be present, after your death, in the everyday memories, thoughts, and feelings of your loved ones, because one sense brings up the rest automatically, in a wave of sensation and experience.

Taste As An Example In Synaesthesia

Some of the iconic foods for the sense of taste for each generation that trigger emotion and memory for each generation might be:
1. Depression era, WWII Generation may remember tasting egg crèmes, making tomato soup out of ketchup, bacon, salted and smoked meats, Jell-O, marshmallows, boxed cake mixes, salt water taffy, rock candy, jelly beans, candy corn, cotton candy, Necco Wafers, M & M's, Jaw breakers, or canned Spam.

2. Baby Boomers born in the late 1940s and later might have their sense of taste triggered by peanut butter and jelly sandwiches on

white Wonder bread, TV Dinners on foil trays, hamburgers, bubble gum, candy hearts, candy cigarettes, Pixie Sticks, or the orange flavored drink called Tang.

3. Y Generation in the 70's and 80's might be triggered by fondue, crock-pot meals, Pop Tarts, Pez dispensers, Swedish fish, Jolly Ranchers, or Pop Rocks, that they remember as the taste trigger for them.

4. The Millennial Generation might have their sense of taste triggered by Pocky Sticks, Red Vines, Gummy Bears, Skittles, Peeps, Reese's Pieces, or colorful cupcakes that look like artwork.

More than generational foods can trigger the five senses. Culture, family tradition, rituals, holidays, and family favorites can trigger them too. There are many ways to relate your core life message. What you want to look for when layering your core life message with taste is something that is not only layered with Synaesthesia, but piggy backing on vivid memories already in place that you have experienced at holidays, cultural traditions, or rituals that are repeated daily, monthly, or yearly. Vivid is the key to selecting one that fits into the Five Senses Grid.

Combining the five senses in layers is what embeds the experience of your core life message legacy into your loved one's memory, by compressing and binding the five senses together. Then when one sense is triggered, all senses bound together with it are automatically triggered too, all at once. One sense triggers all of them.

ECHOLOCATION

Another way to determine your core life message through the reverse idea of what you think you are, or by the silhouette of your being, can also be through your body's taking in information through the sense of sound; what you hear and what you do not hear. Echolocation is one example of determining who you are by who you are not and where you are not.

CHAPTER 3: STEP 3

The quickness of the click, click, click of my word processor tells my loved ones when I am excited about the thoughts pouring out of me as I type. They also know when the clicks are far and few between, then I am struggling with a thought. The yawn they hear tells them I am determined to capture the thought before it vanishes forever and I fall asleep.

I remember when I was younger and fell asleep in front of the television, only to wake up to the drone of a buzzing sound and a picture of an Indian on the screen. I knew I had gone to bed too late. Yes, a picture of the Indian on the TV screen was a sign that the TV broadcasting had ended for that day! That was when there was no such thing as television-around-the-clock. There was a time when all broadcasting stopped and there was no entertainment on television. It's hard to imagine this today. I also remember the sound of the city wide sirens sounding, as a practice drill, when I was a child in elementary school, as a sign for me to walk to the basement, and cover my head, in case of nuclear attack from the Soviet Union. Again, it's hard to imagine this today. However, sounds also tell you what you are not. Just like tastes, sound can also be associated with generations, cultures, tradition, and rituals. The more vivid the sound or the silence surrounding the sound, the easier it is to embed your core life message for easy retrieval.

Mothers and fathers use echolocation for their intuition in order to pick up when something is wrong with their family. A Mother will say to her spouse, "It is too quiet in there. I wonder what they are up to." I remember when I was pregnant with my first child. I use to always remark to my husband about the kicking of my baby in my abdomen. Then, one day he said, "When was the last time you felt the baby kicking?" He had not heard me tell him about the kicking for a few days. His intuition had noticed what was not there but should have been. It was his listening to what he did not hear, that saved the life of our child. Had he not asked that question, I would never have realized that the sensation of kicking had stopped and our baby was in dire life threatening straights.

Echolocation is hearing through reflected and obstructed sound bouncing off your environment. Dolphins and bats use this method to see their surroundings by listening to the sound reverberate from the environment to create a mental picture of where they are. The blind use this skill by clicking their tongues to find their way because they cannot see. Though sighted, you also use this skill, when you know to stop filling a cup with water so it doesn't overflow when you go to the kitchen in the middle of the night and all is dark. Echolocation tells us shape, distance, pace, and direction. You also know if it is a man or a woman coming down the hall to your office when you hear the click-click-click of the platform heels of your assistant. You know from what direction she is walking, how long it will take her to reach your office and the urgency of the information she is bringing to you. We use echolocation all the time to differentiate not only what something is or is not, but where and how fast it is approaching. This is one reason why many cities have installed escalating chirping noises on crosswalks so the blind know just how much time they have to get across the street. Your sense of sound uses both information it receives, and that which is missing, to determine just how to respond with the information from the outside world.

I keep bringing up ways for you to use the parts of you and your life that are automatically running without your notice. These automatic parts are out of your perception or pervue, but they are running the processes of your life. The automatic, the shadows, the silent, and the silhouette make everything else about you possible.

You might ask why you need to notice the process and automatic parts of your life. Who cares? How does it help you to identify your core life message anyway? Why go through all the trouble? It is hard to look at yourself from the reverse anyway. It is just too much work. You want it easy, accessible, and common. You can do it without information from the shadows. In fact, finding your core life message just through the content of your life will give a more superficial but effective version of your core life message. Many people will opt for the easier. It certainly is an option. In fact, when you try to find a core life message for a loved one who is incapable of getting it for themselves because they've passed away or is too sick to do it, you will have to make their core life

CHAPTER 3: STEP 3

message more common and universal because you are not them. You are not seeing life from their perspective, or from their heart and soul. You will have to do the best you can.

But if you are trying to create a core life message for yourself with all the essence of you that you want to leave for all posterity, the more you include in the processes of your life, the more spot on your core life message will be. You are unique in every way. You most likely will never do a living autopsy on yourself in the mental, emotional, physical, or spiritual way unless you look for your core life message.

You may look at the content of your life, but it is the processes, the prepositions, and the automatic parts of you that hold the most differentiating truth and authenticity of your soul. Whether you use it for your core life message or not, the fact that you recognize your uniqueness in your lifetime, you will feel such a depth of understanding about you and you alone, that everything else by comparison will be put into perspective.

Doctors use 'ruling out' of diseases as a means of determining what disease you have and how to treat you. Teachers give you an A at the beginning of a semester until you give them reason to take away that standing with the inferior work you produce. You know yourself and your core life message by who you are *not*, as well as by who you are.

When my sister was first applying for a job as a supervisor with the airports for Homeland Security, the way they tested her skill and ability to discriminate was to have common items in a box. She was supposed to put her hands and arms in the holes of that box and feel the items to identify exactly what they were. She was supposed to identify them by their shape, texture, and surface. She identified 100% of the items not by what they were, but by what they were not.

You may have known a few pessimists or naysayers in your life. These individuals have practiced the ability to identify what is 'not' in life. However, their skill to use the 'not' solely as their conclusion to what 'is' can also be incomplete. Remember it is the use of both orifices, and the use of both polar opposites, which help to determine what is. You can also use what is not about you as a way to find your core life message in your life and thus tie yourself to the ones you love.

In the next chapter, you will discover how to link an object that best represents your core life message with an everyday physical relic to snap attention to you and your core life message.

STEP 3 LIFE 5 SENSES EXPRESSIONS & 4 RESPONDERS

This chapter identifies HOW you respond to your life. After reading this chapter you can identify whether you are a Thinker, Feeler, Doer, or Dreamer. Once you identify which of these four ways you most often respond to life's challenges, you will then find out which of your five senses is preferred in translating this information into your life experience. You predominantly use one main sense out of the five senses to translate your life and to anchor your core life message into your loved ones' everyday lives. The senses, expressions, and responses you use around them everyday are the ones that single you out, branding you, and differentiating you from others in their subconscious mind. When you combine your key sense, expression, and response along with your one-liner core life message, they have no doubt that it is you who is communicating with them. This four-part combination of one-liner, sensed expression, unique response, along with a trigger symbol becomes the private code that opens the lock and key to their memories, hearts, and lives, insuring a snug Forget Me Knot tie to them.

WHAT YOU'VE GOT:
- You have identified the chief method you use to respond and experience life.
- You have identified yourself as a Thinker, Feeler, Doer, or Dreamer.
- You have identified which sense leads your life: Tasting, Touching, Smelling, Seeing, or Hearing.

WHAT YOU CAN DO WITH IT:
- You can support your communications through your preferred sense organ.
- You can use your preferred sense organ unapologetically to give and receive information, and to make your mark on the world around you.

Heaven has no mouth. It must speak through men.

CHAPTER 4: STEP 4

YOUR ESSENCE

Now is the time to put it all together so you can tie the best of you to them.

You will drill down and turn the essence of your core life message into a one-liner and a symbol through the expression of your leading sense. You will create an easy way to have your signature imprinted on the hearts and minds of your loved ones. By condensing your core life message to a one-liner and linking it through the five senses, future generations can take your spiritual torch as their own and hand it off to the following generations born after them. You will be influencing people you will have never met. If the one-liner and the symbol are simple, clear, and clean, your loved ones will have no trouble knowing, for certain, that you contributed to the richness of their character and helped to guide them in their lives. Your success will be when your loved ones give away to strangers your core life message because they have taken it on as their own, too. Your one-liner constantly hangs itself on an everyday symbol in their lives so they remember you. Your symbol becomes iconic. The trigger symbol anchors your signature character identity to your loved ones everyday comings and goings.

One of the reasons that this combination of a one-liner with a symbol is so effective is that it is similar to the way you remember nursery rhymes and the moral to their story. It is because of the richness of the images with the one-liners. For example, if I say, "Twinkle, twinkle little star...." you can finish the rest. Why? It is the same reason your core life message will also be easily transferable from generation to generation, the images or the five sense triggers automatically link together.

WHY USE A ONE-LINER?

The reason a one-liner works is that it is easy to remember. A one-liner just rolls off the tongue. Trite sayings we all know are one-liners. They are easy to remember and we find reason to use them in our everyday language. It takes a little bit of work to choose only one line that represents all of you, but as we have discussed in earlier chapters, if we choose more than one, it splits the thought, forgetting one and weakening the other. The choice will no longer be yours. Remembering one is to give strength, focus, and intention to the core life message you choose. It does honor to your soul, and the reason you lived fully. You are defining your life your way, even in the end. Your core life message already has the shadow of the opposite within it even without using the words. As we have discussed in Step 2, polar opposites by contrast define each other. They just go together, as night defines day and day defines night, just by being.

After reading this chapter, when you have your own personal core life message linked to a symbol. It will bring clarity and understanding to what makes you tick spiritually, and what your particular fingerprint is on this world. You may have sinned, suffered, and repented, or have been given a second chance at a happy ending, but that is only your story. It is good, but it is not enough for it to last generations. You need to speak your story in spiritual language. Your story does not make the most accessible core life message. Rather, it is the moral to your particular story, and its meaning to you, that sticks in the minds and hearts of your loved ones. This spiritual moral is the one that they can use to apply to their own lives, no matter the era or the life changes each generation must face. Over time, they may forget your story, but will remember the anchored moral to your story.

Perception

If you left the moral of the story to the generations that follow to figure out, on their own, you would leave it to chance how they interpreted your life. They might get it right and they might not. When the police interview different witnesses who saw the same event, their particular take on what happened is varied and they may get many different points of view. As a Homeopath, I have learned never to assume I know what a patient means by any particular word. Therefore, I ask them. Time and time again, a patient reveals to me their meaning of a word that has nothing to do with the English definition of the word, or anything I recognize as synonyms. A patient's perspective reveals their state on which I must then prescribe a remedy. The pattern that runs their state is what determines their meaning of a particular word, and how they see the world, themselves, and others at large.

I have often noted how my daughter's generation views the Baby Boomers at her same age. Her interpretation of my generation looks nothing like what I have experienced. Even genre movies written about lives and stories during the Baby Boomer era, by writers too young to have lived through the times do not reflect the truth as it was at the time. Celebrities, whose lives are reviewed by the public, after they have passed on, are often a mixture of the public and private life of the celebrity. The authentic spiritual language these same celebrities spoke is privy only for their inner circle of loved ones. I often wonder if what I learned in history really reflects the viewpoint of the person who wrote the book rather than life as it truly was. That said, it is up to each one of us to insure that our spiritual language is passed on in the way that we mean it to be, rather than by the interpretation of another.

Wabi-Sabi

Incorporating Wabi-Sabi into your core life message will delight both you and your loved ones. Wabi-Sabi sets you apart from all others on the same life path. Wabi-Sabi is a Japanese term that means taking joy and delight in the transient, imperfect, and incomplete, in an aesthetic way. Wabi-Sabi tweaks your attention to that which is out of place, incomplete, or makes you stand out. You notice the transient, imperfect, and incomplete when it is set against the canvas or your idea of 'perfect'. In perfectly raked Japanese sand gardens, with the symmetrical lines in curved patterns on white refined sand, the Japanese methodically place a large dark stone in a place within the white refined sand where they want you to look and pay attention. The contrasting obstruction is purposeful. The dissonance, imperfection, and incompleteness is placed there to create attention to that which is not what you think it is. It makes you look again, think again, and ponder longer. The obstruction will make you ponder on the polar opposite so you will see the perfection differently had the obstruction not been there at all.

Human Wabi-Sabi is taking joy, delight, and curiosity toward that which is transforming within you, as you learn and evolve in your lifetime. Your incompleteness, imperfection, and changes are interesting to the rest of us. It delights us by what makes you so unique. When you delight in your own incompleteness and evolution, like the Japanese gardener, you place the dark stone of obstruction or adversity with intent in your life so you can see, for yourself, by contrast, your own perfection in a new light. Then, you will experience your life differently. You will observe yourself evolving while at the same time experiencing your life. It is as if you are seeing with two eyes at the same time without judgment or discernment, while observing and experiencing at the same time. It is a lovely place to experience when the two polar opposites do not have a pull on your attention. Rather, it is the dance that they do together, perfect and imperfect, that is more intriguing than naming them. Your imperfections, missteps, and dust-offs intrigue, charm, and magnetize us to you. The idea of 'perfect', while it may be a worthy goal, can be rather boring and off-putting in relationships because there is nowhere for us to connect to 'perfect'. It stands alone away from us.

Some examples of Wabi-Sabi in nature are to see an old tree that stretches up to the skies. On that tree, erosion and weather have made the trunk of the tree knotted and rough but very fascinating at the same time. It snags our attention and makes us share a feeling, thought, or touch with another living thing. A perfect tree trunk without any markings may go unnoticed. Wabi-Sabi can be a rainbow in the middle of a rainstorm, or the endearing rush from us when we see a scrawny kitten that is the runt of the cat litter. Imperfection draws us in. Perfection keeps us out. Flaunt your "imperfection." Your imperfections are really just your marks of where you are growing, learning, and changing. They are as delightful as seeing a baby's first tooth in a gummy toothless smile. If we can embrace these Wabi-Sabi parts of ourselves, we can also use them to communicate our unique core life message to those we love and cherish. They love and recognize our lumps, knots, flaws, and frailties. They love us for who we are. I remember a friend of mine answering so proudly when I asked her why she married her second husband. She said, "It is because he loves me, flaws and all, even when I don't love them myself."

Look for the Wabi-Sabi in you. Fearlessly carry your unique life changes with you, like a baby with a curled and bowed lock of hair on the top of your head. Your loved ones already see your Wabi-Sabi whether you are working hard to camouflage it or not. They see yours and you see theirs like a marquis on a movie theater, like it or not. There really is no hiding your true authentic self no matter how hard you try. It is for that reason I can say to my patients in a health consultation, "You can lie, make it up, guess, or imagine it. It will not matter. You will still provide the pattern that will reveal the state from which I need to prescribe." Revealing your Wabi-Sabi shows vulnerability. It is that vulnerability and truth that encourages others to reveal their own Wabi-Sabi as well. The Wabi-Sabi of you melts the walls between you and others. It automatically sorts out the interested from the oblivious and unqualified from being in your world. It teases out who belongs and who doesn't by the recognition of your Wabi-Sabi. As long as everyone sees your imperfections, or so you call them, you might as well have fun with them. Bring them along and play with them. Including them in your life will make you look more perfect to those who love you by contrast, as well as the permission and freedom for them to play with their own Wabi-Sabi and share it with you too. It can only be good. Put your Wabi-Sabi into the core life message of your life and there is instant recognition of you.

SAME STORY, DIFFERENT MEANING

Many people will have the same life story: financial ruin, divorce, poverty, abuse, war, abandonment, disability, disease, disappointment, oppression, addiction, loss, heartache, death, etc. Nevertheless, each one of us takes away something different from the same or similar story.

For instance, the bank robbers, Bonnie and Clyde, each took away something different from their experience. Clyde (Barrow) said, "Hold on to your hats, it may not have a bottom." Bonnie (Parker's) experience was different. She said, "Never go crooked. It's for the love of a man that I'm gonna have to die. I don't know when, but I know it can't be long." Gracie Allen and George Burns each had their own take on life, through their shared working life together. Gracie said, "Never place a period where God has placed a comma." George had a different take on life, "The most important thing is to be honest. If you can fake that, you've got it made."

WHERE TO SEARCH

In ascertaining exactly which one-liner best identifies you, remember you can always test it out with the preference and aversion meter inside you. You have given much attention, interest, and energy to those things that are most important to you. You might have said one line many different ways in many different situations, but it is coming from the same core belief. Finding that core belief is where there is heat, thought, attention, imagination, desire, as well as avoidance, disgust, hatred, or revulsion. It may be the other side of the same coin. Even the reviled negative things in your life have the same core life message. Where you have passion, you will also be able to say the opposite would be as abhorrent. You will know you have hit the right spot when one idea or premise makes you feel equally passionate and highly charged about the polar opposites of your core life message.

When you are checking a math problem, you have to work backwards. The same is true when you are trying to check your work in choosing your core life message. Do not leave out your aversions. Just as vehemently as you feel about your most important belief, motto, or character trait, so too you will feel just as strongly about the repercussions of the opposite being true.

A good example of this would be with Curtis, my patient. He was a super responsible man in life, as well as in death, by laying to rest five family members for whom he cared for deeply. He saw situations all around him where others were irresponsible, careless, and self-indulged. When Curtis saw irresponsibility, he would go off on a rant at not only the person at fault, but also the person's generation, race, gender, religion, and anything else he could attach to the lack of self-responsibility. He put them all under the same umbrella of irresponsibility. He was passionate about responsibility no matter what side of the coin he spoke on responsibility or irresponsibility.

THE CURSE MEETS THE GIFT

In my Homeopathic practice, I know I have come to the place where I must prescribe on the pattern. This is a place where "the curse meets the gift." My first experience with that concept is when I had a patient, Bridget, who was born without any hair on her body anywhere. It was a genetic mutation. I have already told you that the core life message is in everything we do and all that we choose. Guess what job this patient had most of her life? No, she was not a hairdresser, or selling wigs. She was an electrolysis practitioner. She removed hair for a living.

You might ask yourself just why she would want to remove hair on others when there was a lot of ridicule and attention in her life to the fact that she had none. As I said before, when we set ourselves between two very clear polar opposites we oscillate, express, experience, and evolve. In her case, Bridget, set herself between hair and hairless, or fitting in or not fitting in at all. By helping others not to have hair, she was enlarging her world of 'fitting in'. She was making the hairy more beautiful by making them hairless, just like her. We all go back to where we left a part of ourselves because we know there is a precious piece of the puzzle of our lives we need to retrieve. This was true for Bridget.

I tell you these stories to help you to see things in a different way with a nudge to enlarge your point of view about yourself when you are searching for you own core life message.

Hints

If at this point, you are still confused as to what your pattern or core life message is, I can offer some ways to find the heat and meaning of your being and your essence. It is time that you pay attention to your pattern and the one-liner you want that best represents you and the value you have to pass on to your loved ones. I suggest that you might continue to collect information about what makes you tick. I have listed some uncommon areas that you might also find clues to your core life message. You will be able to see from all this information you collect below, what is your core life pattern and message, and what has mattered to you in your life.

Terms Of Endearment

List the endearing or negative names people have called you. When you collect the endearing names and say them aloud, you will instantly feel something: a part of yourself that you like and can identify.

For instance, my father used to call me 'Aveev-ka-beev'. My sister, Shoshana, had the nickname of Sho from Co-Co-Mo. I smile and feel warm inside when I say these names. No other child in our family, in all of the six children had this nickname. I was unique, and felt special for that name was only for me. To me, it meant love.

CHAPTER 4: STEP 4

My sisters later called me 'Bucky Beaver' for the crooked front tooth in my mouth, or 'Four-Eyes' for the pink sparkly wing tipped glasses I used to wear. I also had a best friend, Julie, call me 'Weirdo', which sort of meant 'Geek' in my day, but was a special secret endearment between the two of us. Another nickname was 'Million Dollar Red Pony' for my red hair and the way I ran five miles a day. I also have been called 'FiFi' for my thick waist long hair that I foolishly permed into poodle curls one year, which became a tightly knotted red-haired Afro after the perm solution was left in too long. Yet another name was Bunny, for my sweet but fierce nature to protect those for whom I cared. My two adult daughters call me 'Mommykins' instead of Mommy. True or not, to them the name gives it a more grown up flair, nurturing, but personal nonetheless.

Each one of these endearing names, bad or good, singled me out from all the rest. I felt valuable, noticed, and that I mattered to the ones I loved. As you can tell just by this *Forget Me Knot* book that I have written, I value the unique and individual spark of life each one of us brings to the world. I want to see it preserved so our spark does not go extinct. Unions, groups, and gatherings are not my thing. I am not a believer in 'strength in numbers'. I value the individual will and soul in each one of us. I do not want any one of us to be 'lost in the shuffle'. As you can see, my pattern is noticeable in the endearing names as well as the derogatory name calling that being unique is our divine right and pleasure in life.

You will have childhood and adult endearing names, sacred names, initiate names, as well as hurtful, even cruel names. Rather than throw any of these names out, or put them in the recesses of your memory, bad or good, use them as indicators of where the heat is for your thought, passion, and energy. A stored fossil inside you is valuable in defining what is most important to you in your core life message. You do not want to miss it.

GESTURES

What are the repeating gestures you use all the time to underscore what you mean or are passionate about? Gestures are very important to a Homeopath, like me. Gestures are automatic movements that express energy without words. They usually tell me where to look for a pattern in prescribing a remedy. We, Homeopaths, know that our body's constitution is very efficient and does not want to waste any energy on a physical, mental, or emotional level. When you use a gesture to be emphatic, it is automatic and without thought. You use gestures to express energy of what your words cannot convey. Gestures are a clue to your pattern, or your core life message.

You can see an example of just how powerful gestures can point to your core life pattern from Kimberly, a patient who had been a child actress. She never wanted to grow up. Even though she was an adult, she seemed to have left something behind in her childhood as a working actress. She was rewarded well for playing a public role that was not authentically who she was. The impact of that public role defined her life and her true unique self was 'lost in the shuffle'. I remember one time, when she would speak; Kimberly would stand and automatically wave her arms in a flapping motion as if she was flying, as she spoke of her greatest fear, her fear of aging. Her fear was that she would not live long enough to express her gift of writing, and giving her true gift. She feared she would die before her time. While she was a woman in her mid forties, she dressed like a pre-teen and hated the idea of aging in any way. It is interesting that the remedy prescribed for her was the Butterfly remedy. Butterflies live only 26 days before they die, a short life span. She often dreamt of feeling as if she was a butterfly in a jar with holes punched into the metal lid. Her physical symptoms showed a constitution that was speeding up, too, with hyperthyroid symptoms on the physical level. Everything about Kimberly was about making sure that others understood her, on her terms, in beauty, gentility, and grand wisdom, in her way, before it was too late.

Kimberly's automatic movement gave me a clue that when she spoke of her greatest fear, she was speaking of her core life pattern. Her gestures of arms flapping directed me to truths that were running automatically underneath her story. Kimberly wanted to give her creative gifts to the world before she passed on to the hereafter. In her mind, as long as she stayed young she would have time to express the wonderful, undiscovered creative gifts she knew she possessed.

Kimberly's core life message might be a quote from Carl Sagan, "We are like butterflies who flutter for a day and think it is forever." Another quote might be from the best selling author, Richard Bach, "What the caterpillar calls the end of the world, the master calls a butterfly." The obvious symbol that will trigger Kimberly's core life message in the hearts and minds of her loved ones is the butterfly. Kimberly will tie her message to her loved ones when they view a butterfly. The butterfly, when they see it in their everyday world, will be a trigger for them to express their gifts right now, and not to delay because the window for its expression has a short time span and there is no time to wait.

Everyday gestures, by hand or foot, twitch or jerk, indicate where there is a large amount of energy or passion. The gestures will not be random. The gestures will be repeated and noticeable to the observant eye. They often connect to everyday rituals in speaking, eating, sleeping, laughing, crying, anger, or other simple actions.

MANNERISMS

Mannerisms are gestures as well. Actors and actresses, while they work hard at extinguishing them for the sake of their art form, and widening the acting parts they can play, their mannerisms creep into their work. Their mannerisms are the authentic part of themselves no matter how hard they try to get rid of them. It is through those mannerisms we come to know, and recognize them and love them. Meryl Streep, Barbara Streisand, and Eddie Murphy all have facial mannerisms that uniquely define them in our minds; no matter how many and varied parts they play. We do the same for the ones we love. Mannerisms can be the way you either look others in the eye or not, or even smile with your eyes. It can be your twitches, the tilt of your head, the sound of your laugh, or the twisting of your hair lock. Mannerisms can be the way you purse your lips when concentrating. Mannerisms can be tucking your thumb under your forefinger in a closed fist when you eat a meal, or your face hovering close to the plate as you bring fork to mouth.

Mannerisms are automatic movements. Because mannerisms are not from thought, we do not know when we are doing them. That is why it is so difficult to extinguish them from our actions. Mannerisms reveal one more place to dig where there is heat. We have energy, attention, and something that has occurred so many times that it has become automatic. Rather than place judgment on whether a mannerism is good or bad, embarrassing or charming, see mannerisms as your custom made emotional beauty marks, emotional tattoos of a sort, that would identify you with those that love and cherish you. It is your Wabi-Sabi.

Heroes And Villains

Who are the heroes you love and the villains you hate? Heroes and Villains are also areas that show you where you have heat and passion. Your heroes have what you know you have too, if only you had the focus and structure to bring your gifts to fruition just like them. Your heroes represent the best in you. You connect with their perfection the way you connect with the perfection in you. Actually, it is much easier to see the best and the worst in another rather than yourself, better out there than inside you. You play pin-the-tail-on-the-donkey game by attaching to another what is really your own. You do that with both your heroes and your villains. You project both the best and worst of you onto another so you can experience the qualities you admire, and the qualities you loathe without having to experience them first hand. Instead of experiencing them, you can observe them and stay emotionally safe out of trial and errors consequences. Your heroes and your villains are really parts of you that you have either to put on a pedestal above or cast as a leper below. In both cases, it is pretense to think that these heroes or villains do not carry the heat of your passion, energy, and attention. Your heroes and villains can be used as polar opposite ways to find your core life message.

What are the qualities you love or hate specifically? These are the ideals you carry, and the spiritual language you speak. Use your heroes and villains as surrogates of what you hold dear, as well as the polar opposite of what you hate. Take both your heroes and villains back, and decipher what is your core life message. Your heroes and villains house your passion. Therefore, it is with them that you can take back what is true for you. A thank you goes out to your heroes and villains for being a receptacle for your ideals and perceptions, preferences and aversions, passions and deterrents. Let your preferences and aversions return home to you. Every single one of them is the opposite of what you love and prefer. You need the polar opposites to have any of the good and beautiful you so desire. Welcome them both.

PREFERENCES AND AVERSIONS

What are the preferences you crave in your life and aversions you avoid at all costs? You have preferences and aversions all day long that have become automatic for you that will give you clues to your core life message. They may look like small choices, but when you add them up, they become very indicative of what makes you unique. As a Homeopath, I hear things like this:

"I like to sleep with my foot out of the blanket at night because it is just too hot."

"I like to sleep with the window open without air conditioning because I cannot breathe."

"I like to go window shopping but don't have to buy anything."

"I like to drive in a convertible with the top down and wind in my hair because I feel free."

"I like to shake my foot when I am bored. It seems to soothe me."

"I like to shake my head when I listen to music because I just can't help it."

"I hate slimy tasting things like okra or oysters because the texture is disgusting."

"I hate dry weather because it makes my skin so dry and cracking it bleeds."

"I hate people to get in my body space. When they come too close to me, I feel violated."

"I hate loud noises and am very sound sensitive because it grates on my nerves."

"I hate strong smells, especially hugging someone who wears cologne; it wears on me."

"I hate tall buildings when I look over the edge, because oddly, I feel like I will jump."

As you can see these quirks are for a reason. They support the core life message if we take the trail and dig down deep. To follow the preferences and aversions is like running your hand over the lines and crevices of the bark of your own character tree. It is the way you respond to the world and whether you involve yourself or retract. It defines your being and hints of your core life message.

You find other preferences and aversions in your favorite food and worst food aversion. It is not just your likes and dislikes, but the reason why they are so which will give you a clue to what makes you tick.

Your preferences and aversions to help you find original information, for your core life message might be:
  Your favorite poem
  Your favorite and least favorite comfort food or recipe ingredient
  Your favorite and least favorite food spice or seasoning
  Your favorite and least favorite perfume
  Your favorite and least favorite natural wonder
  Your favorite and least favorite manmade construction, expression or art piece
  Your favorite and least favorite animal, plant, mineral
  Your favorite and least favorite weather, climate, season, time of day

Ask yourself, why do you love or hate it? You can ask yourself what is your favorite or least favorite clothing, toy, or book, and why. When you do this inventory, you will start to see a pattern. This pattern will lead you down a trail. You will see what makes you tick. You will also see what is relevant to your core life message. I have found, as a Homeopath, the earlier in your life you find the preference or aversion, the easier it is to dig down to the core life pattern and message. So look for your earliest and most sustained preferences and aversions.

Gather your preferences and aversions to guide you to your core life message. Everything that indicates polarity within you will help to clarify your core life message. Nothing is wasted. Nothing is accidental. Like a good archeologist, follow the thread to its end and you will find a fossil of great value that will reveal the more original part of you, the part that makes you unique in all the world. It is a curious and interesting study of you. You will enjoy the course of study on you.

REPEATED WORDS

What are your favorite words you repeatedly use and those you would never say?

Another area to dig for your core life message is the words you repeatedly use. I am not talking about colloquial terms like 'cool' or 'like'. I am talking about words that give you a clue about what is important to you.

For instance, I have had patients talk about the words 'scattered' and 'together,' which seem like ordinary words we all use. But when they are repeated over and over again, you will find that they mean more to you than what the dictionary tells you, especially when the exact opposite has as much passion as its counterpart when spoken.

For my 7-year-old patient, Carrie, she not only used the words scattered, but her actions showed discomfort with anything scattered in her everyday world. Carrie would collect her sister's toys. She organized her toys and similar objects in nice orderly piles. In addition, when Carrie drew a picture for me, she drew her sister, mother, and father bound together. She also drew a monster separating her from them with one of her arms stretched elongated extra long trying frantically to grab for her mother so they could be together. Carrie would run from the presence of any new person and hide behind her mother's skirt. She would wail in fear of being taken from her mother, including me, when I first met her.

When she finally warmed up to me, she would take all my pens, put them together with a rubber band, and then do the same with my pencils. That day, Carrie was wearing a costume over her clothing that was two sizes too small. She liked it that way. She liked tight clothes. The one great indicator of her remedy state was when I bid her and her family good-bye. I walked Carrie, her mother, and sister to their minivan. Carrie's mother started to buckle Carrie in her car seat. As her mother buckled her in, Carrie asked her to tighten the safety belt tighter and tighter. I could not fathom anyone wanting to be that tightly held in. It was so restrictive. Carrie, however, wanted it tighter. Carrie's mother said that request was common for Carrie. Even when her mother tucked Carrie in at night, she had to tuck the sheets, blankets, and duvet in very tightly so Carrie could sleep soundly. Oftentimes Carrie would wake up her mother in the middle of the night when her blankets would loosen, just so her mother could tuck her back into her bed safely, to get a good night of sleep.

I prescribed a remedy that was in the pea pod family for Carrie. Imagine opening a pea pod and all the peas scattering all over the ground? That feeling of scattered is what Carrie felt all the time; fallen out of her pod, her family's safe bond. She felt separated, like a pea from her pod, so she tried to secure the world on the outside so she could feel the bound feeling on the inside. She craved and needed to be bound to her parents and sister so she could function in the world she lived. Her words like scattered and together represented her core life meaning, and the pattern in her remedy state. Carrie needed to be part of her family group to feel safe in the world. This is an example of why repeated words become great clues to what is important to a person. Even in adults, the same holds true. The words you use repeatedly are clues to what is important to you. Repeated words can give you an indication of where to look for your core life meaning, and the most important message we leave to those we leave behind in passing.

For Carrie, even as a child, her core life message might be:
"We are like two peas in a pod."
"Me without you is like shoes without laces."
"What's mine is yours."
"There is no place like home."

Of course, Carrie's symbol might be an open sleeve of a pod with a group of peas on a line.

What Are You Known For?

What do others know you for being, doing, saying, or standing for in your life? Have others teased you over the years for things you do or say? It could be a mental idea that sets you apart: Maybe 'Ditz' is your nickname because you wander and are scattered in your thoughts when you speak. It could also be an emotional feeling that sets you apart: You might have been told you have a bladder behind your eyes because you 'Cry at the drop of a hat'. Do you have a physical trait that is different from others? Maybe others call you 'Mr. Ed', the horse, because you have large 'horse teeth' and a big smile. It might be an endearment. Maybe people call you 'Dinner' because you are always late for it.

Do others know you for something special that you do or say? My daughter is well known for the phrase, "Wait, wait, I have a question!" Everyone uses that saying to imitate her. I am not suggesting you look for the obvious, but rather use it as a starting point. Take for instance, Kobe Bryant, known for masterful basketball. People also know Kobe has a disciplined work ethic. Some know him for "suicide push ups," where at the top of the pushup, he launches himself off the mat so hard that both his feet come off the ground and his hands slap his pectoral muscles on his chest. Kobe's 'suicide push ups' represent his drive for excellence in his work. Asked how he wants others to remember him, he stated, "To think of me as a person that's overachieved, that would mean a lot to me. That means I put a lot of work in and squeezed every ounce of juice out of this orange that I could." The area people know you for is a good clue as to where you spend your attention, energy, and life force.

My patients know me for sending them a comic strip and a small apple eraser with every remedy they receive in the mail. They have come to know that I want them to have the apple of health and a giggle or two to shake up the symptoms that bind their health. I was surprised to visit a patient's work to see he had collected all the apples and the comic strips over the years of treatment. I smiled. I had no idea of the impact I had made beyond healing his health.

What do people know you for that you do repeatedly? You will find that you repeat things that have meaning to you, and thus give meaning to your core life message. Your hobbies have meaning. You might ask yourself why is this so? Only you will know why you spend hours of your life force on that hobby. It will give you a clue to your core message.

WHAT ATTRACTS YOU?

The books you like to read, especially the earliest books in your life, give you a clue as to what might be your core life message. Again, it is not necessarily the story but the moral to the story that will give you an idea of how it relates to your core life message. Fairy tales with their moral message are good ways to discover what spiritual language for which you have an affinity. Do you use proverbs, trite sayings, or parables throughout your daily life? These sayings are also clues to your core life meaning.

By the same token, early writings in a journal or diary, or even a story or poem you wrote and saved from a long time ago often holds the essence of your core life message. Try sorting through some of your old letters and written treasures to find what is so important to you in your life.

Other areas that can help you to discover the key to your core life message are the areas of your life that you would rather not even have to think about. Yet, these areas may be the clearest and easiest to point you to your essence. These areas are usually the oldest and clearest parts of you. The areas of denial, hidden, and taboo, hold many secrets about you. As I have said before, the areas of you that hold the most heat are where you store and spend the most energy of your being, physically, emotionally, and mentally. You also will find your core life message. Do you hate to see begging children in the streets when you travel? Do people who swear make you think they are classless? Do you think most people with handicap placards are using them to get preferential parking? Notice where you judge others, gossip about others, and avoid others. There is heat there. It is a good place to dig and ask yourself what makes you feel so vehemently?

Achilles Heel

If you are honest with yourself, what is your Achilles heel or your greatest weakness? What are your deepest confessions and long held secrets? What is your kryptonite that, when you are around it, you are defenseless even with all your self-restraint and compensations? What are your secrets, confessions, and greatest fears? These taboo areas, even to you, have strong reasons associated with your core life message. From these queries, you can reveal to yourself the two polar opposites that you find yourself moving between throughout your life. Are you hiding something like the fact that you were adopted? Perhaps you have had an abortion? Perhaps you were born from a parent out of wedlock? Perhaps your parent is schizophrenic, or you failed algebra in high school, or you lied on your resume? These secrets hold heat. These secrets hold you between two polar opposites. You can dig and find some truths about yourself if you were to look there.

Addictions

People with addictions will find this area very helpful in discovering their core life meaning because these thoughts, feelings, and memories run automatically underneath all the addiction. Addictions do not define you. Addictions cannot extinguish a core life message either. Addictions are only compensations that artificially seem to help. People with addictions spend a great amount of energy to sublimate those cast off feelings and thoughts that make them feel uncomfortable. It is not impossible to find your core life meaning by looking at the underside of life. As I said before, if it has heat, it is a clue, even if society or you do not judge it kindly.

The addiction does not hold your core life meaning. The addiction is the compensation and the energy spent for cover up. Your core life meaning can very possibly be the reason you seek the addiction. Ask yourself then, for what does this addiction successfully or unsuccessfully enable you to cast aside so you can pretend to live without it? That which you have cast off is really running in default underneath while you perceive you are hiding from its truth. Addictions seem successful to the addict. That is, they seem successful until the addiction destroys the organism, himself or herself, instead of the thought or feeling the addict has been trying to destroy.

The idea of seeing life from the underbelly, or addiction side of life, is to see what imperfection looks like. Consider the reverse of the usual Japanese garden: when you place a stone of perfection in the middle of the garden for beauty and attention. It sounds a little counterintuitive but picture in your imagination, not the usual refined white sand in the immaculately raked Japanese garden. Instead, imagine jet black, sparkly sand instead of the white refined sand in the garden, like the metaphor of the underbelly of life. Imagine it raked erratically, but in an even noticeable pattern, all by itself. Then, imagine that you place a brilliant large white stone, instead of a dark one, for contrast, right in the middle of the jet-black sand to take your attention to the obstruction in the black sand garden. Your attention goes to the light white stone because of the contrast it provides. It is the same contrast as a typical Japanese garden, only in reverse. In an odd way, that is why people who live their lives on the underside of life, learn as much as those living in the light do. These people learn from contrast, but it is contrast between the same two polar opposites. It is the same experience as those from the topside of life learn, except in reverse. In the example of addictions, it is about destruction of the unwanted feeling, idea, or event that the drugs are to suppress. Nevertheless, along with

CHAPTER 4: STEP 4

destruction of the unwanted thoughts go all others as well, eventually destroying the organism too.

As an addict, you will still learn about yourself by seeing the lightness in your life, even if they are few and far between. The large white stone allows you to compare your addiction and chaos to the purity and beauty you possess. It reminds you of who you are not by your addictions themselves, but rather by what is not about your addictions, your original purity, and beauty. The contrast represents both sides of you. An addict would like to see life as all black or all white so he or she can put the reason underneath his/her addictions to rest. The addict can call him/herself a loser, or in some cases a recovering loser. However, neither is the case.

Addicts get to learn about their core life message by coming from the underside, a different and often dangerous way of experiencing their life. The negative print of a photograph still has the same imprint as the photo itself, only in reverse. The addict is experiencing his core life message from a reverse position, but the value is there nonetheless. The difficulty with learning about one's core life message is that addictions can destroy you before it ever destroys the thought or feeling that lies under the addiction. Addicts can have just as clear core life messages as anyone else, if they look to the areas that they play in their life: secrets, taboo, denial, and the hidden. Addicts know very well about lepers, cast-offs, judgment, denial, and destruction. They often do it to themselves.

A family friend, Tom, was an addict of all kinds of substances, mostly legal doctor prescriptions. He was an intelligent, compassionate, kind soul who eventually died in his sleep from an overdose, after going to an emergency room for a doctor's prescription for pain medicine. Everyone knew Tom would end up dead from his addictions. He seemed like a cat with not nine lives, but more like eighteen lives. It was just a matter of when, not if it would happen. Somehow, Tom always landed on his feet and never fully paid for the consequences of his choices and actions until his untimely death.

Tom was a clever, charismatic, bright engineer for both the aerospace and automobile industry. At the time of his death, his life was subdued and simple. He was an onsite plant manager for an assisted living facility. He made the facility clean, beautiful, and kept it running problem-free. While outwardly, things for Tom were orderly and flowing, inwardly things were chaotic and suppressed. Tom had numerous jobs, surgeries, wives, homes, and dogs. He was a functioning transient, who was on the run from feelings and thoughts that ran him from the underneath. Tom sabotaged every relationship that supported him in his life. Even though Tom was a charmer and liked people, he felt he was alone and abandoned his whole life. Tom was the child of an alcoholic father for whom he was the scapegoat for all that had gone wrong.

Tom was supposed to stop the damage created by his alcoholic father and make it right for his mother and brothers. Unfortunately, he never had the power to do so. Tom looked like his father and had some of the same natural gifts as his father, as well as the same curses. Tom could see many of the same characteristics of destruction in his father that he saw in himself, as well as his intelligence, good looks, athletic ability, and loyalty to family. If only Tom could destroy the part of himself that was similar to his father, that part that shamed and destroyed the love in his family, he could redeem his family. He could keep his promise and complete his role in his family for his mother and brothers. However, no matter how Tom tried to destroy the thought or feeling, he ended up destroying himself, just as his father had.

As much as Tom wanted to be different and better than his father who had been an addict, he went to the place where he left something in his childhood. That place was addictions. The very way he wanted to be different, he ended up being the same. He was an addict just like his father. Even so, as he looked for his experience from the underside of life, he learned compassion for his father in his addictions. He learned forgiveness and generosity, even with self-loathing and destruction. He learned what his own mother learned in the light of day without being an addict. She learned generosity

CHAPTER 4: STEP 4

and forgiveness too, for both Tom and Tom's father. One learned it from the topside of life, the other from the underside by walking the same path—same polar opposites, same lesson, and expression. We evolve between two polar opposites.

Tom's courage to bring his family peace and hope, though not accomplished, was his core life meaning. No matter how self-destructive his path, Tom always returned to his mother's home to help her in any way he could. Tom was there for his ailing mother to her very last breath. As a plant manager of the assisted living facility, he looked after the environment of patients who could not fend for themselves. In his last days, he was the one person that brought light and hope to the disabled, ailing, and dying people in the assisted living facility for which he managed. By comparison, Tom saw his core life meaning by looking at his life landscape in reverse. The addictions and suppressions were the canvas by which he could see the goodness of his soul. He wanted so badly to be like the savior that his mother so fervently prayed to in church every week. He just couldn't do it consistently no matter how he tried. Tom's core life meaning might be:

"A rebel adult often seems like a glorious savior, whereas a rebel child often seems like a little devil."
"Secrecy, once accepted, becomes an addiction."
"Addiction is a symptom of not growing up."
"Before you can break out of your own prison, you must realize you are locked up."
"A habit is a shirt made of iron."
"Habits are first cobwebs, then cables."
"Daisies of the world unite. You have nothing to lose but your chains."

The trigger symbol for Tom at his funeral was a chain of simple daisies, with one given to each of the mourners to pick the petals, saying, "I love me, I love me not. I love me, I love me not."

While Tom and other addicts use drugs to suppress that which they cannot change or affect, you may have simpler addictions that also hold the heat of contrast where you can find your core life message. Could it be your aversion or craving for food? Could it be your obsessive control of cleanliness? Could it be your need to fill every moment of time on your calendar? It might also be your need to exercise for hours a day, or the need to avoid carbohydrates as if they are poison. Look to where there is heat in how you think of addictions whether they are for your "good" or "bad." Use these areas to dig for your core life message.

THE COMMANDMENTS

The rules, laws, commandments, and edicts you use to keep yourself on the straight and narrow to stay true to your core life message are good places for you to find where you house your core life message. Which of the seven deadly sins have you experienced in your lifetime? In addition, which of the seven heavenly virtues have you strived to live by in your lifetime? As you can see these are two extreme polar opposites. You can use the sins and virtues to see where you place yourself so you can find your core life message. For your review, here are the Seven Deadly Sins and Seven Heavenly Virtues:

Seven Deadly Sins	Seven Heavenly Virtues
Lust (Excessive sexual appetite)	Chastity (Purity)
Gluttony (Over-indulgence)	Abstinence or Temperance (Self-restraint)
Greed (Avarice)	Liberality or Charity (Giving)
Sloth (Laziness/Idleness)	Diligence (Zeal/Integrity/Labor)
Wrath (Anger)	Patience or Forgiveness (Composure)
Envy (Jealousy)	Kindness (Admiration)
Pride (Vanity)	Humility (Humbleness)

Which of these have you strived to live your life for or have avoided at all costs? The Seven Deadly Sins and Seven Heavenly Virtues are common polar opposites that are the bookends of your core life message. Examine just how much passion or heat you have for any of the sins or virtues listed above. Vehemence about any one of these on the list may indicate the necessary heat to identify your core life message. They contain the spiritual language you might like to use to make a one-liner for which your loved ones can remember you. You might have your own personal commandments or list of sins and virtues. You might want to be creative and come up with your own that fits your personal core life message.

What are your favorite religious parables or proverbs? These lines of thought can also indicate where you house your core life message. If these thoughts or ideas have stickiness so you remember or live by those words, they may house your spiritual language for your core life message.

LAWS, AXIOMS, MAXIMS

Some people live by rules, axioms, or what looks like a contradictory conundrum in an oxymoron. They can be the core life message that you live by and want to leave to your loved ones as a connection to you. The rules may be simple. These laws, axioms, or maxims most often come from your own personal experience in your life. You may want to make up your own law, axiom, commentary, paradox, fallacy, postulate, aphorism, adage, formula, dictum, precept, debate, dilemma, motto, philosophy, equation, truths, theory, inversion principle, observation, corollary, rebuttal etc. when you construct your own core life message. You may want to name it after yourself so others never forget it came from your legacy. All you need to do is add your name to a truth from your core life message and it becomes your unique stamp on the stream of logic in the world. Here are some examples:

Murphy's Law: "If anything can go wrong it will."
The Peter Principle: "In a hierarchy, every employee rises to his level of incompetence."
Match's Maxim: "A fool in a high station is like a man on the top of a high mountain; everything appears small to him and he appears small to everybody."
Iron Law of Distribution: "Them that has, gets."

Harris's Lament: "All the good ones are taken."
The Army Axiom: "Any order that can be misunderstood has been misunderstood."
Truman's Law: "If you cannot convince them, confuse them."
Boren's Law: "When in doubt, mumble. When in trouble, delegate. When in charge, ponder."
Frothingham's Fallacy: "Time is money."
The Golden Rule of Arts and Sciences: "Whoever has the gold makes the rules."
Segal's Law: "A man with one watch knows what time it is. A man with two watches is never sure."
Miller's Law: "You can't tell how deep a puddle is until you step in it."
Trischmann's Paradox: "A pipe gives a wise man time to think and a fool something to stick in his mouth."
Churchill's Commentary on Man: "Man will occasionally stumble over the truth, but most of the time he will pick himself up and continue on."
Fowler's Note: "The only imperfect thing in nature is the human race."
Cahn's Axiom: "When all else fails, read the instructions."
Jones's Motto: "Friends come and go, but enemies accumulate."

OXYMORON

An oxymoron can be a memorable core life message because it combines two normally contradictory terms yet somehow it makes sense. An oxymoron will make people ponder because it contains two superficially opposing points of view, but the views share a truth. An oxymoron is like the Japanese garden with the stone as an obstruction. Oxymorons make people think twice and question their logic. You can use others as a core life message if it pertains to you, or you can make one of your own. Here are some examples:

"Agree to Disagree."
"Adult Children."
"Alone in a Crowd."
"Almost Done."

"Born Dead."
"Definite Maybe."
"The surgery was a success, but the patient died."
"Free advice is worth what you paid for it."
"I used to be indecisive, but now I'm not sure."
"Always be on the lookout for the obvious."
"I can't remember having a more memorable time."
"The point is there ain't no point."

Oxymorons are interesting ways to communicate your core life message. They have an impish, tongue-in-cheek way of making us take a double take, because at first glance it doesn't make sense. If you have an impish way and want to make sure the legacy you leave matches you, having an oxymoron will fit nicely as your core life message. You can also create a motto, a promise, a mission, or a mantra.

MOTTOS

A motto is a short sentence or phrase chosen that encapsulates a belief or ideal that guides an individual or institution. You might have one that has been the pointer in the compass of your own life. It may be the magnet to your core life message. Here are some examples of others mottos. Perhaps some of them will trigger a creative idea of your own that will encompass your core life message.
"Old enough to know better, young enough not to care."
"One world, one future."
"Don't eat yellow snow."
"Carpe Diem."
"Just do it."
"Hakuna Matata."
"It's not what you know, it's what you do with what you know."
"Double Amen."
"Sharing is caring."
"Live Fast, Love Hard, Die Young."
"Yesterday you said tomorrow."

Mantras

A mantra is any sacred word or syllable used as an object of concentration and embodying some aspect of spiritual power. A mantra is ones own personal prayer for self that keeps you focused. You can make your own or you can borrow from another. Here are some examples of others mantras:

"The best place to find a helping hand is at the end of your own arm."
"Keep your head up and your heart open."
"Don't sweat the small stuff."
"Don't cry over spilled milk."
"One day at a time."
"Haste makes waste."

Golden Rules

There are universal golden rules, religious golden rules, and many others. Nevertheless, you too can make up your own personal golden rule, just as I did. It can be your mantra, your motto, or your core life message. There are at least two dozen religious versions of the Golden Rule:

1. **The Baha'i Faith**: "Ascribe not to any soul that which thou wouldst not have ascribed to thee, and say not that which thou does not." Or "Blessed is he who preferreth his brother before himself." Or "If thine eyes be turned towards justice, choose thou for thy neighbor that which thou choosest for thyself."

2. **Brahmanism**: "This is the sum of Dharma (duty): Do naught unto others which would cause you pain if done to you."

3. **Buddhism:** "A state that is not pleasing or delightful to me, how could I inflict that upon another?" Or "Hurt not others in ways that you yourself would find hurtful."

4. **Christianity**: "Therefore all things whatsoever ye would that men should do to you, do ye even so to them: for this is the law of the prophets." Or "And as ye would that men should do to you, do ye also to them likewise."

5. **Confucianism**: "Do not do to others what you do not want them to do to you." Or "Do not impose on others what you yourself do not desire." Or "Try your best to treat others as you would wish to be treated yourself, and you will find that is the shortest way to benevolence."

6. **Ancient Egyptian**: "Do for one who may do for you, that you may cause him thus to do."

7. **Hinduism**: "Don't do things you wouldn't want to have done to you."

8. **Islam**: "None of you truly believes until he wishes for his brother what he wishes for himself."

9. **Jainism**: "Therefore, neither does he, a sage, cause violence to others nor does he make others do so."

10. **Judaism**: "Thou shalt love they neighbor as thyself." Or "What is hateful to you, do not to your fellow man. This is the law: all the rest is commentary." Or "And what do you hate, do not to any one."

11. **Native American Spirituality**: "Respect for all life is the foundation." Or "All things are our relatives; what we do to everything, we do to ourselves. All is really One." Or "Do not wrong or hate your neighbor. For it is not he who you wrong but yourself."

12. **Roman Pagan Religion**: "The law imprinted on the hearts of all men is to love the members of society as themselves."

13. **Shinto**: "The heart of the person before you is a mirror. See there your own form." Or "Be charitable to all beings, love is the representative of God."

14. **Sikhism**: "Compassion, mercy and religion are the support of the entire world." Or "No one is my enemy, none a stranger and everyone is my friend."

15. **Sufism**: "The basis of Sufism is consideration of the hearts and feelings of others. If you haven't the will to gladden someone's heart, then at least beware lest you hurt someone's heart, for on our path, no sin exists but this."

16. **Taoism**: "Regard your neighbor's gain as your own gain, and your neighbor's loss as your own loss." Or "The sage has no interest of his own, but takes the interests of the people as his own. He is kind to the kind; he is also kind to the unkind: for Virtue is kind. He is faithful to the faithful; he is also faithful to the unfaithful: for Virtue is faithful."

17. **Unitarian**: "The inherent worth and dignity of every person." Or "Justice, equity and compassion in human relations…" Or "The goal of world community with peace, liberty, and justice for all." Or "We affirm and promote respect for the interdependent web of all existence of which we are a part."

18. **Wicca**: "And it harm no one, do what thou wilt."

19. **Yoruba (Nigeria)**: "One going to take a pointed stick to pinch a baby bird should first try it on himself to feel how it hurts."

20. **Zoroastrianism**: "That nature alone is good which refrains from doing unto another whatsoever is not good for itself." Or "Whatever is disagreeable to yourself do not do unto others."

21. **Scientology**: "Try to treat others as you would want them to treat you."

22. **Followers of Seneca**: "Treat your inferiors as you would be treated by your superiors."

23. **Followers of Socrates**: "Do not do to others that which would anger you if others did it to you."

24. **Followers of Epictetus**: "What you would avoid suffering yourself, seek not to impose on others."

Perhaps you have your own personal Golden Rule or some other rule that you live by in your life. I have lived by one myself. I call it the Flight Attendant's Golden Rule: "Do unto others what first you would do unto yourself." Perhaps you would rather live from your own set of commandments, a set of beliefs that determine your standards and beliefs.

Religious Affiliation

It goes without saying that some devote their entire waking life to the spiritual side of themselves. Your core life message may be in the Holy Scriptures woven throughout your daily life. If this is the case for you, there are probably parts of your Holy Scriptures that are your favorites, or even parts you do not like. If so, this is where your heat is located, and perhaps, your core life message. Throw your fishing line in where your own personal fish are swimming to go deep and find that core life message you would want to be passed on, in your stead, generation after generation though you are not in physical form to give advice or direction. Let your core life message ping the conscience of your loved ones.

Other areas that encompass the beliefs that make up your core life message are where you learned them as children. You might have formed your beliefs from nursery rhymes, children's songs, Grimm's Fairy Tales, myths, or Aesop's Fables. You may have formed your beliefs and that which you plant the red flags of polarity for yourself with stories handed down from your parents, grandparents, or other influential people in your life. Use these stories to capture your one-liner moral of the story. You can use this one-liner as your core life message.

THE MORALS OF AESOP'S FABLES

A bird in the hand is better than two in the bush.
A fine appearance is a poor substitute for inward worth.
A man is known by the company he keeps.
Avoid a remedy that is worse than the disease.
Beauty is only skin-deep.
Better be a certain enemy than a doubtful friend.
Birds of a feather flock together.
Choose the lesser of two evils.
Clothes do not make the man.
Contentment with our lot is an element of happiness.
Count the costs before you commit yourselves.
Do not attempt too much at once.
Do not hurry to change one evil for another.
Do not count your chickens before they are hatched.

Exposure to Aesop's Fables affects us all in one way or another. This partial list is just a few of the beliefs about self and humanity that are an excerpt from those fables. Investigate the entire list and see if one of the morals aligns with your own perception and spiritual language that sings true to your heart. Select one that sounds true to you and personalize it to make it your own with your voice and intent.

MORAL TO YOUR STORY

What is the moral to your own story that rings truest for you? Remember the favorite year of your life and the reasons why you feel that way. Ask yourself, what is your best or your worst life memory? What is your best or your worst adversity? What did you get out of that adversity in the end? What is the moral to your own personal story? What is your perception and your point of view? By the same token, what do you consider your special gift that is an 'open sesame' to your life because 99% of the time it falls your way? My own father used to have a parking angel that got him a space right in front of any venue in which he arrived, even if he was running late. It worked every time. I also have a special gift of winning contests for my loved ones and myself. I have won many things in my life with this special gift. What is your special gift or windfall in this lifetime? Does that influence your core life message that you want to leave behind?

What are the genie-in-a-bottle wishes for which, if you could, you would love to grant people's wish? Ask yourself these questions to help you find your core life message in the memories, morals, mottos, edicts, commandments, rules, laws, and rights of your life. We all have them. We run our lives by these beliefs whether we are conscious of doing so or not. These thoughts drive the compass that directs our actions and deeds.

ASTERISKS, FOOTNOTES, POSTSCRIPTS, AND AFTERTHOUGHTS

Sometimes it is the first or the last thought that has the most power or potency of any interaction. Ask the TV character *Detective Colombo, Investigator Clouseau,* or any other detective why they save their last revealing question just as they are leaving the room as an afterthought, "Oh by the way..." The asterisks, footnotes, postscripts, and afterthoughts have the punctuation point or clue to your core life message. They are powerful and indicative to your last word, the last statement, thought, or feeling. In my experience as a Homeopath I have found that sometimes the first and the last statements in a health consultation are the most important to define the patterns of the patients remedy state on which I can confirm their prescription. The same is true for you in trying to discover your core life message. Look to the beginning or the end. They often match by coming full circle. Where full circle meets, is where powerful energy and transformation happens.

Proverbs, Quotes, Sayings, Song Lyrics, And Poems

Once you have clarified your core life message but are not sure how to put it in one concise, memorable line, you can find your one-liner stated in a way that condenses it. Proverbs, quotes, pearls of wisdom, sayings, even trite sayings, rhymes, song lyrics, and poems are excellent sources for trimming the idea, thought, or feeling into a one-liner while preserving the precise meaning. That is why these remain classic in literature and music, and are easy to remember. The very best one-liners come from the combination of experience and expression. As I stated earlier, you can speak and pass on your experience and expressions of your spiritual language for generations. Following are some examples.

Proverbs

What you see in yourself, you see in the world.
A beautiful thing is never perfect.
The believer is happy; the doubter is wise.
It's not enough to know how to rise. You must also know how to fall.
Where there is a will, there is a way.
Two wrongs don't make a right.
No man is an island.
Better late than never.
Keep your friends close and your enemies closer.
There is no such thing as a free lunch.
The early bird catches the worm.
Actions speak louder than words.
Practice makes perfect.
You can't judge a book by its cover.
Honesty is the best policy.

Do your homework and see if sages or wise ones who have lived before you have not already said what you think is your most important core life message. Chances are your core life message has been the message of another who also made a one-liner. The reason for this

CHAPTER 4: STEP 4

is that proverbs speak a spiritual language from experience and expression. You remember their words because they are universal and speak to your heart. This spiritual language will never go out of style or cause misunderstandings, no matter the language, the country, or the culture. Put your spin on it to carry your own voice and your own life experience.

QUOTES

Quotes and sayings are another lovely way to turn your core life message into a one-liner. They also come from the mouths of experience and expression. You may find a quote from a hero or villain that speaks your one-liner more clearly than you could ever have said it yourself. Discover the flair and fun that can come from another's communication.

"It is never too late to be what you might have been."
- George Eliot
"The best way to predict the future is to invent it." - Alan Kay
"Life is 10% what happens to me and 90% how I react to it."
- Charles R. Swindoll
"If you cannot do great things, do small things in a great way."
- Napoleon Hill
"You miss 100% of the shots you don't take." - Wayne Gretzky
"An obstacle is often a stepping stone." - Prescott
"You make a living by what you earn; you make a life by what you give." - Anonymous
"Luck is a dividend of sweat. The more you sweat, the luckier you get." - Ray Kroc
"Do not let what you cannot do interfere with what you can do."
- John Wooden
"A journey of a thousand leagues begins beneath one's feet."
- Lao Tzu

Sayings

"Even the inside of your own mind is endless. It goes on forever, inwardly."

"No Rain. No Rainbows."

"The Sun loved the moon so much he died every night to let her breathe."

"Normal is an illusion. What is normal for the spider is chaos for the fly."

"Anybody remotely interesting is mad in some way."

"Never say Goodbye because saying goodbye means going away and going away means forgetting."

"Stop wearing your wishbone where your backbone ought to be."

"One day, in retrospect, the years of struggle will strike you as the most beautiful."

"Don't judge someone just because they sin differently than you."

"The greatest thing you'll ever learn is just to love and be loved in return."

Song Lyrics

Song lyrics have an uncanny way of reaching our hearts and triggering our emotions to make us feel what the lyricist translated in the human experience. Song lyrics are an excellent place to discover your core life meaning. Below are a few examples of popular song lyrics used as core life messages:

"You may say I'm a dreamer, but I'm not the only one."
- John Lennon

"Freedom's just another word for nothing left to lose. Nothing ain't nothing, but it's free." - Janis Joplin

"I'd rather be a hammer than a nail." - Simon and Garfunkel

"They paved paradise to put up a parking lot." - Joni Mitchell

"I'd rather laugh with the sinners than cry with the saints. Sinners are much more fun." - Billy Joel

"I'm just a soul whose intentions are good. Oh Lord, please don't let me be misunderstood." - Joe Cocker

"Every breath you take, every move you made, every bond you break, every step you take, I'll be watching you."
- Hugh Padgham
"With every wine you taste, with every song you sing, by now you may have guessed, I hope you get the best of everything."
- Fred Ebb
"Someday I'll wish upon a star and wake up where the clouds are far behind me, where troubles melt like lemon drops away above the chimney tops, that's where you'll find me."
- Yip Harburg
"Unforgettable in every way, and forever more, that's how you'll stay." - Irving Gordon

I remember teaching my toddlers to know their name and address by superimposing the information on the melody of Twinkle, Twinkle Little Star. Later, as they got older, I also put their eating prayer on the same melody so they could remember that as well. If you choose to state your core life meaning with melody, you need not have to make up your own. You can take a riff or a stanza from a beloved song and put your own one-liner to it for your loved ones to remember.

POEMS

Short poems or parts of poems are another way to make your core message into a one-liner. You can collect a thought from those that are written either in books, magazines, or online, or you can make a poem of your own. Below are a few that come from children's books.

"Yes, we'll walk with a walk that is measured and slow, and we'll go where the chalk-white arrows go, for the children, they mark, and the children, they know the place where the sidewalk ends."
- Shel Silverstein
"Black Jelly Beans are best, I let my brother have the rest."
- Grace Andreacchi

JOKES AND RIDDLES

Jokes and riddles are fine ways to consolidate your core life message. They combine the seriousness of your core life message with a lighter feel of humor and laughter so it makes it easy for your loved ones to give it away to others. My own father has a trick riddle that to this day no one knows the answer. We all have tried to answer it in every way possible. My father promised to leave the answer to the riddle in his will. We have had many family outings and meetings where we debated the answer to my father's "A man had a dollar" riddle. This riddle is his trademark and has become part of his core life message. The riddle goes something like this:

"A man had a dollar. He bought a drum for ninety cents and two drumsticks for a nickel. With the remaining nickel, he paid his fare on the bus, when the fare was still a nickel. He rode one block and the bus driver threw him off. Why?"

People knew my father for leaving a joke with every doctor and nurse he ever visited. This was his way of saying thank you, by leaving them with something happier than the sickness they faced all day long. You too may have a joke or riddle that becomes your trademark and relates to your core life message.

Examples of riddles:
"There are ten people in a house. Everybody wants to make a hand shake with only people shorter than themselves. Assume everybody is different in height. How many shake hands?
Answer: Zero, because a taller person wants to shake hands with a shorter person. However, the shorter person doesn't want to shake hands with him.

"One morning a man is leaving on a business trip and finds he left some paperwork at his office. He runs into his office to get it and the night watchman stops him and says, 'Sir, don't get on the plane. I had a dream last night that the plane would crash and everyone would die!' The man takes his word and cancels his trip. Sure enough, the plane crashes and everyone dies. The next morning the man gives the watchman a $1000 reward for saving his life and then fires him. Why did he fire the watchman who saved his life?"

Answer: He fired him for sleeping on the job.

Jokes are also a wonderful way to leave your core life message. The joke can be simple and appropriate to your core life message. Here are a few examples of jokes that can leave a giggle for your loved ones when you pass on before you leave for the hereafter:

"I went to the zoo the other day. There was only one dog in it. It was a shiatsu."

"Dyslexic man walks into a bra."

"Slept like a log last night... Woke up in the fireplace."

If you are an impish person or a practical joker who always brings laughter to life, you may want to use a joke to carry on your core life message.

RHYMES

Rhymes are another catchy way to leave your core life message. Think of how easy we remember nursery rhymes. "Baa Baa Black Sheep..." Or "Do you know the muffin man?" Or "Do the Hokey Pokey..." etc. Rhymes make it easy for your loved ones to remember. They are very useful tools to house your core life message.

Dr. Seuss was a master of rhyme. Some of Dr. Seuss's rhymes for example are: "The more you read the more things you will know. The more that you learn the more places you'll go." Or "A person's a person no matter how small." Or "Today was good. Today was fun. Tomorrow is another one." If you can't think up your own, you can borrow from children's books and change it up, or give the author credit as being your favorite.

Symbols, Icons, And Relics

When we think of relics, we think of religious relics like the bones of saints. However, everyday relics for the common man or woman have a similar function. Their job is NOT to minimize the life of a deceased down to one material object to collect and revere, but instead to link and anchor your core life message bringing it alive and making you heard even though you have passed on to the hereafter.

The function of a relic, symbol or iconic form is best described in the book, *Rag and Bone*, by Peter Manseau, where he describes a conversation he had with Mother Elizabeth Romaniva who was explaining the importance of the relics of St. Elizabeth's bones. She said, "When you venerate, kiss, or show reverence to an object or the body of a saint you give that veneration not to the body itself, but to what the body represents. Just like a photo of your mom or dad, or someone you love. You don't talk to that photo, but that photo helps to translate your thought to that person. That is what we do with relics. We don't pray to St. Elizabeth's bones. We pray to live the kind of life those bones did, and to die her kind of death."

She continued, "I liked St. Elizabeth's boldness, her character. She was just so sure of her path. She didn't go around things. She went through things. I admired that she could put everything else aside and tried to see what truth was, even in death. Even after being thrown down a mineshaft she found a reason to sing."

Relics turn a life into an object that was once useful to an individual that then becomes useful to an entire community, and perhaps humanity. For you, it will be a way to create a vehicle to pass on your core life message from generation to generation.

In most religions, it is strictly forbidden to sell sacred relics. However, the loophole is if someone gives it as a donation, the gift is acceptable. Therefore, it goes that the relics that do not have a price tag are the most expensive of all. By giving your loved ones an object or relic that represents the core life message of your character or values, you are leaving for posterity a very rich intangible legacy they can then nourish their own next of kin's character and self esteem in the many generations to come after you. It is a gift of the highest order to give to the ones you love.

BLONDE AND PERFECT BRAIDS

During the Holocaust, there was the story of Lily Hersh and her blonde, perfect braids. Before going to the concentration camps, Lily's mother cut Lily's braids and placed them inside a velvet bag that usually housed a Jewish prayer shawl called a Tallit. The fringes on the prayer shawl are made with eight threads tied with five knots each, totaling 613 knots. These knots correspond to the 613 commandments in the Torah, the holiest book for the Jewish people. The Tallit underscores the central doctrine of Judaism, that the Lord is One.

Because the Nazis forced Lily and her mother to leave their home, Lily's mother, a devout Jew, knew she would not be able to care for her daughter's perfect long blonde braids. Therefore, she chopped off Lily's two long perfect braids. She tucked them into the velvet Tallit pouch and gave them to neighbors for safekeeping. Within six weeks, the Nazis murdered Lily and her mother in the concentration camp at Auschwitz.

Lily's braids are the relics of a memory that one cannot take away: one's spiritual beliefs whether we live or die. Lily's braids symbolize the knots on the Tallit, as well as Lily and her mother's spiritual language: the unity of pure hearts, with devotion and determination. When we see Lily's braids, as a relic or symbol, we feel connected in our heart to all others with compassion. Lily and her mother passed on with their signature of love, compassion, and the courage of their spiritual beliefs in the face of destruction. We pass onto others the story of Lily's braids as her core life meaning and she lives on in us. Lily's knotted braids and core life meaning are one more example of the *Forget Me Knot* book's method of attaining a core life message.

What Is A Symbol, Relic, Or Icon?

A symbol is something that stands for something else, especially a material object that represents something abstract or invisible. Another word for a symbol might be an emblem, token, sign, or image. A relic is an object that has survived from an earlier time, especially one with a sentimental interest. Another word for relic might be artifact, antique, or holy piece. An icon is a person or a thing regarded as representing a symbol of something.

In choosing a symbol or icon for a core life message, it is best to think very simply and uncomplicated. The simpler the symbol not only is it easier for your loved ones to remember, but it allows them to fill in the spaces of your core life message with a little bit of them. In doing so, this is how they will translate your core life message and allow it to live on. Remember, the simpler, the more your loved ones will feel. The more complicated, the more your loved ones will think. The choice is yours.

If you were to think of symbols, relics, or icons in a more religious or cultural sense, you might think of heretics because of their external images of devotional tools to the Devil's craft. Some perceived that this type of devotion misleads or distracts from true devotion to God. On the other hand, people believed the ancient idea of symbols, relics, and icons would bring spiritual benefits including indulgences that could influence moral development. People also thought relics, symbols, and icons capable of invoking heavenly intercession against discord, plague, or bad weather.

Nevertheless, for the purposes of our core life message, we are not necessarily connecting the anchor that triggers your core life message as a religious connection, even though it usually speaks a type of spiritual, universal language. The symbol, relic, or icon is just a representation in physical form of your most important and precious character trait, value, or belief that you want handed onto others in future generations.

CHAPTER 4: STEP 4

Such simple core life message symbols might be a paper clip, a key, a feather, a needle, a paintbrush, an apple, a watch, a bottle cap, a pink crayon, a treble cleft symbol, etc. The simpler and the more common the symbol in everyday use, the better. Because if it is an everyday object, the more often your loved ones will be triggered to have you tied to their everyday world.

For example, one of the friends of the late actor, James Gandolfini, said at his funeral was that James, the lead actor in the TV series *The Sopranos*, was "a real eagle perched at the top of the church, looking out over all of us, just as he had done in his life." Eagles can be the symbol, relic, or icon for James. Another friend said James was "just like homemade wine." However, we wonder what James himself would have wanted people to know him for. His son said he was a spontaneous practical joker who "looked all grown up and responsible, but he was really just one big kid." His son remembers him at a street intersection. When the signal light turned red, his father James would spontaneously jump out of his car and run around the car. He would then dance in what some called a "Chinese Fire Drill." James was having childlike fun. Red lights are the trigger to James' son that he is around him all the time. His core life message is to stop and play when everything looks so heavy, responsible, and serious. He said, "Add a smile, smirk, or a joke to life when everyone least expects it."

Since James Gandolfini was never very clear about his core life message, others came up with their own perception of what James was all about. This, unfortunately, is more often the rule rather than the exception. It is for this reason that I strongly suggest you make your Forget Me Knot core life message now, while you have the wits and health to do so. This is how you can say, "I love you" after you have passed on. You emanate your core life message all the time, in everything you do. This is how you can pull their heartstrings from the ethers, reminding them of what is important when there is no mouth to speak the words, and give a hug or plant a kiss on their forehead. This core life message is what you would say to them, in your last breath, on your dying deathbed. It is the "I love you" of forever-and-a-day that will be the mobile memory of a souvenir for your love of them.

You might want to have a few examples of relics and icons that can trigger your core life message if you are a thinker, feeler, doer, or dreamer. Here are a few ideas:

Thinkers: books, slide rules, rulers, compass, tools, nails, paper clips, duct tape, #2 pencils, glue, and chalk.

Feelers: corks, balloons, daisies, four leaf clovers, thermometers, stamps, matchbox, Sharpie, nail polish, walnut, push pin, maraschino cherry, seeds, and handkerchief.

Doers: chewing gum, perfume, tennis or golf balls, shells, fishing hook, rubber band, dollar bill, and lipstick.

Dreamers: tea bag, tarot/deck of cards, star, and moon.

You can favor the symbols that are more congruent with your nature matching your favored sense whether it is Sight, Smell, Touch, Sound, or Taste. Here are some examples of relics, symbols, or iconic forms for your core life message:

1. **Visual (Sight) symbols**: tossing hair in a sprightly dance, crisscrossing of shadows on a rug from French windows, pair of black thick coke-bottle eye glasses, rainbow, red apple, domino cube, holey socks, punctuation point, a cross pen, light bulb, crystal on a chandelier.

2. **Auditory (Sound) symbols**: sound of a train on a track, crack of branches on a tree, sound of the ocean in a shell, tick of a clock, clicker to lock a car, rain on a tin roof, baby's first giggle.

3. **Olfactory (Smell) symbols**: salt/pepper shaker, smell after a new rain, dirty laundry, brewed coffee, cologne, soap, socks, deodorant.

4. **Kinesthetic (Touch) symbols**: bed linens, puzzles, pats on the back, handshake, nail biting.

5. **Gustatory (Taste) symbols**: fork/spoon/knife, spice, bean, seed, food, gum, toothpick, chopsticks, ice cube, stir stick, coaster, corkscrew, cork, lemon twist, measuring spoons.

Now is the time for you to be your own archeologist looking for the fossils for your own personal core life meaning. As you do your research, you will be discovering what makes you tick. I believe you will find just how interesting, unique, and special you are to yourself and to all of us. When your study goes inward, you are bound to stumble upon your own spiritual language. There is nothing better than to understand and accept yourself. What you find is when you understand and treasure all that makes you so unique, others will, by osmosis, seem to feel the same way about you. You will feel treasured by all.

This experience can only come from your internal journey. So many people do research into their ancestry and their genetic line finding out who their relations are and what their family name stands for in life. However, few do the same research going within to find the byline or hash tag of their own life. I hope you choose to be one of the few who travel inward to your truth. The journey has the rewards of bridging your physical existence to your spiritual ascent. The wake of your uniqueness will allow your loved ones to follow, taking your core life message as a permission statement for them to do the same for those they love too. Thus, many more will speak the spiritual language of loving than is now, in our everyday world.

Unite The 5 Senses

Synaesthesia

Synaesthesia In A Core Life Message One-Liner And Symbol

Synaesthesia is the uniting of the five senses, as I mentioned in the previous chapter. This idea is very useful when anchoring and embedding your core life message into the hearts and minds of your loved ones. By combining your five senses, layering, and embedding them, your loved ones will have an experience so it will seem like you are with them, in the moment. Each of the five senses is that powerful by itself, but layering them together has a synergistic effect making your core life message stick to them like Crazy Gluing it right into their hearts and minds. It is uncanny when you witness it for yourself.

The more senses you use to layer your core life message, the more bound, and anchored you are to your loved ones lives, experience, and memory, so you automatically trigger in their memory. Your loved ones respond as if you are right there with them in the moment. It is almost as if it is a time released 3-D experience. If one of your loved one's senses is triggered, like the whiff of freshly baked chocolate chip cookies right out of the oven, so too they'll be caught in the net of experience and memory of you with all their other senses.

One of the ways you can anchor your five senses is through a physical symbol, relic, or icon that already houses and triggers memory, feelings, and sensation. Hijack the repeated memories made from everyday symbols and layer your own memory right on top of them. Mrs. Field's cookies are such a symbol. Her cookies are iconic. The average person can have the same effect as Mrs. Fields in the hearts and minds of their loved ones.

When you lay down a memory with Synaesthesia, you also lay down sound and its opposite, the sounds of the silence that surround the memory of sound as well. When you recognize a memory by comparing the sound to its surrounding silence, you are using the skill of echolocation. We all have that skill to some degree or another. You can practice it to get even better at recognizing what is there by what is missing in the sound.

You can use the Five Senses and Four Responders Grid in Step 3 to combine the five senses by layering and embedding your life experience, or reinforcing your core life message with your trigger, symbol, or relic. By doing so, you compress and bind the five senses together so you have certainty that you will not be forgotten. Then, when one of the five senses triggers your chosen symbol, in your loved ones left behind, all the senses bound together, trigger as well, all at once. One sense triggers all of them. They are an embedded team. All the senses layered together then become your emissaries to remind your loved ones of you in the goings and comings of their everyday lives. The more often your loved ones see your symbol in their life, the more often all the senses that are bound together by the hormonal oxytocin or vasopressin bond, it will instantaneously come forward into their attention, along with your core life message. Message, senses, and symbol all choreograph as a team that work together to bring the memory and essence of you into the lives of your loved ones.

STEP 4 LIFE PATTERN ONE-LINER & SYMBOL

This chapter helps you to match your core life message to a snappy one-liner. It also helps you to match your one-liner to a common symbol, relic, or object that best represents your core life message. Combining your one-liner with a symbol makes it easy to embed and trigger your core life message into the everyday lives of your loved ones right NOW. The matching symbol could be a sound, gesture, scent, or taste. The more simple and common the symbol, the more often they will be reminded of you and sense you in their lives now as well as when you have passed. You go where they go. It is the combination of the snappy one-liner, anchored and embedded by the five senses, and all wrapped up in a relevant symbol that triggers your core life message. Then, in that very moment, they can garner their emotional inheritance from you with this portable, timely one-liner legacy. They can use your legacy to create a more authentic life experience for themselves. At the same time, by triggering and anchoring your Forget Me Knot tie you have recharged the spiritual bond between both of you, so you live on in them.

WHAT YOU'VE GOT:
- You have a snappy one-liner linked to a symbol, relic, or iconic trigger that relates to your core life message.
- You know how to use Synaesthesia to bond your core life message.
- You know how to use the 5 Senses/4 Responders Grid to bond your one-liner to your loved ones.

WHAT YOU CAN DO WITH IT:
- You can use it all the time, everywhere, and with everyone who is important to you.
- Draw attention to it. Reinforce it. Leave one with everyone you meet. Let them associate the symbol with you every time they see, hear, taste, smell, or touch it.
- Give it as a gift. Mention it in your conversations, letters, stories, and even your last will and testament.

Unpolished gems don't glitter.

CHAPTER 5: STEP 5

MAKE YOUR MARK!

Did you ever carve your name on a tree, (you +) in a heart shape? Did you ever doodle your name on a text or library book, even when you knew you would pay the price? Did you ever graffiti a public place like a bleacher seat, a telephone pole, or a bathroom wall? Do you find you like to have monogrammed towels, shirt cuffs, luggage or day planners? If so, you will love this chapter. It shouts MAKE YOUR MARK! You get to put your mark on the physical world. You get to have the last punctuation mark on your life expressed and exclaimed your way. Having spoken to freeway graffiti taggers, one told me the unspoken rule among taggers is that all is fair in making your mark on public property, but private property is off limits. This is your turn to be a tagger on your own private property, your life. Make it a double take. Make it beautiful and unique. Make it last over time. This is a Doers delight. However, it is for all of us to have our last say and put our own last nail in our own coffin.

This final step in the Forget Me Knot experience is for you to bring all your senses into play, or at least the main method you use to respond to the world and leave that imprint for your loved ones. This is a 'doing' step, a type of homework. It bridges your experience of this book from being something intellectual, heady, and nice to know, to being something for your loved ones. They can use your

Life-o-graphic™ at your funeral, and beyond. A Life-o-graphic™ is fun for you to make. It speaks your one-liner without words. It is an art piece and an all-encompassing symbol of your core life message in the method you usually respond to in the world. It brings the core life message to life and movement with the five senses. To make a Life-o-graphic™ is to bring culmination to all the five steps to tie you to them.

YOUR LEGACY IN A SNAPSHOT

Most of you, by yourself, cannot afford to leave your legacy and put your name in perpetuity by setting up a foundation, funding a wing to a hospital or university, setting up a scholarship fund, or a trust fund for a non-profit cause. Yet you still want to make sure your life mattered and you have contributed to humanity. Well, not only money makes a legacy. In fact, it is the small simple way in which your mark can be felt that affects the most people and resonates the highest in their hearts.

Having spoken to many spouses who have lost their loved ones, I often hear what they miss most are "the little things." Maybe the endearing name, the toast and tea with the morning paper ready on waking up, or the way he hung his nightshirt on the hook. It is not the big vacations, the audit from the IRS, or the dent in the new car that rings truest and makes the tears roll. It is in "the little things" that reveal the void and the loss felt.

That is why it is important to make your own version of YOU with a Life-o-graphic™. A Life-o-graphic™ is the common man's wing on the hospital, scholarship fund, and personal foundation. A Life-o-graphic™ is the testament to your core life message, and to what is truly important in life. It is a creative venture on your part made from your own head, heart, and hand. If you have ever received a homemade card, a homemade afghan or quilt, homemade jam or cookies, or a homemade sweater or slippers, you know what a treasure that is for you. You also know just how it stirs your heart. A Life-o-graphic™ is the key to the representation to what is important to you, and how your life mattered. A Life-o-graphic™ is your legacy stated your way in a personal, authentic, and vulnerable way.

REASONS TO MAKE A LIFE-O-GRAPHIC™

There are at least thirteen reasons you would need a Life-o-graphic™:
- To use it as a physical bonding tool, to bridge your physical existence to your loved ones heartstrings with Synaesthesia.
- To make sure they know there is no doubt what was important to you and what made your life matter.
- To make you come alive like a 3-D movie where they can touch and feel something of yours, since they can't hug you anymore, when you are gone.
- To ping their memories that you were more than your accomplishments, bio, and your adversity.
- To show the authentic, vulnerable sides of yourself that will make them wish they had gone deeper with you when you were still alive.
- To give them something to share with their children, and a prop to share stories about you with the next generation.
- To help them heal the void of you with something other than the heaviness of grief and loss.
- To remind them to think of you the way you want, and not to rewrite history to fit their perspective.
- To personalize your signature and mark on this earth with what mattered to you most.
- To have fun making your own bohemian creation of you, for all of posterity.
- To put your core life message in a time capsule for 100 years from now.
- To love and honor yourself, your individual spark, what you did with your piece of God in this lifetime; and to be grateful you were you, and that you mattered.
- To shout to the world, "I was here!"

WHAT IS A LIFE-O-GRAPHIC™?

A Life-o-graphic™ is a living expression that houses the core life message of an individual, their developmental life timeline, their favorite colors, tastes, smells, sights and images and sounds. A video, a collage, a song, a recipe, an act, a special scent, story or dance, etc. can show the expression of this message. The form is not as important as the expression of the essence of you, your core life message. A Life-o-graphic™ can house as many of your five senses as you currently use to express yourself in your everyday life. When you let your favorite leading sense be your guide, the format of your own personal Life-o-graphic™ will become clear.

For instance, if you are foodie, and taste is your leading sense, then maybe a recipe will be the format for your expression. Maybe you will leave a favorite recipe for all your loved ones with an expression of your meaning, why you chose this recipe, and how it relates to your core life message.

Say for instance, if you use sign language for the deaf, have a great affinity for the deaf culture, and touch is your favorite sense organ; you might use a hand sign for a word most precious to you, like 'Love'. Perhaps you use hand mittens with the tips of the fingers bare in the shape of the hand sign for love, and teach it to all you know. As you say hello or good-bye, you sign the word love and have your loved ones return the sign back to you.

A Life-o-graphic™ is a multimedia expression, like an art piece, a movie, photo, quilt, animated flip tablet, postcards, toolbox, matchbook cars, baseball card collection, favorite sweatshirt, baseball cap, hunting gear, gun collection, clothing, and collage. It expresses the most important parts of your whole life, using the same colors, symbols, shapes, and images that you prefer, and support your core life message.

The making of a Life-o-graphic™ is a healing experience. It is a type of love letter to yourself and to those you love. It is a type of eulogy

CHAPTER 5: STEP 5

without words. It is an honoring and a last physical experience in mutual understanding between you and those you love. It is the surrogate for you when you are no longer present.

A Life-o-graphic™ is not an infographic, although it has information in it about you. It expresses your feelings, perception, vulnerabilities, and decisions, as well as what interested you in your life. It is not just a graphic, even though it can have symbols, words, form, and color. It is a synopsis of your life. It is about the life choices you made and those you let go. It is a celebration and an acknowledgement. It can be fun and it can be somber. It can be creative and quite simple. However, what it does have are two or more senses involved. A Life-o-graphic™ is your own personal sized metaphorical statue, monument, and inscription on the wing of your metaphorical, symbolic 'life building'.

THE FOOD PORTRAIT LIFE-O-GRAPHIC™

One Life-o-graphic™ creator, named Marcus, made a handmade portrait of him, and then layered on top of the portrait all the comfort foods that his girlfriend had taught him to make just after he went to college. He matched the colors of his face to the various foods. He had fried chicken wings for the red color of his hair, barbequed pork chop bones for his eyebrows, and sweet and salty almonds for his eyes. The portrait was stunning far away, and even more interesting close up. Marcus took a photograph of his creation and gave it to all his friends and relatives.

Marcus was a good cook and took pride in his comfort food. The core life message for the impish Marcus was, "All food to me is comfort food, or maybe I just like to chew." Marcus was a problem solver and born into a family of engineers. He loved to take his time when presented with a problem, chew up an idea, break it into parts and figure out the best way to not only make things whole, but to bring a bright and creative zing to the answer. Marcus had in him part Eagle Scout, part computer wizard, and part innovative artist. Food was just one more canvas for Marcus's unique way of expressing himself. Marcus loved to take the simplest of ideas, turn them upside down, and make them fun, interesting, and new. Marcus, a thinker, who led with his sense of taste, had a childlike pure spirit that believed in the good in all he met. Anything unlike that goodness, he just let roll off his back and out of sight. Marcus's symbol was a Goldfish to demonstrate the bright simplicity of life with color, fluidity, and observation from inside the bowl, looking out. Marcus's core life message, above, has the same simplicity, lightness, and fun as his symbol and Life-o-graphic™.

Another example is with Page. Page Hodel makes a heart Life-o-graphic™ every Monday to her beloved Madelene Rodriquez, who she lost to cancer over 18 months ago. Every Monday, Page creates a heart out of any material she finds around, and forms it into a heart for her beloved, who loved hearts herself. Page feels the love she puts in her hearts will affect others and spawn love in their hearts too. If you want to receive a unique Monday heart email of one of her Life-o-graphic™ hearts of every shape and color, send her an email at http://www.mondayheartsformadelene.com. This Life-o-graphic™ is a living breathing love and connection affecting lives all over the world. This is what Page said: "When Madalene died, for me, there was an avalanche of grief I didn't think I could possibly endure. My little soul just didn't feel strong enough. There was something about the continuation of making these hearts for her...that was not only my desperate effort to keep my connection to her alive in my physical world...they are also an intuitive yet unconscious act of self preservation. I could keep her alive in my heart and mind...if I could make her a heart then she must still be with me. When I originally got the 'message' (idea) to start sending them (the hearts) out in the world, it was to express this profound love that had nowhere to go... It is seriously healing my heart. I know Madalene is smiling BIG, BIG, BIG, and I know she is as honored as I am. She CAN see us all down here from heaven...I believe it..."

Others have made Life-o-graphics™ out of maps, postcards, phrenology-mapped brains, x-rays, socks & shoes, tissue boxes, or baby teeth. The possibilities are endless. Your creativity will guide your core life message, and the way you express yourself with your leading sense.

CHAPTER 5: STEP 5

When you can visually see, where you have been and the choices you made in your life cycles by looking at the snapshot of your Life-o-graphic™, it is similar to seeing your own name on the wing of a hospital or university building. Your life decisions, patterns, and core life message become clear. When your core life pattern is clear, then a theme emerges and all your expressions can build around your core life message theme.

WHERE CAN YOU USE A LIFE-O-GRAPHIC™?

You will see Life-o-graphics™ at funerals, yahrzeits, or death anniversaries, birthdays, and celebrations, after you have passed, to include you in the family memories and activities. Your family can use the pictures of your Life-o-graphic™ as a memorial program either paper or online, e-mails, Instagrams, or thank you notes. Your family can send your Life-o-graphic™ among family members to recall a memory with you once you have passed on, or to share with the children or grandchildren along with stories and memories. Life-o-graphics™ can be mobiles hanging in a home, framed on the wall, made into a placemat, mug, or a T-Shirt. You will find Life-o-graphics™ on websites, or made into an interactive app for the mobile phone. The possibilities are endless, and the only limit is the creative mind.

HINTS AND TIPS FOR A PERFECT LIFE-O-GRAPHIC™

When you are making your Life-o-graphic™ remember to Imagine-Look-See-Tell. To begin and to make sure you are on the right track, making the most out of your experience, ask yourself these questions:

IMAGINE

- What is the best, fastest, richest, and most believable way to get an idea from my head to yours so it is vivid and unforgettable?
- Make sure the core life message is simple, clear, illuminating, sharp, discoverable, dispelling, or debunking; NOT boring,

complicated, cluttered, foggy, missing, obfuscated, rotten, or diverting.
- Make sure your vivid ideas have shape. Fit in a nutshell. Look familiar. Seem complete but not done.
- Include your core life messages with its polar opposite.
- Make the invisible become visible. Look for the hidden framework.
- Make sure everything matters to YOU.
- Make sure your core life message is universal and in the language of character.
- Show your favorites.

LOOK

- Use trial and error until it hits the spot: Idea-Iterate-Revise-Reconsider Options-Try-Modify.
- Like a garage sale: First, know what you've got.
- Know when you have enough to look at.
- Use segmentation to contrast unity.
- Where will you have them look first?
- Show things in a triage. It is easy to remember.
- Show things in a structure of Width/Length/Depth.

SEE

- Lay it all out side by side. Define the system to give clear orientation and position.
- Cut ruthlessly that which is irrelevant. Filter for relevance. Make sure there is no clutter.
- Landscape your work.
- Keep your work odd numbered so they ponder longer.
- Maybe add '½' to numbered ideas, so they stay confused. Leave a place for them.
- Collect and merge. Use asymmetry.
- Show Proximity. Size. Shape. Color. Direction. Orientation. Shading for aesthetics.

CHAPTER 5: STEP 5

TELL

- Include what you are thankful for in your life.
- Use analogies. Pattern. The obvious.
- Make connections. Rearrange.
- Clump creatively. Remember your priorities.
- Throw them off just to put them back on your track as a surprise.
- Make things repeatable.
- Show your improvements.
- Make sure you highlight your fundamentals.
- Decipher for them so there is no doubt in their minds. Use basic shapes.
- Use Tactics and Strategies.
- Name everything when you display it.
- Use the Who-What-When-Where-How-If method to bring clarity.
- Remember to Look-See-Imagine-Tell so the story of your core life message lives on.
- Show a Before and After, or a Beginning and End.
- Show comparisons.
- Show your pieces.
- Let them Imagine you, and what makes you feel good.
- Once you are sure, bond the idea.
- Link the idea. Change both after linking. Make sure it matches as an Inward/Outward core life message idea.

WHAT DO I NEED TO MAKE ONE?

When you have finished plotting your timeline for the Life-o-graphic™ you should have these parts to work with in constructing your Forget Me Knot tie to your loved ones:
- Your one-liner key core life meaning. It comes from your 9-Life Segments and three major life decisions: 27*, 54*, 81*years-old.
- Your type of response: Doer, Thinker, Feeler, or Dreamer.
- Your favorite Leading Sense of all the five senses by using the Five Senses Grid.

- An everyday symbol or relic that best represents your core life meaning.
- Supporting clues to what makes you tick: humor, color, gestures, sayings, dress, etc.

SIMPLE CORE LIFE MESSAGE AS THE THEME

Don't forget to keep things simple and straightforward. Your family will remember the simple, clear messages best. There is an ancient story about this very concept.

Two hundred years ago, a wealthy patron commissioned a Japanese Zen monk and artist Sengai to produce a work of calligraphy. Sengai delivered his work to the patron. Sengai wrote in elegant calligraphy, "A parent dies, a child dies, and then a grandchild dies." The patron was furious over this simplistic and obvious message. However, Sengai gently rebuffed his complaints, "There can be no greater happiness," he said, "than to live a life that follows the natural order of things."

When making your Life-o-graphic™, use some of the principles of Wabi-Sabi aesthetics. Leave space for others to join you in your Life-o-graphic™.

Use asymmetry. It makes things loose and spontaneous.

Use simplicity, sparseness, freshness, and neatness over the cluttered so you leave a place for them to enter your world in their imagination and heart.

Be austere and reduce it down to the nub, the essence, and the nut.

Use the natural; the common things around your world that let go of any pretense or self-consciousness.

Use shadows, subtlety, mystery and the unexplainable to make your loved ones stay awhile and wonder.

Have movement in your work that is without stagnation or obstruction so it plays with light and possibility.

Embrace a calmness that happens when things change in polarity like dawn to dusk, autumn to winter, happy to sad.

CHAPTER 5: STEP 5

Now you have enough pieces to construct a Forget Me Knot Life-o-graphic™ and embed your core life meaning into the hearts and minds of your loved ones. Make sure all your materials and tools are ready as you prepare your Life-o-graphic™.

THE DIFFERENT TYPES

Life-o-graphics™ can come in the oddest and most interesting of packages. Here are a few ideas used by others that might inspire you. Use the structure of Thinker-Feeler-Doer-Dreamer as a base, and put your theme, core life message, layered five senses, the way you respond, and anything else that marks your personality and temperament on it. Below are items used to create a Life-o-graphic™ and some examples of how others have used them.

THINKER

Timeline. Book. Booklet. Mind map. Instructions. Money/coins. Compass. Tape. Where you came from/Your Geography. What applications & uses you have created in your life. A globe. A gavel from a judge. Rules. Nails. Safety pins. Straight pins. Lock and key. Steps. Stamps. Checklist. Graded test. Newspaper. Morris Code. Apps. Periodic Table. Chemical Formula. Mathematical Equation. Problem to solve. Road Signs. Duct Tape. Book cover. Arguments/Counter Arguments. Debates. Self-drawn animated flipbook. Route. Treasure Map. Puzzle Riddle. Portfolio. Resume. Epitaph. Obituary. Biography. Curriculum Vitae. Dominoes. Lego's. Head Phrenology Picture.

> **Chart.** One sailor used a navigational chart to show the places on the global waters he found himself "Dead in the Water", with instruction on what he did about it using his core life message.

> **Old Dictionary.** A writer used an old Dictionary and a red Sharpie to circle his most important words, philosophies and ideas that made him write his various articles and books. He circled the words that made up his core life message.

IRS 1040 form. A businessman who had claimed bankruptcy three times used this form to leave caveats of what *not* to do so you do not leave this world owing anyone. He made that his core life message.

Tools. A craftsman used his toolbox and etched advice on each handle of each tool. For instance, he put a tag on his hammer with his core life message: "If you only have a hammer, you tend to see every problem as a nail."

Animated Flip Book. A 9-year-old boy used a small index-card-sized blank white tablet pad. He drew animated stick figures at the very bottom of the pad that moved when you flipped the pages with one thumb. It became a moving cartoon. He drew a picture of himself hugging each one of his family members with a big "I love you" just before "The End." It was like a small little movie.

Safety Pins. A young mother of three children used safety pins to pin a handkerchief folded into the shape of a baby diaper. Written on the handkerchief in magic marker pen was a personalized love letter to each and every child telling them what part of her they carried forward.

Periodic Table. A chemical engineer used the periodic table to select out the traits he had in common with the elements, metals and gases on the table. For instance, for the element Ferrum or iron, he wrote his core life message, "Resolve to perform what you ought. Perform without fail what you resolve."
– Benjamin Franklin

Phrenology Map. A brain surgeon used a side view of an image of an empty head. She put her thoughts, ideas, and feelings in each part of the of the brain that she thought was important about lessons she had learned in life, including her core life message.

CHAPTER 5: STEP 5

Feeler

A pocket. A Portrait. Flow Chart. Napkin. A teacher's lesson or corrected paper with red marks. Your specifications and details. What Ingredients you're made of. A Doctor's Prescription. A Mortar and Pestle. A sheet of music. A box of assorted chocolates description. A plant. Toothpicks. Chopsticks. Sweet and Low packets. Pictogram. Film Script. Teeter Totter. Drips of a faucet. Parts of a Hershey chocolate bar. Pessimist/Optimist. A Club Oath. Gift certificate. Flowers in a Garden. Roots of a tree. Pie. Popcorn. Nature. Soup. Coffee/Tea. Candy. Nuts. Vitamins. Forest for the Trees. Hidden Picture. Draw a picture. Kissing. Joke. Trading Cards. Postcards.

Postcards. One world traveler put words of wisdom on the back of twelve postcards, one for each month of the year. For instance, on the back of a postcard that had a photo of Paris' Eiffel Tower she wrote, "The real voyage of discovery is not seeing new landscapes, but it is having new eyes." - Marcel Proust. She put the twelve postcards hanging as a carefully balanced mobile flowing in the wind.

Candy Kisses. A thirteen-year-old girl used chocolate candy kisses. She made her own one-liners and replaced the tag hanging out of the chocolate with her own wisdom. One silver candy kiss had this tag hanging out of the top: "Kiss a Boo-Boo. It makes the pain go away."

Sheet Music. A musician used sheet music to write a refrain, especially for his 3-year-old son. He used it for a nighttime prayer before going to sleep. It went like this, "Tuck your giggles in your cheeks, it's time to go to sleep. Collect your curious looks and curl them behind your lashes. It's time to go to sleep. Cover up your listening with the wiggle of your ear lobes. It's time to go to sleep. Snuggle your sniffing nose so it can snooze. It's time to go to sleep. It's time to put the sunny day to sleep and let the nighttime play its own way. It's time to go to sleep."

Doctors Prescription pad. A doctor used his prescription pad to give his core life message for a happy life with the dosages and refills.

Forest for the Trees. A gardener left her core life message by stating it on the bark of one of the trees in a tiny forest of trees. She had made a miniature Bonsai tree garden with three trees. One tree had engraved her core life message on the trunk of the tree. It read: "Life without love is like a tree without blossoms or fruit." –Khalil Gibran.

Soup. A woman who was an avid cook and a motherly type, gave her prize chicken soup recipe with a small bag of the secret ingredient that made her soup taste different than any other chicken soup. She had her own chicken base called "Glace de Poulet." She gave her recipe, secret ingredient, and her core life message: "I live on good soup, not on fine words." - Moliere

Napkin. A salesman wrote his one-liner on a white paper napkin in pen. He wrote, "Things do not change. We change." - Thoreau

An Oath. A Shriner wrote his own oath for his children to follow. It said, "I promise to help the child who is always within myself, to always walk and run free among all men and women." He had it printed on a red ribbon bookmark that had the yellow Shriner's tassel dangling off the end.

DOER

Roulette. Checkerboard. Anthropomorphize anything. Linen. Pillowcase. Swiss Army Knife. Plate. Cup with tea leaves. Knife-fork-spoon. Pizza. Show and Tell. Hand. Foot. Fingers. Body part. A track or path. Your footprints. A medal. An animal. Bobby pins. Poker hand. Poker Face. Playing cards. Games. A bumper sticker. Contests. Baby diaper. Egg carton. Bathtub. Insects. Spiders. Tricks. Face/Mask. What is buried? Trophies. Bird gets the worm. Beach ball. Training wheels.

CHAPTER 5: STEP 5

Bobby Pins. One fashion hat designer put her one-liner core life message on a silver ribbon attached to a bobby pin. It said, "There is beauty in imperfection. Remember to tilt it."

Poker Hand. An actor glued together a straight flush out of a deck of cards. He wrote his core life message in black across the fan of cards, "God does not play dice with the Universe."
- Albert Einstein

Egg Carton. A farmer put one egg in the carton and wrote on the top of it, "Don't count your chickens before they hatch." When you open the carton he had written on each eggshell (with the yolk carefully blown out) having an important message for each month of the year from the Farmers Almanac.

Bumper Sticker. A car salesman wrote his core life message on a bumper sticker: "Find the joy in the journey."

Bird gets the worm. A bird watcher hobbyist handed out candy gummy worms with a ribbon attached. It said, "The early bird gets the worm, but in the end, the worm gets the bird."

Mask. A religious woman who went to Mass every Sunday used a mask to reveal all her fears, adversity, and mistakes. She made it into a collage of pictures. Across the forehead, she wrote her core life message, "Virtue has a veil, vice a mask."

Plate: A grandmother used a white paper plate. She used an Exacto knife to cut out a portrait of herself and her core life message, which is a saying she said all the time, "There is always food for one more." She mounted it on a black background and placed it in a frame. The family used it at her funeral.

Roulette: A young man who was adept with technology created an app that was a roulette wheel. When the person's spin stopped on a particular number, it produced an idea, thought, or belief that meant something to the young man. The collection of thought provoking ideas was important to him in his life.

Dreamer

A Doodle. Map. Pathway. Edges and limits. John Lennon's glasses. Pack of cigarettes. Lines and arrows. Doctor's monogrammed lab jacket. Stethoscope. Hieroglyphics. Treasure Map. Bulls Eye. Clouds. Yin Yang Symbol. GPS. Light bulb. I Ching. Connecting numbered dot-to-dot picture. Photo negative. Evolution of man from ape. Parachute. Colliding with what? Title wave. Pyramid. Stopwatch. Bubbles. 3-Legged Stool.

> **A Doodle.** A songwriter took all the doodles he had collected when he had 'brain locks' and couldn't come up with any ideas for his songs. He put the doodles in a frame with his core life message, "Turn your cant's into cans and your dreams into plans." – Kobi Yamada.
>
> **Treasure Map.** A teacher used a treasure map of the city to lead others to a concrete park bench that had his favorite core life saying chiseled into the seat.
>
> **Light Bulb.** An electrician used a bouquet of twelve different colored light bulbs with green cords attached to the bulbs like stems on a flower. Each cord had its own plug. There was one for each month of the year. When plugging each bulb into the socket, the bulb's message was written across the bulb so you could see it. It looked like an art piece imitating a vase of flowers.
>
> **Tarot Deck.** An astrologer used the Tarot Deck to tell the story of her life. She took out the cards for the major turning points of her life, wrote on the cards the key points, and the meaning of her journey.
>
> **3-Legged Stool.** A handyman used an old three-legged stool. He gave away identical wooden legs (a fourth leg) to all his loved ones with the etched words, "Be the leg of stability. Always stay grounded." He put the same thing on the seat of the three-legged stool.

Bull's Eye. A hunter made a wallet sized round bull's eye target in white, black, blue, and red with yellow in the center. He made it for his family to carry with them always. It had his core life message inscribed on it, "Aim above the mark to hit the mark."

Hieroglyphics. A language interpreter used hieroglyphics to share her core life message. She put it on yellowed stained paper. She rolled it up like an ancient papyrus document. She first put it in hieroglyphics, then with an equal sign she wrote in English, "Don't let love get lost in translation."

Clouds. A poet put cotton puffs in small plastic snack bags. Inside each baggie was her core life message with a handful of white cotton puffs, "Reach for the stars. If you miss, then grab a handful of clouds and rise up to dream even bigger."

Response Words That Might Be Helpful

When you are thinking of the theme movement and words you might use in your Life-o-graphic™, I have listed some words that might help to consolidate and formulate the clarity of your core life message. These words can make your Life-o-graphic™ interactive. Many of these words can add a bit of whimsy and surprise, make your loved ones smile and delight them:

Thinker: Connect, bridge, cross, protect, pull apart, barrier, climb, ascend, descend, trend, link, chain. Balance, scale select, delineate, standardize, measure, compass, ruler, data, number. Complicate, watch, mechanism, security.

Feeler: Leverage, influence, expand, drip, ration, allocate, flexibility. Distribute, filter, funnel. Safety, uncertainty, certainty, vulnerable. Heat, flame, fire, energy, burned, willingness, potential, open door.

Doer: Influence, patriarchy, trade offs, move, sail, travel, freedom, detect radar, warning, stalking, tracking, hide, temptation, close, cage, protect, trap.

Dreamer: Surprise, pop, bubble, direct, compass, course, GPS fly, balloon, vision, Universe.

5 Senses Movement

Putting movement into a Life-o-graphic™ helps to take it out of being a static noun and changing it to something that has vibrancy. When you add movement, verbs, and interaction to your Life-o-graphic™, you allow your loved ones to co-create and participate in experiencing what you meant by your core life meaning. You can get your loved ones to feel your message becomes their message when you take it out of static form: reading, hearing, or viewing. When you let them touch, feel, talk in unison, draw, sing, copy etc. your core life message goes deeper. It is the Synaesthesia effect. Some people have made their Life-o-graphic™ small enough to put in a wallet so their loved ones have to take it out every time they count their money, comb their hair, or look in the mirror. Doing it this way reinforces their core life message in everyday tasks. This brings your core life message to life in a fresh way. To make sure there is movement and life in your Life-o-graphic™, you might want to look around you for something moving that catches your eye. Below are a few of these metaphors, from Nature, that have been used in the making of a Life-o-graphic™.

Thinkers: Transporting, distributing, constraining, destroying, knowing, memory, longevity, threatened, ignoring, willful, work, industrial, no support, no backing, no capacity, rejection, collapse, and struggle.

Feelers: Sensitivity to change, grow, root, branch, family, network, shrink, nut, compact, hardened, ever changing, weird, strange, bewildering, crying, laughing, nodding, ah-HA, Shhhh, eenie-meanie-miny-mo, irregularity, aesthetic, emotional, and feeling hurt.

Doers: Feed, falling in love, capitalism, survival, defense, protection, aloof, not good enough, winning, feeling split, surviving, quirks, eccentricities, ritual, custom, prop, gesture, competition, aggression, sexual and sensual, being looked down upon, being attacked, pet peeves, animated, attention seeking, charming, alert, and excited.

Dreamers: Calm, opportunity, potential, overwhelm, unprepared, love, inspire, peak, ascent, guru, terrifying, chaos, fluidity, time, streaming, melting, endless, serene, dissolving structure, eroding, completeness of existence, bound and released, breaking free, escape, impulsive, letting things out, global, universal, expanding, "Run in feet, dream in miles."

The intent in sharing these ideas is to stimulate your mind to choose what is most relevant to the key decisions in your life that make up your core life message.

What Are The Steps?

Here are the simple steps in creating a Life-o-graphic™. Slow it down. Make it fun. This is all about you. You are fun. You are precious. You matter to all of us.

- Your best decisions happen at the beginning when you sit down to work. The best intuition happens at the end when you come to completion.
- Have your core life message one-liner.
- Compile all the senses you would like to layer in your Life-o-graphic™.
- Use the 5 Senses/4 Responses Grid.
- Decide what form and medium you want to use, and what design.
- Get to the point. Tell the truth. Make things work together. Sketch out the complete idea.
- Use sticky notes to find your inspiration. It requires time and focus.
- Familiarize yourself with the theme you are after.
- An image is worth a thousand words, so make it clear.
- Make a focused decision and see where it leads you.
- Start with a plan. Be ready to modify it as you make it.

- Have a list of the items you want or need along with measurements.
- Have a tape measure/ruler, notebook.
- Pick the right tools for the job.
- Have samples of fabric, swatches, photos, images, symbols, and relics.
- Reveal yourself through design.
- Assemble your colors.
- Determine, identify, and order the elements with meaning in your Life-o-graphic™.
- Determine the location, structure, space, white space, and light.
- Determine if it will be flat or raised, and the background.
- Love your creation in the end.
- When completed share and promote it. Have an unveiling of your Life-o-graphic™.
- Take a photo of your Life-o-graphic™. Share the photo.

CAT IN THE HAT EXAMPLE

As an example, with tongue in cheek, I have used a Life-o-graphic™ to plot the life and accomplishments of The Cat In The Hat. His creator, father and author-mentor, Theodore Geisel or Dr. Seuss, had a big impact on his life. It is an example of just how valuable a Life-o-graphic™ can be.

With The Cat In The Hat, I plotted his life segments on the Life-o-graphic™ Template. The Cat lived 34 years, from 1957 to 1991, just a portion of his father, Dr. Seuss's 87-year life. His legacy lives on today. On the Life-o-graphic™ template, I plotted all his decisions on the graph for each of his developmental segments: 0-27-years-old, his youth; 28-34-years-old, his power. Since his legacy lives on, I decided to plot his legacy up to today to see what decisions have been made during his wisdom years between 54-81-years-old. The life decisions that happened from 27-29-years-old were pinnacle for The Cat. He went from being a static book character to going international in Russia and becoming a musical star on Broadway. The Cat In The Hat became a global phenomenon.

CHAPTER 5: STEP 5

Nevertheless, even as he chose to entertain and educate on a larger scale, the roots of who he was never changed. He was a visionary with children's literature, making it fun to read while letting children's minds and imaginations travel and take risks into thought and places unknown. The Cat remained colorful, playful, and interactive. He loved children and their innocence. He remained polite and respectful while being impish and curious. He loved making fun with whatever was at hand. He took responsibility for his mistakes and made right what he had wronged.

You can see this clearly in the pinnacle choices at each 9-year segment. We also see from the graph that he was a big 'Doer'. He didn't have to talk, plan, or feel. He just had to do and see where cause and effect would take him. He died in his power segment of his life after recording on audio. He had finally gotten his voice lifted from the static printed page of the book.

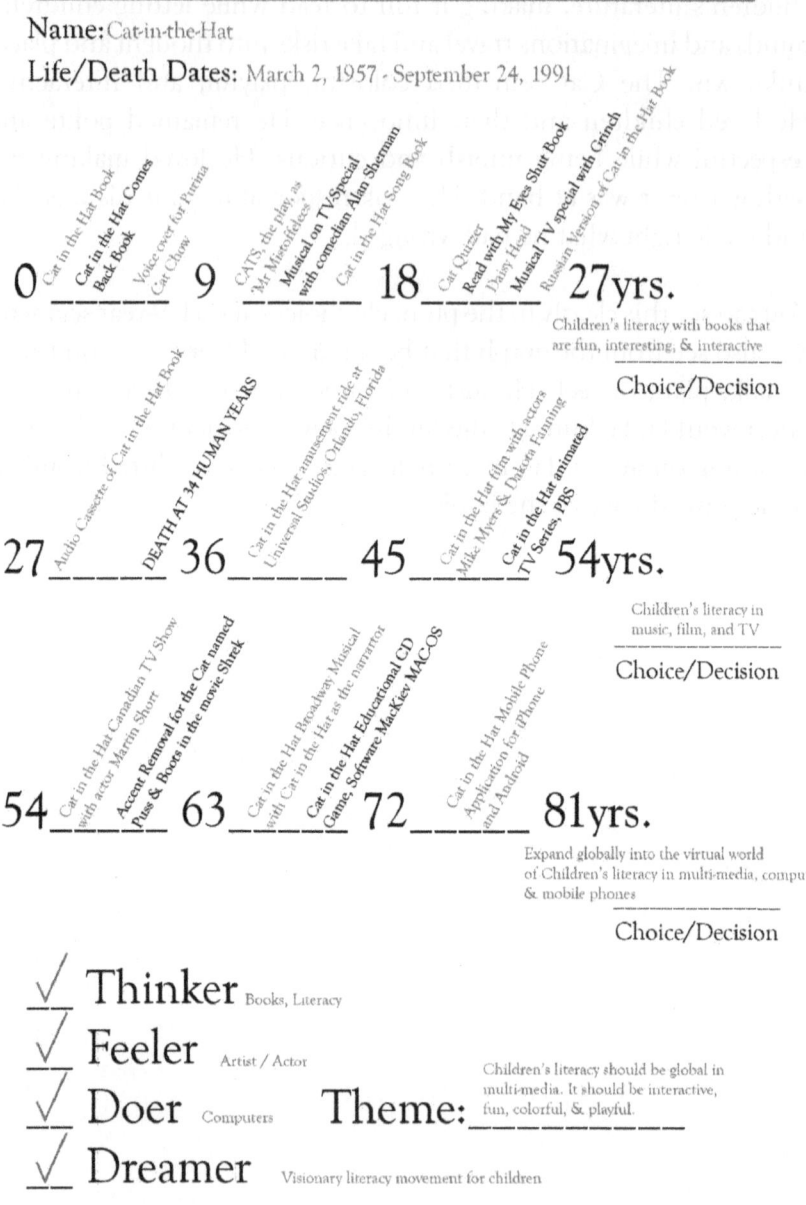

LIFE-O-GRAPHIC TEMPLATE

Name: Cat-in-the-Hat
Life/Death Dates: March 2, 1957 - September 24, 1991

0 — *Cat in the Hat Book* — 9 — *Cat in the Hat Comes Back Book / Voice over for Purina Cat Chow* — 18 — *CATS: the play, as "Mr. Mistoffelees" / Musical on TV/special with comedian Alan Sherman / Cat in the Hat Song Book* — 27yrs. — *Cat Quizzer / Read with My Eyes Shut Book / Daisy Head / Musical TV special with Grinch / Russian Version of Cat in the Hat Book*

Children's literacy with books that are fun, interesting, & interactive

Choice/Decision

27 — *Audio Cassette of Cat in the Hat Book* — 36 — **DEATH AT 34 HUMAN YEARS** — *Cat in the Hat amusement ride at Universal Studios, Orlando, Florida* — 45 — *Cat in the Hat film with actors Mike Myers & Dakota Fanning* — 54yrs. — *Cat in the Hat animated TV Series, PBS*

Children's literacy in music, film, and TV

Choice/Decision

54 — *Cat in the Hat Canadian TV Show with actor Martin Short / Accent Removal for the Cat named Puss & Boots in the movie Shrek* — 63 — *Cat in the Hat Broadway Musical with Cat in the Hat as the narrator / Cat in the Hat Educational CD Game, Software MacKiev MAC-OS* — 72 — *Cat in the Hat Mobile Phone Application for iPhone and Android* — 81yrs.

Expand globally into the virtual world of Children's literacy in multi-media, compu & mobile phones

Choice/Decision

✓ **Thinker** Books, Literacy
✓ **Feeler** Artist / Actor
✓ **Doer** Computers
✓ **Dreamer** Visionary literacy movement for children

Theme: Children's literacy should be global in multi-media. It should be interactive, fun, colorful, & playful.

218

CHAPTER 5: STEP 5

Life-o-Graphic Template

Name:
Life/Death Dates:

0 _____ 9 _____ 18 _____ 27yrs.

───────────
Choice/Decision

27 _____ 36 _____ 45 _____ 54yrs.

───────────
Choice/Decision

54 _____ 63 _____ 72 _____ 81yrs.

───────────
Choice/Decision

__ Thinker   Theme:_____
__ Feeler
__ Doer
__ Dreamer

By doing a Life-o-graphic™, you learn about The Cat In The Hat's life decisions, his color, pace, intensity, and desire for entertainment. It was a theme throughout his life to mix entertainment, interaction, and education. Literacy was his vision. Making literacy fun for children was his goal. The Life-o-graphic™ helps to clarify the expression of the Cat's core life meaning, and how best to symbolize the core life meaning for his legacy.

There are template instructions for filling out the three parts of a Life-o-graphic™. The blank template makes it easy for you to see what the patterns are in your core life meaning, by the decisions made in each of your life cycle segments. There is a thread that repeats in each one of these segments no matter how much transition or challenge has presented itself.

Make sure you plot such items as: education, experience, skills, interests, connections, languages, awards, honors, travels, creations, health crisis, divorces, moves, losses, victories, hobbies, unions, deaths, spiritual moments, etc.

After you have plotted everything on the Life-o-graphic™ timeline, search for the pinnacle decisions at the key years, 27-29-years-old, 54-years-old and 81-years-old. Notice the thread or the pattern. Decide on the key core life meaning from looking at the timeline. Notice if there are any other clues about how you used your senses, colors, shapes, everyday relics, words, sayings, or gestures, which were your unique fingerprint signature.

More Examples

What is an example of a Life-o-graphic™? I chose The Cat In The Hat because he is an iconic figure that makes it simple to show how easy it is to make a Life-o-graphic™. I am using the principles listed in this book.

CHAPTER 5: STEP 5

- First, finding the core life message from the three major decision-making times of his life, at 27-years-old, and 54-years-old. He died before 81-years-old.
- Choosing his key way of responding: Thinker-Feeler-Doer-Dreamer. The Cat In The Hat is a Doer.
- Choosing his major favorite one of the five senses: Taste.
- Use what personality he had and make it come to life, make it move, and become vibrant and interactive: He rhymes. He loves fun. He loves the colors blue, red, white, and pink. He loves his imagination. He likes to move. He loves red bow ties, white gloves, and a tall red and white top hat. He loves exits and entrances.

TASTE: If the Cat's favorite sense is the sense of taste, he could make his Life-o-graphic ™ with a pink frosting cake or red velvet cake. He could put his core life message on the cake's top. He might write, "Don't cry because it's over. Smile because it happened!" He could make the shape of the cake in the shape of a tall red and white striped top hat or the shape of a red bow tie, which are the symbols of The Cat In The Hat. Each loved one could have a recipe for the red velvet cake with pink frosting wrapped in a scroll, tied with a red tie, and tucked in the left white cotton glove (the right glove had gone out with the invitation). The flowers next to the cake might be a Cat-O-Nine Tails.

CAT IN THE HAT PINK FROSTING CAKE

INGREDIENTS
2 ½ Cups All Purpose Flour
2 Cups Sugar
1 teaspoon Baking Powder
½ teaspoon Baking Soda
1/8 teaspoon salt
1 1/3 cups Buttermilk
½ cup Butter
1 teaspoon Vanilla
4 Egg Whites
Pink or Red Food Coloring

DIRECTIONS

Preheat oven to 350 degrees F.

In a bowl, combine flour, sugar, baking powder, baking soda, and salt.

Add buttermilk, butter and vanilla.

Beat with an electric mixer on low speed for 30 seconds. Then beat on high speed for 2 minutes.

Add egg whites and beat for 2 more minutes.

Add a few drops of food coloring to desired color.

Pour the batter into the greased and lightly floured baking pan.

Bake for 40-45 minutes or until a toothpick inserted near the center comes out clean.

Cool on a wire rack for 10 minutes. Remove from pan. Cool thoroughly.

While the cake is cooling, you can prepare the frosting. Add a few drops of food coloring to already prepared white frosting. Mix thoroughly.

TIPS AND TECHNIQUES

You will need 1 medium sized mixing bowl, 1 mixing spoon, 1 electric mixer and one 13 X 9 X 2 inch baking pan.

HEAR: If the Cat's second favorite sense was the sense of hearing, we can use Synaesthesia to layer his core life message. We could recite some of his rhymes, or pretend to have his niece and nephew, Thing 1 and Thing 2, read the eulogy below at a memorial.

TOUCH: We could layer in the sense of touch with Synaesthesia, making the core life message interactive. We might teach all his loved ones the hand gesture he used frequently. We would teach them to twiddle their thumbs whenever they were thinking of a new idea, and when they finally came up with their answer we would teach them the gesture of TA-DAAAA! The Ta-Daa hand gesture is one with his hands flipped out, fingers slightly bent backwards with thumbs up. Maybe for a dramatic effect we would have them wear white gloves while they do the gesture.

CHAPTER 5: STEP 5

SIGHT: If we want to layer in the sense of sight with Synaesthesia, The Cat In The Hat books and literacy are the theme. The Geisel Library in San Diego, whether in person or online, is a wonderful way to reinforce the theme of the importance of making children's literacy global, playful, and fun using multimedia and interactivity.

A POSTSCRIPT

Most of us are not 81-years-old who are reading this *Forget Me Knot* book. Nevertheless, that does not mean you cannot be wise and imagine what it would be like. What if you were 81-years-old at the crossroads of choosing between the three choices before:
- Becoming dependant on another in senility or dementia,
- Dying, or
- Being an honored or respected elder who blessed others just by being in their presence?

Which would you choose? If you chose to be a wise and respected elder, wouldn't it be nice to have your core life message ready to hand out to all who cross your path? Wouldn't it be rewarding to make sure the hard knocks you faced in your life will have had some value for those that come after you? Won't it be comforting to share the wealth of your spiritual connection in loving generosity? A Forget Me Knot experience will have a ripple effect not only on you, but also on those that you love, right now, *before* you pass on into the hereafter. Then you can be at peace, knowing everything after this moment is just a cherry on top. Life is just your little extra zing!

THE CAT IN THE HAT EULOGY
BY THING ONE

My brother is not much of a talker, so I am speaking for the both of us – The Cat In The Hat's niece and nephew, Thing One and Thing Two.

We adored our uncle, The Cat In The Hat, God rest his soul. He was an impish trickster who always made chaos look fun. He stretched out the elasticity in what the rest of the world calls rules. In addition, he was constantly playing tug-o-war with gravity, oftentimes by juggling this object on top of that. With his signature red bow tie and his red and white striped top hat, he had a dignified flair with his imagination and extravaganza. No matter where he was, he could take the mundane, simple, and yes, even boring, and within minutes, mix it all up, and make life itself seem new, interesting, engaging, and exciting. It was never a dull moment with Uncle Cat.

No, No. Never dull with Uncle Cat. At times, it was REALLY hard just to keep up with him. He wasn't the preachy, moral-of-the-story advice giver kind. That wasn't his style. He saw a moral coming a mile away. Instead, he lived by example. He moved. He laughed. He not only juggled objects but also words to express his imagination. He lured us in with his topsy-turvy, inside out, upside down kinda ways. He lived life full on through his imagination, his daydreams, and his sense of make believe. Life just looked so much brighter, more fun, more doable, more possible, and happier, when he was around.

Uncle Cat had two gestures he used to do with his hands that pretty much were his signature statement: One of the hand gestures was his "Voila" or his "Ta Da" with his hands flipped out, fingers slightly bent backwards with thumbs up. When he completed his masterpiece, he would fling his hand out in full showmanship – Voila! Sometimes even bowing to his own creation.

His other gesture was a more introspective gesture. He usually used this hand gesture when he was cooking up a new thought, an

CHAPTER 5: STEP 5

outrageous new idea, or a new move. He would "twiddle his thumbs," with his fingers interlocked, thumbs always moving. He would twirl and twiddle until the imagination would come to a complete halt. Then a grin would emerge, a twinkle in the eye would glean, and it was as if the sun had just come up and a grand surprise was just ahead. The butterflies and excitement would begin.

Uncle Cat loved the mind to stretch, jump, move, and make unexpected, unpredictable turns. Those people, things, or circumstances we all took for granted in our daily lives, all of a sudden would look brand new and enticing. His enthusiasm was contagious. Before we knew it, just being around Uncle Cat, we started using our own imaginations in wild, unexpected ways too.

Uncle Cat's native language was called a poetic language *Anapestic Tetrameter* where two weak syllables are followed by one strong syllable as if on a beat, like music. As he repeated his words the sound of the beat made us know that playfulness and fun were about to begin.

I think it only proper to set the record straight. Even though my Uncle Cat was a celebrity in his own right, in books, film, and photographs, the rumor is NOT true that at one time he had really big ears and hid them under his tall striped top hat. No he did not have plastic surgery on his ears to make them look more normal, and though they look small for his stature, the scalpel did not "cut too much off" and create one more Hollywood horror story. As a matter of fact, all of our family has small ears and very, very long eyelashes. We also are all a little on the droopy side and rounded of stature. Thankfully, we have no signs of Osteoporosis, and perhaps that is because of all the crème we eat, from organic grass fed cows.

Moreover, since we are talking about rumors, it is all just scuttlebutt about my Uncle Cat hating technology and computers being the ruination of small minds. He would probably own a Kindle Fire or iPad just like the rest of us. Yes, he loved books, words, and thoughts best because he believed our imagination kept us young and was an investment in the fingerprint of each one of our spirits. He believed a good imagination could cross all boundaries, all cultures, all bias, all fears, all ignorance, and all imperceptions. He believed reading could take you places with your mind that may not be possible with the body. He also used technology, like the rest of us, but using it as a servant and slave rather than the master of our time, attention, and resources. He used machines and technology in order to speed up things, clean up, and to give clarity to logical things and rules. He used reading and imagination for just the opposite: freedom, feeling unlimited, color, spice, and fun.

Uncle Cat never had a problem in saying "No" to things he did not want to do. Everyone knew "he was dexterous, he was deft, and never mixed his right foot with his left." Children loved him. Adults loved him. Animals loved him. His devotion to improving literacy won him Academy Awards, Emmys, a Peabody, and a Pulitzer Prize. Now he stands immortalized in the National Memorial Sculpture Garden in Springfield, Massachusetts. He may be a celebrity to you, but to my brother and me as Thing One and Thing Two he will always be the fun, daring, and our imaginative Uncle Cat In The Hat.

Therefore, I urge all of you to celebrate your imagination on one special day a year: that would be my Uncle, The Cat In The Hat's birthday, March 2, 1957. Set a place mat at your dinner table. Have a piece of Red Velvet Cake with fluffy pink frosting. Let it topple over, kind of messy-like, and get frosting on the tip of your nose while you read a book out loud. Use your imagination and celebrate the flair and "TA-DA" or "Voila" in your life, just as Uncle Cat would have wanted. Give the gesture and flip your hands backwards. And by doing so, you will keep his name, his vision, and his legacy alive, as well as putting elbow grease to shinning your own imagination and keeping it vibrant and new. That would be a great happy birthday for The Cat In The Hat, and at the same time, his subversive, impish little gift to you. So, let's all eat cake!

STEP 5 LIFE-O-GRAPHIC™

This chapter brings it all together. It is the final step in tying you to your loved ones. This is your chance to expand on your one core life message and premise of your life. You finally get to really explain it, your way, with a Life-o-graphic™. A Life-o-graphic™ is a tangible multimedia expression of just how your core life message gave your life meaning in a fun and creative way. You can now share how it can bring meaning to your loved ones as well. When you make a Life-o-graphic™ you clarify the meaning of your core life message and also show how it evolved in your life. Your Life-o-graphic™ is your chance to make sure you communicate clearly the most important bit of wisdom you want to leave for your loved ones so they can impart it to their children and future generations. Your Life-o-graphic™ is your own personal 'wing' on a hospital or scholarship to the University of Life. It is a bequeathing from the everyday man to humanity. A Life-o-graphic™ is an act of love and exemplifies the details in your personal life experience and expression that has made your life worthwhile and meaningful. Your Life-o-graphic™ reminds your loved ones that they too can build a happy and authentic life using the premise of your core life message as a precious life prompt.

WHAT YOU'VE GOT:
- You have a multimedia example of your character, personality, wisdom, and life expression, your way, without misunderstanding.
- You have a Forget Me Knot tie to your loved ones, so you live on in them.

WHAT YOU CAN DO WITH IT:
- Share it with all you know. Use it at your funeral. Take a photo of it and share it on your memorial program, emails, Instagram, Pinterest, birthdays, and death anniversaries. Make it part of the décor of your home, work, or everyday comings and goings. Make it so that your Life-o-graphic™ is what you are known for.

FORGET ME KNOT
5 STEP GUIDE
TO TIE YOU TO THEM

Step 1 – Life Cycles

| Youth 0-27 yrs | Power 27-54 yrs | Wisdom 54-81 yrs |

_____ Theme

Step 2 – Expression

Thinker   Feeler   Doer   Dreamer

_____ Favorite Expression

Step 3 – Senses

Taste   Touch   Smell   Hear   See

_____ Favorite Sense

Step 4 – Symbol

_____ Theme Symbol

_____ Everyday Symbol _____

Step 5 – Life-o-Graphic

0_____ 9_____ 18 _____ 27yrs.
27_____ 36_____ 45 _____ 54yrs.
54_____ 63_____ 72 _____ 81yrs.

_____ Choice
_____ Choice
_____ Choice

CONCLUSION

The dead bear leaves its pelt. Man leaves his reputation.

CONCLUSION

You are probably feeling pretty confident now, not only about your skill with your Forget Me Knot tie at death, but also in how much more alive, unique, and clear you are about what makes you tick in your life. You know where they stop and where you start. You might be really proud of the spirit that lives in your skin now, and the sovereignty you recognize you have over your soul's experience and expression. After taking the five steps, you may feel that you have done a pretty darn good job with the life you are living and everything after this is extra credit, or a cherry on top.

Maybe you are feeling that you are wealthy of character and generous about sharing your spiritual wealth, your fluency in spiritual language with others. I say, go for it! Make this new found skill something you pass forward so others can experience your Forget Me Knot tie while living and breathing. Imagine leaving a Forget Me Knot tie when you break up with someone, or even divorce. What a precious gift to help them heal and move on. What if you gave a Forget Me Knot tie away as a graduation present, or at a baby's birth? What if you gave your symbol and one-liner at every one of your birthdays and layered it with synaesthesia to insure that you would make a bold italicized Forget Me Knot tie?

SECRET TOOL

There is responsibility for a person who holds a secret like a Forget Me Knot tie. Like all secrets, it has heat and takes a lot of your energy to keep it under wraps. That is why most people cannot keep secrets. It requires too much of them to hold it in, no matter how much they promise they will never tell. Remember in Step 2 how "Nevers" are words of destruction and hold the red boundary flags of the life game within which you play? So I say, honor your core life message and spill the beans, everywhere, anywhere in an unapologetic way. Share the Forget Me Knot tie secret and get others skilled with the tool you are now adept. Let's all be just like our five senses emissaries with the 'all for one and one for all' to connect our message via our loved ones bonding hormones. The Forget Me Knot tie message insures that you can become immortal with your bonded core life message, one-liner of character. Let's use ourselves, and our core life message with synaesthesia, to make certain a spiritual/character part of us lives on forever. Let's lift all of our near and dear loved ones by intertwining us with our Forget Me Knot tie; binding us together, in a web of a different kind, a spiritual web. That way we can all raise each other at death back into oneness.

Try bringing your core life message everywhere you go just like you do with your cell phone. Like the taggers on the freeways, leave your mark everywhere you go, unapologetically. Like I said earlier in this book, my father would leave a joke with the doctors and nurses at the clinics and hospitals every time he would go to leave his mark. He was known for lifting everyone's serious nature. Make sure you are known for something. Leave a wake, a scent, a feeling of yourself when you leave a room. Leave your silhouette, your shadow, and a hint.

PRACTICING CONSCIOUS DYING DAILY

Whether you know it or not, you have been practicing dying every day of your life, all day, every day since the day you were born. Every decision or choice you make practices death. We have discussed the power of "No" and the Boxer Leg-A-See Formula in Step 1, so you know your "Nos" left behind leave a trail of legs. By the time you come to the final choice, the last powerful choice of life, saying "No" to being physical and saying "Yes" to being fully spiritual, at death, you are skilled like an Olympic athlete. You know you've got this down, this Quality of Death thing. You don't need to learn anything new. It is your divine experience and part of the joy of being a piece of Oneness, and a piece of God.

Revel in your differences, your personal response pattern, your "Nos" and all the ways to access your Wabi-Sabi and shadow side. You might try to consciously notice yourself saying "No" to some and "Yes" to others. To be conscious about death on a daily basis makes for a grand exit on that final choice. It will look and feel familiar on your deathbed because you have been practicing it your whole life. Eek every drop out of your polar opposites right up to your last breath. Practice death consciously. You know too much now to pretend you don't. You cannot 'unknow' that the polar opposites you have used to play between in your own game of life. You know now they have both created a valuable, rich life experience for you.

How Will They Actually Feel When I Die?

While knowing your loved one is accessible with a core life message, symbol, and synaesthesia, it does not relieve them of their sense of humanity at your death. A Forget Me Knot tie fosters the healing journey that restores them to their mental, emotional, and physical homeostasis, while at the same time including grief and loss as the catalyst and healing agent of change for them. Even if I could, I would not want to rob them of the pull of your bonded heartstrings, even if the bond included grief and loss. Actually it is those bonded heartstrings that we are using to bring you alive in their grieving heart, mind, and life. That is exactly why a core life message in a Forget Me Knot one-liner is different than a quote or a book. It is the Forget Me Knot bond that brings you to life in them, and vice versa. But that same bond flows both ways. It keeps feelings, memories, and responses alive between you both, including grief and sadness. When grief is fresh they feel it. But they will also feel the bond shifting from a physical one to a spiritual one with you because of a Forget Me Knot tie. Otherwise, your core life message one-liner would just be some clever quote on a bookshelf or on the Internet. Furthermore, their sadness and grief is linked with the salty, oceanic waters of tears that cleanse, heal, and transform their relationship with the deceased into a new form, a spiritual form. They need their tears and their sadness. It heals them. They can then form a new bridge between you, the departed, and them. It is all part of the healing process, with a Forget Me Knot tie or not.

NEED FOR SURVIVAL

The psychologist and scientist, Abraham Maslow, explained why we do what we do so clearly in his 1943 paper, "A Theory on Motivation"[1]. Maslow's hierarchy of needs also applies to death and dying, as well as the healing of grief and loss. Maslow states that if you are in the first stage of needs, the survival stage, you will have physiologic needs like the need for water, air, food, and sleep. These basic and instinctive physiologic needs require immediate attention. At death, most of your loved ones will feel the need to survive as the waves of sadness wash over them and remind them of their own mortality.

If they are in the first stages of loss and grief this stage may apply to them. They may only care that they can get sleep and escape from the grief. They do not feel like eating, drinking, or even going outside for fresh air. The idea of a core life message may be the farthest thing from their mind. They just want relief from the incessant thoughts and feelings of grief that are overwhelming and paralyzing. They may feel this is not the time for recognizing a core life message. They may not be ready to hear your core life message immediately after you have passed, even if you may be trying to wake them up from across the ethers. That is not only fine, it is appropriate. Your Forget Me Knot connection will wait until they are ready to access it. And there *will* be an opening. There always is.

Many times it is the Forget Me Knot symbol and trigger that wait for your grieving loved one's attention and recognition, and when they finally receive your one-liner and everyday trigger symbol, it actually helps to speed up their healing in the natural human oscillation of the waves of grief. So when they are ready, your Forget Me Knot

CONCLUSION

tie is waiting to help them through the first stage of survival needs. Honor their pace and intensity of healing. That is one important valuable reason a Forget Me Knot tie is created; to help them to move through the hierarchy of needs quickly.

Once they are in the third or fourth stage of the hierarchy of needs they may want a Forget Me Knot core life message and everyday symbol for themselves so that when it is their turn for others to grieve for them, it is easily accessible just like your Forget Me Knot tie is needed for them in the moments of fresh grief. You must really understand just how hard it is sometimes to be able to see beyond grieving tears. But also know that an everyday symbol trigger can snap them out of a heavy sad funk and speed up the healing of grief, moving them from the first survival level in Maslow's hierarchy of needs. Those who mourn for you later, in a delayed fashion, will also need what the grieving and forlorn need right now; a bonded connection to you, the deceased.

I have had many patients reveal to me, even when in fresh grief, how a dream, or a sign from the environment seemed like a communication from their lost loved one, even when they had not created a Forget Me Knot tie. It gave them hope, peace, and closure. It soothed their soul. Those dreams are powerful and similar to a Forget Me Knot tie, except that they are only a one time shot. Remember, when your grieving loved ones move to the third or fourth stage of the hierarchy of needs, after grief softens, and they are ready to make a Forget Me Knot tie for themselves, it is their way of further healing their own grief as well as leaving an emotional first aid kit for the hearts and minds of the loved ones that *they* leave behind at their own death. A Forget Me Knot tie will soothe their loved ones' souls even more so than a dream because it is not a one time connection. It is available everyday, all day.

They might even wish they had a Forget Me Knot tie for a faster healing of the angst of their own grieving heart, even with the dream. But when they are ready to do it for themselves, they will find the *doing* of a Forget Me Knot tie is also very healing to a heart still fresh from grief.

Then, when it comes to their turn, when they pass and their grieving loved ones open their Forget Me Knot emotional first aid kit with an everyday symbol and their trigger all around them, even though grief stricken, their one-liner will eventually heal them.

And so the shifting and healing around death mitigates the tsunami of grief that is sweeping the earth. The Forget Me Knot tie heals like a human hot chain link because of the subconscious pre-arranged and embedded bonding links from synaesthesia. You might suggest your loved ones go through the *Forget Me Knot 5* steps with you right now so that there is a strong reinforced bond between you in life as well as death.

Doreen, a grieving patient, was in the first survival stage of Maslow's hierarchy of needs when she called about the loss of her husband. There was no Forget Me Knot tie that had been created by her husband who had recently passed. She said this to me: "I also want to honor my husband in some way so he can live through me and beyond me. I want to create something not only with his motto, 'Where there is love there can be no fear.' I want to create some sort of foundation in his name as well. However, my grieving just seems to get worse as time goes by. It will be three months tomorrow. I understand this grief may last for years and I can't even fathom that. I know he is with me, and trying to help me, but nothing can seem to penetrate my grief because I am so alone, and he was my entire world. I am just so lonely without him. I haven't looked into any of my ideas to have him live on because the grief and sleep deprivation has me paralyzed. I think I need to help myself get through this before I can devote any energy to preserving what he stood for."

If Doreen's husband had done his work to create a Forget Me Knot tie with an everyday trigger symbol, during his life, making sure Doreen knew she would not be alone, he might have left a way for her to heal more rapidly. But, that alone would not have stopped Doreen's grief. Doreen's grief is natural, healing, and necessary. For Doreen it may have taken all her energy to grieve and cry. Her grieving and crying is building a spiritual bridge between her and her husband, where a physical one once connected the two. She was healing at her pace and time and in her way, just like your loved ones will heal. A Forget Me Knot tie could have been a buoy, a lifeline, or an emotional first aid kit that might have made her healing occur faster. Doreen needed the oxytocin bonding with her husband so she could soothe her aching heart and shift from a physical to a spiritual format. Remember, a Forget Me Knot tie uses an oxytocin bond to connect the living to the dead, as well as being the bonding hormone of falling in love. For Doreen it could have been a 'twofer'. A Forget Me Knot tie from her husband could have been running simultaneously along side Doreen's physical grief, waiting for an opening in Doreen's attention or consciousness to receive his spiritual core life message along with a trigger symbol, as well as to feel his love. Then a new kind of bond might have been available between them, reconstructing a different and new way of their being together.

Doreen knew, "I know he is trying to help me." If only Doreen knew *how* he was trying to help her, she could have most likely moved through her grief without paralysis, or sleeplessness. He may have been trying to connect with her spiritually all along as Doreen's intuition was telling her, but Doreen had no way to understand or access his efforts. And so it goes that his healing help went on deaf ears. Lorraine DiGiovanni, a well-known Energy Healer/Intuitive, suggests that spirits from the other side "feel so thwarted that their loved ones cannot receive their healing communications of love and guidance." A Forget Me Knot tie solves that dilemma.

Tear Remedy For Grief

To help your loved ones with their grief, I will share with you a ritual I have with my daughters to heal our own sadness. It might help your loved ones and give them some solace if you share it with them in advance. When my daughters and I cry, we automatically touch our forefinger from our wet tear stained cheek to our tongue to taste the salty fluid. Our tears become the perfect homeopathic remedy that we need in that moment. It is said by the sacred elders that tears are created from the large collective grief of mankind. By crying, our tears are the method by which we are getting the soothing and healing from the community of all humanity, and all who have come before us, who have grieved and cried. They are coming to our aid to help us to join them in the evolution of man. Many people can attest to the fact that they feel better after they 'have had a good long cry'. If you are one of those who are trying to create a Forget Me Knot tie and at the same time healing from grief and sadness, then I am so sorry for your loss. And I hope that your creation of a Forget Me Knot tie helps to heal your own heart, as well as in the future, those who you love too.

NEED FOR SECURITY

The second need on Maslow's hierarchy of needs is the need for safety and security. Though security is not as demanding physiologically as survival, it still presses your grieving loved ones to stay safe by avoiding more personal feelings and thoughts of grief in favor of security. Security can be translated into the need for a steady job, health care, a safe neighborhood, or shelter from the environment. If your loved one, who you have left behind, has been dependant on you during life for security, they might be asking themselves, "How will I pay the mortgage or rent?" Or "How will I handle the inheritance taxes due?" Or "How can I go to work when I feel this sad?" Your loved one may be facing many changes in safety and security because of the sudden loss of you, just like Doreen. It may seem like it is not the time for them to make a Forget Me Knot tie to help them to get through the need for feeling unsafe and insecure, but it *will* help them. Responsibility and adapting to new changes and the relentless number of necessary decisions may seem overwhelming to them after your passing. It may take precedence over their creating a core life message. But then again, maybe not. You see, if they had a Forget Me Knot tie created by them for you, in your stead, you would still have a way to give direction and guidance to them across the ethers through an everyday trigger. That way when they come to a crossroads, indecisive as to what to do next, your everyday symbol would come into view and remind them of your core life message.

CONCLUSION

They could feel the bonded connection from you, and know the next best thing to choose.

With a core life message and an everyday anchor/trigger symbol they just might not feel like they are all alone in trying to make decisions or finding a safe place to heal all by themselves. Creating a surrogate core life message for a deceased loved one might help them to heal faster. They can create a Forget Me Knot tie on your behalf so they can feel supported and assisted by you after death. Yes, it would have been better had you done the necessary work for yourself, but this is a second best way that could help them to find their way through to security. Taking out an old photo album just so they are connected to you for one fleeting moment will only give them temporary relief. It just isn't enough. So, as best they can, they can go through the same five steps for you, as you would have done for yourself in the *Forget Me Knot* 5 steps, so that they will have some way to access your previous heart connection with them and feel the bond again with their own oxytocin hormones connecting them to you. So it is nice to know there is a second way, a type of bypass, to help the grieving to set up a way to create a Forget Me Knot tie, even in absentia, even after death. If Doreen would create a Forget Me Knot tie for her husband, she would feel better.

It is not so difficult to cut a path for a deceased loved one, in absentia, with this *Forget Me Knot* 5 Step Guide. After creating a Forget Me Knot core life legacy message from the deceased loved one's point of view, all that is necessary is to look around for a matching everyday trigger symbol so that their bonded five senses will show them the way to security. Later after the grieving get their bearings in survival and security, it is time for them too to create a Forget Me Knot tie for the loved ones who will have to grieve for them at *their* passing. A premade, pre-embedded core life message can go a long way. It is unwise to make the same mistake of leaving others insecure when death comes. A Forget Me Knot one-liner can make lives easier whether it is done before or after death. It makes healing more expeditious at death.

Now that you know what it is like for your loved ones to be left feeling so insecure, you can make sure you prevent this by following through with all the five steps in making your Forget Me Knot tie before you pass on to the hereafter. You can help to heal their grief while guiding and overseeing them through the security need. They will still feel connected to you sensing you are guiding them in their decisions and choices with a Forget Me Knot tie.

In the case of Doreen, if she were able to access her husband's motto, "Where there is love, there can be no fear," then she would not be so scared that her grief would go on forever. Her husband had left her his motto/one-liner, but he had missed leaving her his symbolic anchor and trigger. He had also missed bonding and layering the one-liner with her five senses. It is like giving her the menu with no way to deliver the food. Therefore, Doreen went hungry, and felt a little crazy for it. Doreen can create a Forget Me Knot tie on her husband's behalf by completing the five steps. She is way ahead of others in making a surrogate Forget Me Knot tie because she has his clear core life message already. The remaining steps should be relatively easy for her to complete for him.

NEED FOR BELONGING

Maslow's third stage of hierarchy of needs is the social need for belonging, needing love, and affection with friendships, romantic attachments, family, community, and the need for companionship and acceptance. For many in the grieving process this stage is the hardest, especially for the senior population whose relationships are longtime commitments and many of their friends and relatives have already passed. For many, they have built their world around the one person who they've lost, so that it means they will have to reconstruct a whole new community, when in fact, in grief, they have the least motivation, energy, or interest to do so. These seniors want it just the way it was, and that is impossible after death. If only they had a Forget Me Knot tie they would feel the hormonal bond and feel the relief with some connection. Again, if you are a senior who is tightly connected to your spouse, position your own core life message with a symbol or anchor in your loved ones everyday life while you are living. It will soften this third stage of belonging for your beloved.

You will be with them, helping them to construct a completely new physical way of belonging to the world.

Marie did not have a Forget Me Knot tie when her husband Mark passed away after a sudden heart attack. It was a second marriage for the both of them and their marriage was only 3-years-old. They were both seniors. Marie was devastated, heart sick, and hit the wall of grief hard. Responsibly, it looked like she moved through the safety and security stage successfully, but she did so by suppressing her feelings the entire time. By her heeding Mark's wishes in his will and trust, she kept busy, and it was one way she still felt connected to Mark. However, after handling his affairs, Marie took an emotional turn for the worse. Marie moved to a remote town and lived by herself with her cats. She became more and more reclusive and unresponsive. Her grief and loss became all encompassing. Mark had left no core life message, anchor, or trigger. At the time of their marriage, he felt like a young man in love, and death was far down the road for him. Marie had put all her eggs in Mark's belonging basket, leaving go many of her old friend relationships for the special one called Mark. So, when he passed, so did her sense of belonging. Had Mark left a core life message with an anchor to trigger her sense of knowing that he was beside her, she could have risked again by entering a community where she could feel a sense of belonging once again. She was dying of a broken heart unnecessarily.

NEED FOR PERSONAL WORTH

Maslow's fourth stage of hierarchy of needs is the sense of self-esteem and personal worth, social recognition, and accomplishment. You may be one of the lucky ones whose loved ones are more resilient and are fluent spiritual/character speakers. When you make sure that your loved ones know you are with them, then you can use your core life message not only to have them benefit from your wisdom, experience, and healing, but they can also share your core life message with other people so that you can be actively kept alive in the hearts and minds of many others. Nancy Reagan did this for her husband President Ronald Reagan with the Reagan Presidential Library.

Dana Reeve, wife of the movie version of *Superman*, Christopher Reeve, did that for her husband, too, with the Christopher and Dana Reeve Foundation.

It is not necessary for you to build a foundation, library, create a cause, non-profit organization, or build a wing on a hospital or university to further your core life message for your loved ones. It is a lot simpler than all that, and even more effective and accessible when your core life message is embedded into their lives. When you create your own Forget Me Knot tie, all that is necessary to carry forward your core life legacy message is for you to share your character, right now, along with your one liner to everyone you meet, but especially to your loved ones. Make sure you include your everyday symbol in conjunction with your actions, responses, preferences, aversions, thoughts, feelings, and life itself so that everyone, including your loved ones, know with certainty the two go together and represent you. In life and in death, it will trigger thoughts of you automatically whenever their senses are triggered. If a core life message and symbol had been put in place, Doreen could have acted like she was strong and fearless in accomplishing her dreams while sharing her husband's core life message with others, without having to start a foundation.

NEED FOR SELF AWARENESS

The last of Maslow's hierarchy of needs is the need for people to be self aware, concerned with personal growth and less concerned with the opinions of others. When people are more concerned with fulfilling their own potential, they have a stronger self-esteem. When you have reached this level of need it is the perfect time to create your own Forget Me Knot tie. That is probably why you purchased this book. You are most likely at the self-esteem level of the hierarchy. To create your core life message and symbol in advance of your survival needs of ill health, when death is looming, places you at the top of Maslow's hierarchy of needs. By making your core life message in advance and tying that message from your heart and mind to them, is to be self-aware and fill your human potential. By creating a Forget Me Knot tie *before* you are too sick to do so, when survival becomes the need of your day, it makes the end of your life one more grand adventure rather than a clean up of the unresolved loose emotional ends.

Having a living, breathing core life message that you carry around with you and embed in all that you do and all that you know is to be living from the highest level of hierarchy of needs with a strong self-esteem. You have arrived. Your life will seem full and meaningful. Your will and intention will be toned and vital. Your soul and spirit will have a cleanliness and purity about it, not only from your own assessment, but to those around you too. Your authenticity will allow others not only to feel vulnerable around you but also to give, receive, and interact with you in an authentic fashion. Your relationships and interactions, both positive and negative will feel real and delightful. You will feel a strong sense of peace.

Not A Stair Step Hierarchy

My personal opinion is that Maslow's hierarchy of needs is not like a stair step that you either go up or down or are one level or stage at any given moment in time. I believe the stages can be simultaneous. You can be in love and hungry at the same time. You can want shelter and be part of a community at the same time. You can grieve and feel connected at the same time. Which need takes center stage is mutable, and depends on your will and intent. More than one need can be present at any given time and have some of your energy attending to that particular need as required. That is why you can have sadness and grief while at the same time fulfilling your potential with the help of a Forget Me Knot tie.

I feel this way because I observe this in nature. Children grow in spite of the fact that they are abandoned. Trees grow even when there is a season of drought. With that said, I would say to Doreen, Marie, Nancy, and Dana the same thing, "Let your loved one stay by your side just as you would have wanted to your dying day, only differently. The difference cannot be closeness in a physical body that you can recognize, but with an anchored trigger, you will know when the alarm goes off that his/her spirit is side by side with you and you are not alone." Knowing this will be comforting, healing, and make the process of urgent change easier in a world where all of Maslow's needs seem too much to handle. A core life legacy message with a trigger will make their lives just a little bit easier, brighter, and hopeful.

FORGET ME KNOT TIES ARE RECHARGEABLE

Don't forget another reason why a Forget Me Knot tie is so unique is that it is rechargeable just like a battery. Every time your trigger symbol snags the attention of your loved ones and instantly brings up the bonding through all the five senses, it reboots and strengthens the memory of you, your core life message, and of course the bond. It shines up the memory of you. Oxytocin bonds last about twenty-one days without any other connection. When your every day trigger symbol is all over your loved ones daily comings and goings, it re-stimulates and reignites you in them through this bond. Gone are the possibilities of forgetting you after two years of not visiting the cemetery, or remembering you only on your birthday, holidays, or death day. Instead you have become their shadow glued to the hormones in the posterior pituitary of their brain.

A Forget Me Knot tie is a spark of light to reignite your passion for living, bringing that light to your being. Take it. It is yours. It is an act of love from across the ethers. It is a gift and connection from them to you and from you to them. A Forget Me Knot tie connection traverses all time, place, and circumstance. You have the secret sauce now. You know more than most people and you can't unlearn it. Knowledge IS power, spiritual power in this case. You are different for having read this book, so spread your word, your core life message by living it. You have only to see for yourself the power of a Forget Me Knot tie. Now, go and tie your own knot to those you love, so that you live on in their hearts forevermore and never go extinct.

[1] Maslow, A.H.(1943). A Theory of Human Motivation. Psychological Review 50(4), 370-96. Retrieved from http://psychclassics.yorku.ca/Maslow/motivation.htm

CONCLUSION

~The End~

ACKNOWLEDGEMENTS

These precious souls gave me some of my life's greatest healings. I treasure their pearls of wisdom that I proudly hang around the neck of my spirit. With the deepest of heartfelt gratitude, I want to thank these generous souls. I share with you the wisdom they shared with me:

Chelsea Spann
"No one hears the flat notes when you sing your Life's song. They are too busy being emotionally transformed by your melody."

Kent Hewitt
"Just *do it your way* in life, with no regrets. Your way is the only way."

Lindsay Spann
"After you have done it all for everyone else, you have had very good practice. Next step is to do the same thing for you; this time applying all that wisdom you gained from practice."

Nadia Eagles
"What you eat and digest in your mind and heart ultimately eats you, transforming and evolving your spirit."

Hoda Meisamy
"Bring to fullness or drain to empty here and now to heal."

Miriam Sobel
"Nature is your first and best teacher. Study with her everyday."

ACKNOWLEDGEMENTS

Joan Rosenberg
"To change your paradigm, take thoughts stuck together with feelings and separate each of them to stand alone. It opens up all kinds of options and possibilities."

Trish Mathews
"Take sovereignty over your destiny and direct your soul's evolution right NOW."

Kay Mitsunaga
"The battle you so passionately fight today will have little relevance tomorrow. So keep a perspective of the bigger picture. Some of the best victories are the battles you never fought."

Harry Boxer
"The sword cuts both sides. Fair is when you can gladly take either half of the pie."

Aaron Boxer
"The epiphany of universal perfection is when it's revealed it was a gift disguised as a struggle all along. You are perfection."

INDEX

5 Colors 134, 135
5 Directions 125
5 Elements 125
5 Emotions 134
5 Life Cycles 125
5 Seasons 125
5 Senses vii, li, 146, 195, 214–215
5 Senses and 4 Responses Grid 215
5 Senses Correspondences 130
5 Senses Synaesthesia 242
5 Tastes 125
7 Deadly Sins xl
7 Heavenly Virtues xl
9 Year Segments 5, 43-45, 80
9/11 xix, xxii

A

A.R.E. 3, 7, 27, 120, 172
Achilles Heel 165
Acupuncture Points 37, 55, 117
Adage 171
Addictions 165–170
Aesop's Fables 177–178
After Thoughts 179
Akashic Records 19, 22
Always and Nevers 123
Alzheimer's xxxi–xxxii, xxxv
Anchors 87, 113, 126, 147
Antique 188
Aphorism 171
Apple of Eden 81
Artifact 188

Association for Research and Enlightenment 19, 23
Asterisks 179
Axioms 171

B

Baby Boomer vii, xix, xxi, xxiv–xxvi, xxviii–xxx, xxxiv, xli, xlviii, li, 149
Baby Boomer Bulge xix, xxix
Baby Boomer Reality Statistics xxx
Birth xxi–xxii, xxiv, xxvii, xxx, xl, 1, 5, 14, 20, 42, 49–52, 55, 58, 60, 63, 69, 77–80, 90, 93, 229
Birth Dearth xxii, xxiv
Blind xxxvii–xxxix, 11, 30, 61, 64, 101, 114–115, 118, 144
Blindspot 115–116
Bonnie & Clyde 152
Boxer Leg Theory 24
Boy Scout Badge xlviii
Butterfly Remedy 156

C

Candy Lightner 70–71
Carl Sagan 157
Cat in the Hat Life-o-graphic™ Template 218
Celebrities 1, 149
Chine v, 49–55
Commentary 171–172, 175
Compensation 110, 166
Conscience xii, xxv, 10, 16, 19, 41,

INDEX

43–45, 56, 65, 67, 177
Core Life Legacy Message 4, 24, 41, 44–45, 47, 56, 61, 76, 98, 237, 240, 242, 252
Core Life Message ix, xl, xlv, xlvii–xlviii, l–li, 1–5, 11–12, 17, 19–20, 23–24, 27, 29–33, 35–36, 38, 41–45, 47, 50, 55–57, 59–61, 63–65, 67–68, 70, 72, 75, 77, 79–80, 84, 87, 90–93, 95–96, 98, 100–103, 105, 107–129, 131–149, 151–161, 163–165, 167, 170–174, 177–181, 184–191, 193–195, 198–208, 210–215, 221–223, 227, 230–233, 235–242
Corollary 171
Cost of Dying xxxviii–xxxix
Criss Cross 63
Cultural Extinction xxv
Cuttle Fish 59–60

D

Death Anniversaries 203, 227
Debate 171
Decision of No 12
Delusion l
Dementia xxxii, xxxiv–xxxv, 96, 223
Depression Era 141
Dictum 171
Dilemma 171, 235
Disability xxxi, 152
Doer li, 84, 86–89, 99, 101–104, 106, 109, 111–112, 119, 135–136, 146, 190, 205, 207, 210, 213, 217, 221
Dr. Seuss 2–3, 136, 185, 216
Dr. Sidney Yudin xlii
Dreamer li, 66, 84, 86–89, 99, 101, 103–104, 106, 111–112, 136, 146, 182, 190, 205, 207, 212, 214, 221
Dunbar's Numbers xxxii
Dwight L. Moody 21

E

Echolocation 142–144, 193

Edgar Cayce 19–24
Egyptian Huna Tradition 54
Elizabeth Romaniva 186
Emblem 188
Embryo 36, 41
Emotional DNA xlv
Emotional litter xxvi
Equation xxxiv, 23, 171, 207
Eulogy xliii, 79, 200, 222, 224
Everyday Symbol vii, 111, 134, 147, 206, 233–234, 236, 240
Everyday Words of Destruction 68
Expressions v, xlix, 14, 18, 32, 55–56, 73, 99–100, 106, 115, 146, 180, 203

F

Fallacy 171–172
Fantasy xx, xxii, xxiv, 43, 119–120
Feeler li, 84–89, 99, 101–104, 106, 108, 111–112, 134–135, 146, 190, 205, 207, 209, 213, 221
Fibonacci Number 125
Fire Deaths xxxvi
Food Portrait Life-o-graphic™ 201
Foot Soldiers xlvi, xlviii
Footnotes 179
Force to Fit 120
Formula xlii, 36, 38, 40, 42, 44, 47, 123, 171, 207, 230
Fossils xlviii, 10, 17, 35, 40, 43, 72, 116, 122–123, 191
Funeral Industry xxxix

G

Gestures 12, 102, 113, 116, 128, 155–157, 206, 220, 224
Glance xv–xvi, 173
God/Oneness 58, 73
Golden Rule 7–8, 172, 174, 177
Gracie Allen & George Burns 152
Great Generation xxii, xxv, xli
Grief xix–xx, xxii–xxiv, xxix, xxxi, xxxiv–xxxv, xxxix, xlvii, 20, 25, 64, 71,

77–79, 102, 106, 134–135, 199, 202, 231–236, 238–239, 241
Grimm's Fairy Tales 177
Growth 5, 8, 13, 39, 42, 53, 74, 93, 100, 135, 137, 240

H
Habits 51–52, 82, 169
Hall of Records 54–56
Harvest xxxi, xli, 43, 93
Heroes & Villains 118, 158–159
Hieroglyphics 54, 212–213
Hiroshima xxiv
Holocaust xxix, 187
Holy Piece 188
Homeopath xii, xlix, 28, 39, 46, 49, 87, 115, 149, 156, 159, 161, 179
Huna Tradition 34–35, 46, 54

I
Icons 186, 188, 190
Image 21–22, 110, 117, 128–129, 188, 208, 215
Imagine-Look-See-Tell 203
Imperfections 150–151
Indecision 56, 76, 79
Indigenous People xxvi
Intangibles xlvii, 10, 15–17, 24, 34, 43, 65, 67, 72, 74
Intensity xxxiii, 37, 65–67, 105–106, 111, 118–119, 138, 220, 233
Inversion Principle 171
It's a Wonderful Life xlvii
It's Not This, Not That 35, 56, 58–59, 61, 71

J
James Gandolfino 189
Japanese Sand Gardens 150
JFK Assassination xix
Jim Bakker 70
Jokes 101, 184–185

K
Karma 57
Knickpoint 49, 50–55, 82, 84, 93, 96–98

L
Language of Opposites 65
Larry Linville 2
Laws xxxviii, 170–171, 179
Leading Sense 129, 147, 200, 202, 205
Leg-a-see Formula 36, 38, 40, 42, 44, 47, 123, 230
Legacy iv, vii, xviii, xxi, xxviii, xl–xli, 4, 21–22, 24, 35–36, 40–41, 44–45, 47, 56, 61, 76, 91, 98, 139, 142, 171, 173, 187, 195, 198–199, 216, 220, 226, 237, 240, 242, 252
Lepers 64, 167
Lies 13, 43, 65, 71, 78, 119–120, 167
Life Pattern v, li, 1–2, 41, 154, 156, 161, 195, 203
Life-o-graphic™ v, li, 80, 91, 112, 198–203, 205–207, 213–216, 220–221, 227, 246–248, 252
Lily Hersh 187
Loneliness xxxii–xxxv, 78

M
MADD 70–71
Maggots 64, 72
Mannerisms 157–158
Mantra xli, xliv, 59, 77, 173–174
Maslow's Hierarchy of Needs 232–234, 236, 240–241
Materia Medica xlix
Maxims 171
Me Generation xxi
Millennial Generation 142
Misconceptions about Death 79
Misperceptions 79, 119
Modifiers 65, 67, 72, 74
Moral xxv, 77, 98, 148–149, 164, 178–179, 188, 224

INDEX

Moral to the Story 164
Motto xliv, xlvii, 1, 3, 59, 100, 105, 111, 125, 153, 171–174, 234, 238
Mount Everest 101
Mr. Perfect 123

N

Nadia K. Eagles 34–35
Natural Sound
Neilah Service for Yom Kippur 78
Nine Year Segments 5, 43-45, 80
Non-measurables 15–16
Nursery Rhymes 148, 177, 185

O

Observation 171, 202
Occupations 103
One-liner vii, xl, xlv, li, 42, 76, 98, 100, 103, 105, 140, 146–148, 152, 154, 171, 178, 180–181, 183, 193, 195, 198, 205, 210–211, 215, 229–232, 234, 237–238, 252
Oscillation 37, 39, 42, 116, 232
Outcasts 64, 115
Oxymorons 101, 172–173

P

Pace xii, xxxiii, 28, 65, 67, 105–106, 111, 118–119, 121, 133, 138, 144, 220, 233, 235
Page Hodel 202
Paired Organs 115–116, 118
Paradox 171–172
Pearls of Wisdom xlvii, 180, 244
Perception xxi, xxiv, 27, 35, 41, 45–46, 57–58, 63, 67, 72–73, 77, 87, 89, 99, 124, 131, 144, 149, 178–179, 189, 201
Perceptions of Reality and Reaction 87
Peter Manseau 186
Philippines xlvi
Philosophy xiv, 43, 171
Philtrum 61–64
Poems 101, 180, 183
Polar Opposites 10, 14, 38–41, 43, 55, 58, 64, 68–72, 75, 97, 111, 114–115, 119, 123–124, 146, 148, 150, 153–154, 159, 165–166, 169–170, 231
Postscripts 179
Postulate 171
Power xxv, 9, 16, 21, 42–43, 50–54, 100, 112, 130–131, 168, 174, 179, 216–217, 230, 242
Precept 171
Predators 64
Preferences and Aversions 117, 119, 121, 159–161
Premise xliv, 3–4, 12, 17, 20–21, 27, 32, 36, 43, 77, 79–80, 98, 100, 153, 227
Prepositions 25, 112–115, 145
Private Face 2
Proverbs 101, 164, 171, 180–181
Public Face 2, 14

Q

Quotes 101, 180–181, 252

R

Rag and Bone 186
Rebuttal 171
Red Flags 68–69, 71, 75, 107, 109–110, 115, 124, 178
Relic 17, 109, 146, 186–189, 193–195, 206
Religious Parables 171
Remedy xlix, 28–30, 42, 49–50, 59–60, 68, 84, 116–117, 119, 149, 156, 162, 164, 178–179, 235
Repertory xlix
Resistance 121–122
Responses v, xlix, li, 14, 73, 80, 84, 99–100, 106, 130, 146, 215, 231, 240
Rhymes 137, 148, 177, 180, 185, 221–222
Richard Bach xiv, 157
Riddles 184

Ripening 43, 93–94, 131, 135
Rorschach 27
Rules xxiii–xxiv, 53, 69, 71, 75, 120, 170–172, 174, 179, 190, 207, 224, 226
Ruling Out 145

S

Sacred Acupuncture Points 37, 55, 117
Sayings 101, 148, 164, 180–182, 206, 220
Search for God 24
Secrecy 169
Secret Power 21
Selye-Stress Response Chart 15
Sengai 206
Sepia 59
Sexual Differentiation 36
Shadows xlviii, 4, 11, 64, 67, 72, 74, 105, 144, 190, 206
Shape xxii, 59, 61, 70, 126, 128, 139, 141, 144–145, 197, 200, 202, 204, 208, 221
Shhh don't Tell 62
Shifts 11–12, 16, 80, 82, 126
Sight xiii, xv, xxxviii, 37, 125–127, 133, 135, 137–138, 140–141, 190, 202, 223
Silhouette 64, 67–68, 122, 142, 144, 230
Smell 37, 118–119, 125–128, 131, 133–134, 138, 140–141, 190, 195
So Above, So Below 117
Song Lyrics 180, 182
Sound xix–xx, xxxvi, xli, 19, 37, 44, 49, 61, 125–127, 133, 135–136, 138–144, 157, 160, 190, 193, 195, 225
Soylent Green xxv
Spiritual Autopsy 18
Spiritual Language xii, xx, xxx, xlvii, 12, 15–16, 18–19, 21, 25, 34, 44–45, 60, 68, 72–74, 77, 100, 148–149, 159, 164, 171, 178, 180–181, 187, 191, 229
Spiritual MRI 18
Square Peg Round Hole 121
St. Elizabeth's Bones 186
Stephen Wise Temple 78
Storage iv, 43, 93, 132
Substance Abuse xxxiv–xxxv
Sun God 'Ra' 54
Symbol vii, xliv, li, 15, 17, 25, 27, 39, 42, 54, 61, 76, 87, 96, 107–112, 129, 131, 133–134, 140, 146–148, 157, 163, 169, 186–189, 193–195, 198, 202, 206, 212, 229, 231–238, 240, 242, 252
Synaesthesia 138–142, 193, 195, 199, 214, 222–223, 229–231, 234
Synonym 149

T

Tallit 187
Tammy Faye 70
Taste xxi, 37, 125, 127–128, 131, 133–136, 138, 140–142, 183, 190–191, 195, 200, 202, 210, 221, 235
Terms of Endearment 154
The Chinese Cemetery xxvii–xxviii, xliv
The Commandments 170
The Geisel Library San Diego 223
The Narrows xlviii, 54–55
The Portal of Passage 72
The Ruby Red Slipper Effect xliii
Theodore Geisel 216
Theory xxiii–xxiv, xxxii, 24, 171, 232, 242
There is a River, 1942 24
Thinker li, 6, 84–85, 87–88, 99, 101, 103–104, 106–107, 111–114, 119, 132–134, 146, 190, 202, 205, 207, 213, 221
Thomas Sugrue 24
Thread v, 1, 10, 23–24, 47, 90, 92, 161, 220

INDEX

Timeline 80, 90, 93, 95, 200, 205, 207, 220
Token 164, 179, 188
Tone 105–106, 111, 138
Totality of Oneness 14, 16, 24–29, 31–35, 37–39, 42, 44, 58, 60, 62, 65, 71–74, 100
Touch xvi, xx–xxi, xxix, 37, 54, 61, 65, 102, 112, 125–127, 131, 133, 135, 138, 140–141, 151, 190–191, 195, 199–200, 214, 222, 235
Transition xxxi, xxxiii, xlvii, 11, 16, 43, 54, 80, 93, 96, 131, 135, 220
Triggers 15, 87, 111–112, 126–127, 129, 140–142, 148, 188, 193–195
Tsunami of Death xxxi, xxxviii

U
Unity of the Senses 192

V
Villains 39, 64, 71, 119, 121, 158–159
Volume 105–106
Vultures xxxviii–xxxix, 64, 72

W
Wabi Sabi 73, 149
Where's Waldo 57
Wisdom xiii, xviii, xxviii, xl–xli, xliii–xliv, xlvii, xlix, li, 5, 9, 21, 30, 42, 50–51, 53–54, 59–60, 78, 130–132, 137, 156, 180, 209, 216, 227, 239, 244, 252
Wong-Bakker Pain Rating Scale 15
Word xx, xxv, 18–19, 28, 54, 58, 61, 75, 106, 112, 132, 139, 143, 149, 174, 179, 182, 184, 188, 200, 242
World War xxix

X
X Marks the Spot 40–41, 46

Y
Y Generation 142
Yin Yang symbol 42, 212
Youth xxiv, xxxv, xxxvii, 42, 50–54, 78, 82, 130, 135, 137, 216

Z
Zero Population xxiii–xxiv
Zeroes, Cycles and Circles 25

LOVE MY LIFE-O-GRAPHIC
5 STEP TELEVIDEO COURSE

Want the concentrated juice out of this book?

Now, you probably really want an easy, one-liner core life legacy message. You probably want it today, too. You probably also want an everyday, everywhere symbol that will instantly trigger your loved ones to bring you to mind. And how about that Spielberg bonded feeling that insures they carry you around closer than their cell phone? A Forget Me Knot tie is kind of like putting a GPS tracker on their heart and pinging their heartstrings at just the perfect moment, right?

Enough with tolerating just dust: being some words in some dusty book on a shelf; or forgotten quotes on the Internet; or in a dusty, old dog-eared photo album; or worse, just discardable dust-to-dust. This is your life, your turn, your reason for believing it was all worth it. Let them know it. Heck, let yourself know it. You don't have to be like Dionne Warwick, who sang, "What's it all about, Alfie?" or Peggy Lee, singing, "Is that all there is?" With a Forget Me Knot tie you'll know. They'll know. And you now have the secret sauce to keep your connection with them fresh and accessible, assuring you will always be their loving, honorable mentor.

Want a little help from your friends?

If you need a more personal, get 'er done type instruction with flecks of sacred magi wisdom thrown in, then you'll also want to get the Love My Life-o-graphic 5 Step Televideo course.

Love My Life-o-graphic 5 Step Televideo Course

In each of the 5 videos I slow down the 5 steps and walk you through each step to make sure you have a solid, unique, creative Forget Me Knot tie. Once complete you will instantly be able to share it today and see the transformative effect it has on them while you are still living. You will know, with confidence, the Forget Me Knot tie will only continue to be enriching their lives after you've passed.

If you are interested in this more personal approach, join our community at **lovemylifeographic.com**.

Now, go and tie one on them.

DrAvivaBoxer.com

Elevating and Customizing the End-of-Life Experience

THANK YOU!

Thank you so much for downloading this *Forget Me Knot* book!

I hope you found this book to be a useful guide to finally tie yourself to your loved ones while still enjoying life!

Would you please be so kind as to leave a review on Amazon to share how reading this book affected you personally? It would be very much appreciated. By doing so you can help me to reach more people in my mission to elevate and customize the end-of-life.